WRITINGS ON EARLY
AMERICAN ARCHITECTURE

WRITINGS ON EARLY AMERICAN ARCHITECTURE

An Annotated List
of Books and Articles on Architecture Constructed before
1860 in the Eastern Half of the United States

By
Frank J. Roos, Jr.,
Associate Professor of Fine Arts
The Ohio State University

COLUMBUS
THE OHIO STATE UNIVERSITY PRESS
1943

GRADUATE SCHOOL STUDIES
CONTRIBUTIONS IN FINE ARTS, No. 2

Printed in
United States of America

CONTENTS*

* Cities, towns, and counties arranged alphabetically.

PREFACE

Although published at a time when the world is in flames and many of us have anxiously turned firemen, this book is a product of, and a hopeful preparation for, a time of peace. It started ten years ago as a small bibliographic index for the use of students of early American architecture at Ohio University. The need for such a list of titles was very real since there was available no comprehensive geographic bibliography of the subject. Constantly expanding, it proved so useful a tool to students that we were encouraged to see it through to completion. It is hoped that it will not only prove valuable to those who have projects under way in this field, but also point the way to further subjects that need investigation, perhaps for those who have not previously worked on this subject.

While the list was in leisurely process of preparation, interest in the subject was constantly increasing, with a significant rise in the quality as well as the quantity of articles and books. More well-trained observers have become interested in it than ever before, a phenomenon due in part at least to the increased interest in nationalism, evident earlier in other countries than in America. Indeed, it may be that the greater interest in America and in things American is the defensive result of the central European trend toward a supernationalism. Also, our institutions of higher education have been turning out more and more students, equipped not only with training to do scientific research on non-scientific subjects, but also with the tools to make such studies more effective, such as cameras with which to document buildings on the spot. Many of them were interested in European subjects until, finding that continent closed by war, they looked around for subjects nearer home. Some turned hopefully to Latin America while others discovered fruitful material on their own doorsteps.

As scholarship on American architecture matured and expanded, the need for research tools became more and more evident. This book is an attempt to supply one of them—that means of "searching the literature" so necessary before sound work on historical subjects can be attempted. It could not, of course, have been done without the pioneering of others. Richard Bach between

1915 and 1928, and A. Lawrence Kocher in the 1920's, admirably paved the way, while more recently Dean Rexford Newcomb, Professor Henry-Russell Hitchcock, and Mr. Charles E. Peterson have continued the necessary drudgery—for which this writer for one has been thankful (see titles 24, 2764–66, 2773, 2777, 2779). It seems logical to publish this list now, since no effort has been made to find titles published after January, 1941, when Miss Ruth Cook's excellent list of current titles was started in the *Journal of the American Society of Architectural Historians* (see 2770). We have attempted to fill in the gaps left by the earlier bibliographers, to arrange the titles in a more useful manner, to include notes and cross references where such seemed indicated, and thus to make easier the "preliminary searching" on titles published before the appearance of the lists in the Journal just mentioned.

Such a list as this could hardly be the work of one person. The staff of the Library of The Ohio State University was prodigal of its time. The writer is particularly grateful to Mr. Earl N. Manchester, the Librarian, to Miss Bertha Schneider, Catalogue Librarian, who among other things suggested the form of the entries, to Miss Margaret Oldfather and Miss Maude E. Avery of the same staff, as well as to my wife, Beatrice Adams Roos, and Mrs. Robert MacKellar who also gave much of their time. We are grateful, too, for the encouragement given us by Dean Rexford Newcomb, Dr. Fiske Kimball, and Mr. Talbot Hamlin.

Some of the typing and preliminary searching was done by students working under the National Youth Administration. A generous grant through Dean Alpheus W. Smith from The Ohio State University Graduate School funds made possible the final and detailed checking of the titles as well as the publication of the list. It is a pleasure also to thank Professor William R. Parker of this University for his many helpful suggestions, the numerous graduate students who called our attention to obscure titles and, finally, Professor William Charvat of New York University for his help in making possible the inclusion of some titles from the *Index to Early American Periodical Literature, 1728-1870,* a Works Progress Administration project at New York University.

F. J. R., Jr.

Columbus, Ohio
May, 1943

INTRODUCTION

*The Scope of the List, with
Remarks on Past Scholarship in the
Field and Some Suggestions*

INTRODUCTION

SCOPE OF THE LIST OF WRITINGS ON EARLY AMERICAN ARCHITECTURE

Included are titles of books and articles on architecture of the United States, from the east coast to the western edge of the Mississippi Valley. Not included are titles concerned with architecture constructed later than the Civil War, and architecture in the Far West or the Southwest. It is hoped that someone may subsequently make a similar list for the latter areas.

Types of Titles Included

1. Books and articles on American architecture in which the subject is considered historically.

2. Non-architectural titles that include important architectural sections, e.g., the *Federal Writers' Project Guides*, each of which locates the more important examples and includes an essay on the architectural history of the region covered.

3. Purely historical titles containing architectural material not elsewhere available.

4. Titles concerned with such minor arts as are normally attached to buildings, e.g., wrought and cast iron, and wallpaper.

5. References to descriptions and discussion in some early American magazines, many of which were contributed by the periodical index at New York University, mentioned in the Preface. This group is far from complete and is included here because of its usefulness and because it is not elsewhere available in print. Many other references to magazines and newspaper articles can of course be found in the better documented historical titles included in this list.

6. Some titles that could not, perhaps, be printed today because of their unscholarly nature. They are sometimes included, even though their facts are open to question, when they contain the only information on the subject or when they suggest leads for further investigation.

7. A few titles concerning American Indian structures, since there is evidence that the pioneer was sometimes influenced by the forms he found in the newly settled regions.

8. Some types of structures not normally considered in histories of architecture, such as lighthouses, windmills, and shot towers.

Types of Titles Not Included

1. Histories of towns, counties, and states. Although often a rich source of information they are much too numerous to warrant inclusion.

2. Purely historical titles about places and buildings, except for a few included when they were found to contain pertinent material.

3. Many titles of a purely romantic and antiquarian nature, including those in the picture-book class, even though containing some discussion of architecture. Wallace Nutting's *States Beautiful Series* was omitted, but Samuel Chamberlain's many recent titles were included because of their excellent illustrations and factual accuracy.

4. Handbooks for the use of architects and builders, since this group is well covered in Hitchcock's *American Architectural Books . . . published in America before 1895* (see 2773).

5. With few exceptions, no newspaper articles, even though they are often the only source of information on some subjects.

6. No attempt has been made to include all the editions of popular titles.

Method of Classification of Titles

As nearly as possible all titles are located under specific place names, e.g., if possible under city or county, or failing that, under state or region. Some titles are so geographically inclusive as to necessitate classification by style.

Brief descriptive notes are often included when a title is not adequately descriptive. Included are the dates ascribed to the buildings by the author of the publication.

Parentheses in notes are used to indicate dates derived from sources other than the titles in question.

Multiple title numbers are used for multiple entries. It is intended that the titles be numbered in the order in which they are listed (e.g., 244-51). In several instances, multiple or general entries have been given numbers to facilitate cross referencing.

Cross references are used when titles covering similar material are separated for alphabetical or geographical reasons.

The smallest geographical division here used is the town or city. Near-by buildings are normally included under the name of the nearest urban unit. In Virginia, however, most titles are classified by counties, since this has long been the primary geographic unit used there.

Further Suggestions to the User of This List

The reader is urged to remember that if he fails to find a title for a specific building under the town or county in which it is located, it may be included in a more general title classified under state, region, or style. If the building sought still does not appear, it must not be assumed that there has been no discussion in print. This basic list obviously is not exhaustive; indeed, no such first list could be. A student familiar with any part of the general subject should know of more titles on that part than are here included. Later perhaps, a list of additions and corrections can be collected and made available. It is hoped that the user will be lenient if and when errors are found. The writer takes all responsibility for such and would gladly correct them if he knew where they were. Finally, let the reader beware of the confusion of terminology common in the writings listed here. Such terms as Colonial, Post-Colonial, Georgian, Federal, Early Republican, Classic Revival, and Romantic Revival have had different meanings for different writers. For the benefit of the user of this list, the following classification was before the writer when it was being organized. Not all students of the subject will agree with it, but it will have served its purpose if it leads to further discussion which may bring about a more authoritative classification.

Some Abbreviations and Their Meanings

In the list certain abbreviations occur frequently. They include: ac. (active); b. (born); ca. (about); d. (died); fl. (flourished); n.d. (no date); and n.p. (no publisher).

EARLY AMERICAN ARCHITECTURAL STYLES—EASTERN HALF
OF THE UNITED STATES, TO 1860

I. COLONIAL (1611–*ca.* 1800)

    A. ENGLISH COLONIES

        1. Jacobean (to *ca.* 1725). Seventeenth century type. Sometimes called First Period or Early Colonial

        2. Georgian (*ca.* 1725—*ca.* 1800). Primarily Palladian influence through England. Sometimes called Second Period

    B. OTHER COLONIES

        1. Dutch Influence. Primarily Hudson Valley and Long Island. Usually called Dutch Colonial

        2. German Influence. Primarily Pennsylvania

        3. Spanish and French Influence (before 1819). Primarily Florida, Georgia, and Louisiana

II. EARLY REPUBLICAN (*ca.* 1780—*ca.* 1860). Sometimes called Federal

    A. CLASSIC REVIVALS OR INSPIRATION (1799–*ca.* 1860)

        1. Roman Revival

            a) *Adam Type* (*ca.* 1790—*ca.* 1840). Primarily New England; e.g., Samuel McIntire and some Bulfinch work. Sometimes called Post-Colonial, Late Georgian, Third Period, or Federal

      b) Jeffersonian Type (1785–*ca.* 1840). Some Palladian with more direct Roman and French influence. Primarily Middle Atlantic and Southern states. Sometimes called Republican

  2. Greek Revival (1799–*ca.* 1850). E.g., Benjamin Latrobe and his followers: Robert Mills, William Strickland, and T. U. Walter. National in scope. Modified by Asher Benjamin

  3. Renaissance Revivals

      a) French Type (ca. 1803—*ca.* 1850). E.g., Pierre L'Enfant, Joseph Mangin, and John McComb. Some Bulfinch work

      b) English Type. James Hoban and James Gibbs influence on church spires. The latter a continuation in part of Georgian. Sometimes called Post-Colonial

  4. Egyptian Revival (from 1815). Scattered examples by many architects

B. Romantic Revivals or Inspiration

  1. Gothic Revival (1800–after 1860). E.g., Maximilian Godefroy, A. J. Davis, Richard Upjohn, and James Renwick

  2. Romanesque Revival (*ca.* 1850). E.g., Robert Dale Owen and Renwick. Later popularized by Richardson

  3. Battle of the Styles (after *ca.* 1840). Italian villas, Swiss chalets, Victorian Gothic, French Second Empire, Downing cottages, jig-saw work, etc.

C. Original or Unusual Forms. E.g., block houses, dog trot cabins and other log forms, cobblestone houses, decorative wrought and cast iron, Orson Squire Fowler's octagonal houses, and simplified classic revival of the Middle West

Scholarship on Early American Architecture

In building such a list as we are here presenting, one gets a perspective on the scholarship in the field such as could not easily be achieved in any other way. One becomes conscious not only of the men and the areas of study that have been important in the past, but also of the areas and types of subjects that deserve some attention in the future.

Totals of Titles on Architecture Listed, by Two-Year Periods*

1900–01	21	1920–21	126
1902–03	51	1922–23	138
1904–05	36	1924–25	170
1906–07	65	1926–27	168
1908–09	54	1928–29	160
1910–11	62	1930–31	138
1912–13	80	1932–33	137
1914–15	102	1934–35	146
1916–17	137	1936–37	154
1918–19	105	1938–39	202

* Only titles considering architecture historically were counted.

Production, 1900–1940

As the preceding table shows, interest in early American architecture has been increasing since 1900, but it has not had a steady rise, since from time to time world events have diverted study of this as well as other subjects. We can conjecture at the reasons for some of the hills and valleys in the curve that might be made from this table. The long and fairly steady rise in the number of titles from 1900 to 1918 may be seen, on examination of the titles themselves, to be for the most part the result of the interest of antiquarians and romanticists, sometimes indistinguishable, with a sprinkling of a few architectural historians. The subject matter was primarily architecture in the "Colonial Style," used then in a very loose sense, in New England and a few southern states.

In the number of titles, the first World War brought an inevitable decline which, however, was comparatively short lived, since a new and higher peak was in the making. It may be significant that the totals began to slacken even before the stock market crash of 1929, which produced another depression in our curve. But the new peak of 1938–40 rose higher than ever, partly because of the great number of titles about the Williamsburg restoration. A breakdown of these figures by regions shows that the South in 1935 had twice as many titles as the totals on New England and the Mid-Atlantic states combined. Although this list does not attempt to include titles published after 1941, future listings will probably show a decline in the totals beginning in 1940.

The Antiquarians and the Colonial Style

As might be expected, most of the early writers were interested in the subject because of the age of the buildings or their historical associations, rather than in the architecture as such. They tended to ignore contemporary styles and anything, for that matter, newer than the Revolution. As Hitchcock has pointed out (2773), the first separate publication on Colonial architecture was probably by Nathan Henry Chamberlain, published in 1858 (303). Eleven years later, when the American Institute of Architects was three years old, we find Richard Upjohn, its founder and first president, discussing the Colonial architecture of New York and New England (191). Not until after his death, however, do we find any official expression of the need for study of the Colonial style on the part of that organization (179). The bulk of the early writings was by untrained observers, writing under such titles in the 1870's and '80's as *Nooks and Corners of the New England Coast* (308) and *The Homes of Our Forefathers* (373, 374).

By 1877 R. S. Peabody had added the term Georgian to Colonial in an illustrated article in the new *American Architect and Building News* (366). Between that year and 1891 Glenn Brown and others discussed the Colonial works in Virginia and Maryland (1625, 1627). The next year Joseph Chandler wrote on Maryland, Pennsylvania, and Virginia (153), and Corner and Soderholtz published their first study on the South (1629), to be followed three years later by Crane and Soderholtz' work on Charleston and Savannah (1630). Although the subject was well under way in the South in the 1890's, the bulk of titles was still concerned with New England. There again Corner and Soderholtz were pioneers, with a parallel to their southern work in the same year (347). Not until 1895, however, does there seem to be enough material available for Montgomery Schuyler to attempt what was probably the first history of Colonial architecture (188), preceded by his more general *American Architecture* in 1892 (25).

By the late 1890's the subject had been so well covered that critical articles began to appear, with such titles as the *So-called Colonial Architecture of the United States* (152), *Good and Bad Colonial Architecture* (147), and *The Case for Colonial* (193). In the meantime the romanticists and the antiquarians were adding scores of articles and books which, although they were and are useful, reflected in their titles the authors' primary impulse for writing. Typical are *Some Colonial Homesteads and Their Stories* (209), *Stately Homes in America* (86), *The Romance of Old New England Rooftrees* (350), and *Among Old New England Inns* (377). Even as late as the 1920's such titles continue, with *The Mystery of Early American Doorways* (210) and *Ye Old Picture Wall-papers* (232). Most of the titles of this type appeared in the house and home magazine group, however, and seldom in the architectural journals. Some of the antiquarians were inclined to make sweeping statements that remind one of the recent attempt to find the oldest house in Massachusetts, proving anew the danger in trying to identify "firsts" (2000). These earlier writers, romanticist or antiquarian, contributed much that must be commended, however, for in their writings is considerable material that can still be found nowhere else. And they did describe and illustrate many buildings that have since been destroyed.

Scholarship

We have already mentioned a number of pioneer historians such as Chandler, Schuyler, and Upjohn. The first of them all is, of course, William Dunlap, who seems to have made fewer errors than his prototype Vasari (6). His monumental work in 1834 is still the only source of some material—a fact the more noteworthy because he received little co-operation from some of his contemporaries. The 1860's saw the beginning of formal architectural teaching in the United States, even though Europe was still the primary training ground for architects and historians. The Massachusetts Institute of Technology started a course in architecture in 1865, with William Robert Ware as director, and by 1868 the subject appeared in the University of Illinois catalogue, and soon after was taught at Cornell. William Rotch Ware, just back from the Ecole des Beaux Arts in 1876, was the first editor of *The American Architect,* our first architectural magazine. We have already mentioned the publication of an article there on Georgian architecture in 1877 (366). In 1898 Ware started publication in his own magazine of his important series of measured drawings on the Georgian period, which were to appear later in folio form (28). Montgomery Schuyler broke the spell of the Colonial by pausing to look at our college architecture, starting in 1909 (687), and at our Greek Revival in 1910 (290). He had been preceded in his study of the latter style, however, by W. H. Goodyear in 1892 (283). At this time, too, a number of photographer-writers were working on the documentation of buildings. One of them, Frank Cousins, deserves special mention because of the quantity and quality of his work. The prints produced by these men of the horse and buggy days, with cameras and plates that we would call clumsy and inadequate, deserve all the praise we can give them. One wonders if those of us who photograph architecture today, with our automobiles, good roads, high speed films and lenses, could have done as well in their day, with their equipment. But some of our contemporaries use light and shade and composition in a manner that the earlier men would not have thought possible. Kenneth Clark, Arthur C. Haskell, Samuel Chamberlain, and Frances Benjamin Johnston are a few of the many whom we could name here.

In 1915 appeared Volume One, Number One, of that invaluable *White Pine Series of Architectural Monographs* that continued until recently, through its descendant the "Monograph Series" in *Pencil Points*. Russell F. Whitehead, its editor from the beginning and the editors of *Pencil Points* are to be congratulated for having continued such a useful source of material. One regrets only that the series did not include more material from the South and from states west of the Atlantic seaboard. We cannot proceed without mentioning the measured drawings of early buildings that have appeared regularly in this and the other architectural publications. They were a true labor of love, and the architects who did them deserve the thanks of all later students of the subject.

In the previous year appeared the first of a series of articles, no less monumental, by that indefatigable worker, Fiske Kimball. His research on Jefferson (e.g., 2290, 2702–2706) has done much to establish the latter's reputation in this field. Another important contributor to the general study of the subject is Talbot F. Hamlin, whose *American Spirit in Architecture* in 1926 filled a long standing need for illustrations (12). From the 1920's on, the list of students of early American architecture grows continuously, with useful contributions from Frank Chouteau Brown, Aymar Embury, I. T. Frary, Rexford Newcomb, and William Rusk, to name but a few. That the field had become of interest to university art departments is evidenced by the appearance in 1938 of four doctoral dissertations devoted to the subject (253, 291, 293, 2589).

Nineteen forty-one saw the first volume of the *Journal of the American Society of Architectural Historians* under the energetic editorship of Turpin Bannister. Some of the society's members, with the inspiration of Kenneth Conant, are devoting such time as they now have to the subject.

SOME SUGGESTIONS

All past studies in this field may be said to fall into one of the following general classifications: (1) studies of one structure; (2) studies of one geographic unit, such as town, county, state, or region; (3) studies of a style, type, or detail from one or more geographic units or in a given period of time; (4) studies of architects and their work; (5) studies of source materials; (6) collecting for archives; (7) studies concerning restoration and preservation; and (8) studies of a sociological, critical, or developmental nature.

None of these headings has been exhausted by any means. We shall attempt to identify early studies in each classification as well as point out some of the needs in the following pages.

Studies of One Structure

This type of study is normally the easiest and the earliest attempted. It often may take the form of a simple description of a new building or one that is very old. As far back as the 1790's one finds separate descriptions of newly erected structures, mostly of a public type (244–51). Through the first half of the nineteenth century occur numerous contemporary descriptions of buildings, since destroyed or altered, which should prove a profitable source of information to the architectural historian (e.g., 1508–1510, 1528–29). By 1830 we have what is probably the first separate publication on a building—the recently completed Tremont House in Boston (626). Only four years later comes what may be the first guidebook to a building—by Robert Mills on the Capitol at Washington (1788). By the 1880's building guides were quite common, those of David Scattergood being typical (1606–1607).

Almost any city or town has still much to offer in the way of studies of individual buildings, even such as Boston, New York, Baltimore, and Philadelphia, to say nothing of the smaller towns. The Early Republican and the Romantic Revival styles offer more profit than the Colonial in most regions. The tendency has been to write about the largest, best preserved, or most historical structures, ignoring other examples that are sometimes as good or even better architecturally. Future historians who will further codify our architectural past will be grateful to the student who furnishes them with many illustrations of details as well as the usual photograph of the structure as a whole. The Historic American Buildings Survey has done good work along this line. Particularly important is the availability of these records (57).

Geographic Studies

A geographic arrangement of titles such as we offer here immediately shows up the areas that have apparently not been touched at all or that have not been worked on recently by competent observers. Any student may find these areas for himself by scrutiny of the list.

Virginia might be said to have had a head start in this type of title, since as early as 1853 we find an article concerning the progress of architecture there (2127). In 1877 appeared Westcott's *Historic Mansions and Buildings of Philadelphia,* probably the first of the long list of town studies (1540). The older cities of the Atlantic seaboard have been fairly well covered, although, as we said before, there is still much to do in all of them. A particular tendency may be noted, to write about the architecture of the cities or parts of cities that time has left comparatively intact, such as Charleston, Portsmouth, Salem, and the Vieux Carré in New Orleans. These groups have been of interest alike to the antiquarian, the descendants of the old families, and the historian.

Once in a while one finds an area that was worked on very early and has remained almost untouched since. The Genesee Valley is such a region. Claude Bragdon did some excellent measured drawings there in 1894 which he published in the *American Architect* (1223), and in 1923 a paper by him was published on the same subject. This and other parts of central New York are less well covered than the Hudson Valley or Long Island. It is true, of course, that older structures adjacent to large cities are likely to be covered early.

Much work should be done on the Dutch architecture of the Mid-Atlantic states and more is still possible on the work of the Pennsylvania Germans. New Jersey, too, has much unrecorded material and there is more in Florida than this list would lead one to suppose. Although there have been numerous articles on Natchez since 1930, Mississippi can stand more attention, as can the western counties of Virginia, and West Virginia as a whole.

The Midwest has much untouched material. Our knowledge of the classic revival there has increased since Fiske Kimball first wrote about it in Michigan in 1922. Illinois, Indiana, Iowa, Kansas, Michigan, Minnesota, Missouri, and Wisconsin all have material enough for books on the subject. Although Ohio is the best covered of the states of this region, there are still many unphotographed and unstudied buildings there. In it and the other states mentioned above exist also many local styles, variations of European prototypes built by the immigrant groups, that are not mentioned anywhere but in the *Federal Writers' Project State Guides*. For this region, as for the nation as a whole, we need a geography of architecture as well as a geography of antiques.

Studies of Styles, Types, and Details

As we have said before, of the chronological styles, the Colonial has been best covered. The Greek and Roman Revivals still need considerable codification, especially west of the Atlantic states where

the examples are numerous and often very good. It is hoped that
Talbot Hamlin's work on the Greek Revival will soon appear in
print. The next chronological style or group of styles, the Romantic
Revivals, are practically untouched, although the groundwork has
been laid in a few books and articles (291–94). We can no more
afford to ignore this period than an American Wing could afford
to leave out the horsehair sofa, the rosewood chair, or the whatnot.
If architecture, like the other arts, is the visible index of a cultural
period, then we are doubly bound to study this one if we are to
understand ourselves and our past. The approach to the works
of the Romanticists must be different, psychologically speaking,
from the approach to the preceding styles, but the results can be as
profitable as in any other period.

Grouping by type as well as by style has, of course, also been
common. We find religious and public structures written about
briefly in 1859 (135), but it is rather surprising to find as long
ago as 1865 a large volume on the early churches of even so
important a city as New York (1371). Aymar Embury's work on
churches in 1911 and 1912 is still standard. Public buildings were
discussed as early as 1884 (132) but they are still comparatively
neglected as a group. We have already mentioned Montgomery
Schuyler's pioneer work on college architecture, starting in the
Architectural Record in 1909, but he was not the first to consider
it. The *Yale Literary Magazine* carried a brief note on it in 1853
(256).

Of the other types, military architecture could stand more
attention although there have been a number of good localized
articles on blockhouses, forts, and garrison houses (e.g., 340, 952,
1258, 1491, 2129). Although Henry Chapman Mercer (109)
and Harold Shurtleff have both concerned themselves with log
cabins, the subject warrants further investigation. There are many
types from the Atlantic to the Mississippi still unrecorded. This is
a particularly profitable group to study, since in the log cabin form
we can see native ingenuity at work, often uninfluenced by training.
Further study of the examples surviving will tell us something
about the development of functionalism and, in the mutations of
their types, something about the development of style when un-
hampered by aesthetic considerations. Little has been done except
locally, with such infrequent and minor forms as windmills, light-
houses, and shot towers.

We need, too, a closer study and codification of original details of existing buildings, such as bricks, bonds, molding profiles, muntin details, hardware, heating and sanitation systems, and internal construction generally. We have been too much in the habit of looking at the stylistic proportions of the exteriors and interiors and not seeing the buildings as the builders themselves seem to have seen their handiwork—as a series of details put together to make a whole. One of the useful indirect results of such studies would be better restorations.

George Francis Dow in 1926 did some work on hardware (157) and Henry Chapman Mercer's study of old carpenters' tools is very useful (55). We need more knowledge of wrought and cast iron, the foundries and their molds. Thomas T. Waterman and others have done some good work in this field (1655). When more facts are gathered about such details it will be possible to have more articles like those written by Mercer in 1923 and 1924 on the dating of old houses (107–108). All these studies will be furthered by more photographs, especially of details, with a measuring stick somewhere in the picture.

Color as an architectural factor was practically ignored by the writers until about 1928, when A. Lawrence Kocher wrote about it in the *Architectural Record* (177 and 35). Much more knowledge has come out of the Williamsburg researches, but additional work in this field is needed.

The reader of Giedion's *Space, Time and Architecture* (262) will become aware of a large body of material that Giedion only scratched, and his approach to the study of architecture is itself well worth studying.

Studies of Architects and Their Work

Although the listed writings on architects show much good work done by numerous authors, it also shows that many good architects have been comparatively neglected. The list does not show, of course, those architects who have been completely ignored. Perhaps we should not refer to them all as architects, since many of our early builders were something less than well trained. These builders and architects generally fall into one of five groups.

The *carpenters* were for the most part anonymous and drew upon their memories or the handbooks for their designs. These sometimes excellent craftsmen have been almost completely ignored.

Research in the future will probably reveal a few of them to have been better trained and more influential than we now think. The *carpenter-designers* were a step above the carpenters in both training and ability. Some of them achieved considerable orginality in practice or print while keeping within the bounds of contemporary "good taste" and proportion. One might mention Samuel Rhoads of Philadelphia and William Buckland of Annapolis. Asher Benjamin is also in this group, with the distinction of being the author of the first original book on architecture published in America, in 1797 (2773). The wide distribution of this and Benjamin's subsequent handbooks made him one of the most influential builders in the first half of the century. A detailed study of his and Minard Lafever's handbooks will tell us more than we now know of the psychology and methods of our early builders. A large collection of telephoto pictures of details of buildings will show, when compared with the plates of these and earlier handbooks, such as those by William Pain, Batty Langley, and William Halfpenny, the great use to which these volumes were put. We feel that these books can be shown to account not only for some of the changes in style and for the wide geographic spread of certain styles, but also for the excellent design of many of the buildings, especially in the early Republican period. The carpenter, as long as he sought his inspiration from one book or from plates in one style, could hardly go far wrong stylistically. They not only gave him his elementary mathematics for laying out stairs, trusses, arches, or moldings, but some of them adapted the complicated popular styles to his materials, tools, and abilities. It is significant that these books seldom give full plans and elevations. If the elevations are given, they are often in terms of proportions only, with alternate choice of details given elsewhere. In the arrangement of these details lay the carpenters' opportunity for freedom of choice and originality. Any person concerned with restoration would do well to consult these handbooks, too, since in many cases they make it possible accurately to restore the building as it might have been, if it cannot be done as it was.

Montgomery Schuyler sensed their importance as early as 1906 (187), but he knew of only a few, and as late as 1924 Alexander Wall listed only 21 published before 1830 (2782). We will be surprised if many are found in the future that are not already listed in the co-operative list compiled by Hitchcock (2773). It is a pleasure to observe that many architectural libraries are now collecting them. There should be more reprinting, like Aymar Embury's reproduction of some of Asher Benjamin's plates in 1917 (2665).

Thomas Jefferson is the outstanding name in the third group, which we may call *gentlemen-designers*. Although professionally untrained, Jefferson had considerable influence, partly no doubt because he had a reputation in other fields. In this group might also be included Andrew Hamilton and Dr. John Kearsley of Philadelphia, as well as such men as Maximilian Godefroy, who have not been adequately covered.

Some of the *early professional architects*, such as Charles Bulfinch, our first professional, have been given considerable attention in print. Even he has not been studied much since 1925, although Samuel McIntire has attracted discussion of late. Samuel Blodget, George Hadfield, Stephen Hallet, Peter Harrison, David Hoadley, James Hoban, and others, with varying degrees of experience and training, have been comparatively neglected. Some of them and their followers, the *later professional architects*, were discussed by Rexford Newcomb in a series of articles in *The Architect* between 1926 and 1929. Because of their excellence, one wishes that they had appeared in a publication allowing footnote documentation and that Newcomb had continued the series. Of the men in this group, Mills, Town, and Davis have been well covered since 1935, and Thornton, Latrobe, Walter, and Upjohn have had some attention, although some of them are still not as completely covered as they should be. In several instances, work on them cannot be completed until the necessary source materials become available. Latrobe particularly deserves a large volume, not only because of his work but also because of his influence on other architects. He started both the Greek and Gothic Revivals here. His versatility is evidenced by the fact that he seems to have built the first railway, put the first sheet iron roof on a building when fireproofing was a new subject, and apparently utilized for the first time a steam engine to pump water (2719).

Henry Austin, James Bogardus, A. J. Downing, John Haviland, Minard Lafever, John McComb, James Renwick, Isaiah Rogers, and Martin Thompson invite more thorough study. William Strickland, who practically invented a substitute for the dome by using the "Lanthorn of Demosthenes," and who contributed to progress by using illuminating gas in 1809, should soon appear in print. We are glad to be able to say that some of these men are being given attention by competent students. Lastly, such men as Samuel Sloan, whose influence, although later, was not unlike that of Benjamin, should receive more attention, and although Orson Squire Fowler could hardly be called an architect, his influence cannot be ignored if one will check his book against the numerous and widely scattered octagonal houses. Some of the architects who worked in the Midwest and the South, such as Francis Costigan, John Francis Rague, and James Gallier, deserve more attention than they have had. Rexford Newcomb has given us some material on Gideon Shryock of Kentucky (2740) and both I. T. Frary and this writer have brought some of the early Ohio carpenter-designers to light (2575, 2589).

We have named only a few of the men who seem to merit attention, but there are many more, some of whose names we do not yet know. Ever so often some good architect is suddenly brought to light. Some of them have had their reputations established for posterity by one title, such as Philip Hooker (2698). We confess that we were not familiar with Thomas Tefft before Barbara Wriston's articles on him appeared a few years ago (2747–48).

Studies of Source Materials

Well-trained students habitually gravitate to such source materials as contemporary accounts and manuscripts. Antiquarians have recorded for sentimental reasons much that is useful, but we now need students to sort this mass of information and organize it both for themselves and others. The printed records of such historical societies as those in Cambridge, the District of Columbia, the Essex Institute in Salem, the Society for the Preservation of New England Antiquities, the Maryland Historical Society, the Daughters of the American Revolution, and the art museum bulletins all offer gold for the digger. We need from such records more itemized bills and contracts for building, for example, although George Francis Dow and others have published some from time to time (e.g., 543, 559, 711, 747, 779, 848, 1334, 1972, 1985). Manuscript collections in libraries and museums are also full of these documents, which can be checked against the lists of time to be spent on house details by the carpenter, as published in some of the builders' handbooks. Through such studies we can learn more about the builder and his work, his economic life and his day.

Newspapers are obviously profitable. Dow and Rusk have done some good work with them (307, 580, 1948). The inventories catalogued by the Works Progress Administration and such projects as the New York University periodical index will become increasingly useful as they become better known. Much important material, too, is still hidden away in such publications as the old *New Yorker*, the *Portfolio*, and even in such remote places as the *Coast Artillery Journal* (2129), and architectural historians would be thankful for more titles like Stokes' *Iconography of Manhattan Island* (1295).

More states and cities should collect manuscript histories of houses, as Connecticut has done (417) and Michigan is doing, although the recent accounts must be quoted with some caution, unless double checked or otherwise documented. A typical instance of the usefulness of manuscripts that at first glance would not seem pertinent, occurred recently when we found one in the collections of the Ohio Archaeological and Historical Society by Dr. S. S. Walker entitled *Journey of a Voyage to New England Performed in the Year 1844.* In it he wrote,

It [Bunker Hill Monument] is kept by a man who for a quarter will take you to the top in a steam car, or for a shilling you may have the privilege of walking up a never ending spiral staircase. The ascent by the car is pleasant. You step into a bird cage big enough for six persons to stand at once, and in three minutes you open the door of the cage and walk out upon a floor . . . at the height of 225 feet.

This is obviously the same stone hoist which Wheilden mentions as having been used for a year to carry visitors to the top (2763, p. 246). A minor matter to be sure, but it double checks Wheilden and gives more information than he did, such as the size and rate of climb. And apparently it puts the date of the first mechanically powered elevator used for passengers some nine years earlier than James Bogardus' first proposal, cited by Giedion (262, p. 142).

Archives

The last decade has seen a number of attempts at gathering together in a few places factual material about early American architecture for the use of students, architects, or restorers. Collections of this sort will be particularly useful to the future historians who try to codify further this area of American production and culture. It is interesting to note that the opportunity for beginning two of these came as a result of the Depression in the early 1930's. One of them was started in 1933 by the Civil Works

Administration which, with the co-operation of the seventy chapters of the American Institute of Architects, used unemployed architects and draftsmen to survey and document some of the extant buildings (57). This project eventually developed into the more permanent and invaluable Historic American Buildings Survey, whose records are deposited in the Library of Congress under Leicester B. Holland, Chief of the Division of Fine Arts, who had earlier started to collect negatives and photographs of good examples. Since many students now do their own photographing of buildings, it is to be hoped that more of them will leave their negatives to this Library of Congress collection.

Another product of the Depression was the series of state and city guides done by the Federal Writers' Project. They are invaluable in leading one directly to the structure one wishes to see. Many of us remember the difficulty, before their appearance, of finding the buildings we had heard or read about. Although the information about the individual buildings in these guides is sometimes based on hearsay, the architectural essay in each state volume was written by or after consultation with local historians. These and the mass of material from which they were condensed, as well as the other Works Progress Administration inventories, should offer many leads to work undone and much information to the student who has his problem under way (51).

Restoration and Preservation

Many organizations such as the Society for the Preservation of New England Antiquities, the Daughters of the American Revolution, and the members of the American Association of Museums, to name only a few, have long been concerned with the restoration and preservation of historic and architecturally distinguished houses (e.g., 4, 30, 84, 95). The Williamsburg project is, of course, the most ambitious and best known, and it has received the greatest amount of scholarly attention of all the efforts in this field. But Preservationism, which in Europe had almost developed into a science, has had but scattered attention here until recently. It is now receiving concerted attention from new quarters, as the 1941 numbers of the *Journal of the American Society of Architectural Historians* show. It is to be hoped that as time, interest, and funds become available the suggestions for organized preservation, architectural museums, and research centers can be further implemented (e.g., 59, 2560).

Studies of a Sociological, Critical, or Developmental Nature

Architectural styles or forms do not spring full fledged into being, nor do they develop in a predetermined manner, completely independent of outside influences. Some of us have been too prone to think and write as if they did. Not only do we need more studies of individual examples and groups of examples, but there is an even greater need for studies that relate these examples to each other and to the numerous sociological and physical factors that influenced their form. *Mill and Mansion* by John Coolidge, and John Kienitz' dissertation, are two recent titles in this direction that should be followed by more (764, 293). Van Wyck Brooks's popular *The Flowering of New England* offers the student of architecture much profitable material of a similar sort. It is time now to study further some of the many factors that influenced plans and elevations, such as religious and national habits and backgrounds, laws, geographic distribution of materials, and climate.

Someone could profitably do an analysis of the factors that constituted excellence of design in each period. The Palladian emphasis on minute differences in proportion so varies from our concept of goodness today that two buildings which look much alike to us, were considerably different according to contemporary critics. To our eyes almost all the production in the Romantic Revival styles seems bad. And yet these eclectics, too, had their standards which made some buildings aesthetically better than others. We could find profit also in more studies of the background of our city planning, the relation of the town plan to architecture, and of early attempts at co-operative housing.

Studies could profitably be made, too, of early evidences of factors common in architecture today, such as functionalism, or American ingenuity. Modern American architecture is no more completely a borrowing from Europe than is the contemporary American culture which it expresses. We have had many functionalists in our architectural history, even before the Civil War. Horatio Greenough, our first trained sculptor, in the 1850's had nothing less than a twentieth century attitude toward clipper ships and architecture, and Thomas Jefferson's well-known idea for a serpentine brick wall would do credit to a contemporary of ours. We think today that "the most exquisite ornaments lose all their value, if they load, alter or confuse the form they are designed to enrich and adorn." But this is no contemporary of ours talking.

It is Asher Benjamin in 1814 in his *Rudiments of Architecture.*
His ingenuity in adapting designs from such sources as Stuart and
Revett's *Antiquities of Athens* so that they could be used by carpenters
was a step in what we today would call the right direction. Benjamin
was not only being a functionalist of sorts, but he was also express-
ing an originality that would more readily be accepted in this country
than abroad in his own day. Perhaps we can call it part of the
American Idea.

The man who thought of floating houses from Pennsylvania
to Mississippi in 1836 was probably as far from Palladian and
Periclean thinking as most of our architects today (273). Was the
amazing Orson Squire Fowler (2773) a forerunner of Louis Sullivan, Frank Lloyd Wright, or Buckminster Fuller? They have
much in common with him, although separated from him by almost
a century.

It may have been only boredom with classic forms that
prompted Latrobe, apparently at Jefferson's suggestion, to experi-
ment with indigenous plants such as corn, tobacco, and cotton in
place of the non-American acanthus in his capitals. He did not
create an American Order of course, but he was not alone in his
thinking about this anomaly in our Classic Revival, since he was
congratulated from many sides for his originality—by the members
of Congress, by Robert Dale Owen (1729, p. 9), by James Fennell (*An Apology for the Life of James Fennell*, 1814, p. 415)—
and even the ubiquitous Mrs. Trollope was impressed. Alexander
J. Davis tried out wheat and corn together at Chapel Hill, and
corn and morning glories appear around the middle of the century
on a cast iron fence at 915 Royal St., in New Orleans. Later,
Henry Ives Cobb essayed capitals of fish, eels, frogs, cattails, and
other aquatic flora and fauna on the east colonnade of the Fisheries
Building in 1893 at Chicago, and most of us are familiar with
Bertram Goodhue's combination of corn and wheat with some sus-
piciously Persepolis-like bulls in the north vestibule of the Nebraska
Capitol. These are scattered examples to be sure, but they seem
like the murmurings of a new culture and an ingenuity that in our
day has already given us mass production and produced hundreds
of new synthetic materials for architecture and the other arts, that
will give us architectural forms as true to and typical of ourselves
as the Colonial and Early Republican examples were true to and
typical of their day.

LIST OF WRITINGS ON EARLY
AMERICAN ARCHITECTURE

GENERAL REFERENCES

1 BANNISTER, TURPIN C. Architectural development of the northeastern states. Architectural record. 89:61-80. June 1941. illus.

2 BRAGDON, CLAUDE FAYETTE. Architecture in the United States. Architectural record. 25:426-33; 26:38-45. 1909. illus.

3 CAHILL, HOLGER, AND BARR, ALFRED H., JR. Art in America in modern times. N. Y., Reynal and Hitchcock, 1934. 162p. illus.
Chapter 3 by Henry-Russell Hitchcock, Jr., is a brief history of American architecture before the Civil War.

4 COLEMAN, LAURENCE VAIL. The museum in America. Washington, D. C., American association of museums, 1939. 3v.
List of buildings preserved.

5 DRURY, NEWTON B. The national park service and the preservation of historic sites and buildings. American society of architectural historians. Journal. v. 1, no. 3-4. p. 18-19. July-Oct. 1941.

6 DUNLAP, WILLIAM. History of the rise and progress of the arts of design in the United States. Boston, C. E. Goodspeed and Co., 1918. 3v. illus.
First edition N. Y., G. P. Scott and Co., 1834. 1 v. An invaluable source book.

7 FARIS, JOHN THOMASON. Historic shrines of America. N. Y., George H. Doran Co., 1918. 421p. illus.

8 FEDERAL WRITERS' PROJECT. Catalogue of the American guide series. Washington, D. C., Government printing office, 1938. 31p. illus.

9 ———. The ocean highway; New Brunswick, New Jersey to Jacksonville, Florida. N. Y., Modern age books, 1938. 244p. illus.

10 ———. U. S. one, Maine to Florida. N. Y., Modern age books, 1938. 344p. illus.

11 FEISS, CARL. The heritage of our planned communities. American society of architectural historians. Journal. v. 1, no. 3-4. p. 27-30. July-Oct. 1941. illus.

12 HAMLIN, TALBOT FAULKNER. The American spirit in architecture. New Haven, Conn., Yale university press, 1926. 353p. illus.
Vol. 13 of the *Pageant of America*; a pictorial history of the United States. A general history of American architecture, well illustrated.

13 HUTH, HANS. Observations concerning the conservation of monuments in Europe and America. Washington, D. C., Department of interior, National park service, 1941. 64p. Mimeographed.

14 KIMBALL, SIDNEY FISKE. American architecture. Indianapolis, Ind., Bobbs-Merrill Co., 1928. 262p. illus.
A general discussion; includes bibliography.

15 ———. Architecture in the history of the Colonies and of the Republic. American historical review. 27:45-57. Oct. 1921.

16 ———. The development of American architecture. Architectural forum. 28:1-5, 81-86. Jan.-Mar. 1918; 29:21-25. July 1918. illus.

17 ———. The history and monuments of our national art. Art and archaeology. 4:161-68. Sept. 1916. illus.

18 ———. Three centuries of American architecture. Architectural record. 57:560-64. June 1925.

19 LEWIS, WINTHROP. Our architecture, yesterday, today and tomorrow. Country life. 39:40-42. Apr. 1921.

20 LOCKWOOD, ALICE G. B. (ed.). Gardens of Colony and State: gardens and gardeners of the American Colonies and of the Republic before 1840. N. Y., Charles Scribner's Sons, 1931-34. 2v. illus.
Includes many illustrations of buildings.

21 MERCER, HENRY CHAPMAN. Indian habitation in the eastern United States. American naturalist. 30:430-33. 1896.
Some early reactions to Indians.

22 MUMFORD, LEWIS. American architecture. Freeman. 8:344-46, 394-96, 418-20, 538-40, 584-86. Dec. 19, 1923; Jan. 2, 9; Feb. 13, 27, 1924.
Covers 1620–1890.

23 ———. Sticks and stones, a study of American architecture and civilization. N. Y., Boni and Liveright, 1924. 247p.

24 NEWCOMB, REXFORD. Outlines of the history of architecture. Part 4, Modern architecture with particular reference to the United States. N. Y., John Wiley and Sons, 1939. 319p.
Lists buildings with dates. Bibliography.

(Preservation of historic buildings.) American Society of architectural historians. Journal. Apr.-Oct. 1941.

25 SCHUYLER, MONTGOMERY. American architecture. N. Y., Harper and Brothers, 1892. 211p. illus.

26 SINGLETON, ESTHER (ed.). Historic buildings in America. N. Y., Dodd, Mead and Co., 1906. 341p. illus.
As seen and described by famous writers.

27 TALLMADGE, THOMAS EDDY. The story of architecture in America. N. Y., W. W. Norton and Co., 1936. 324p. illus.

28 WARE, WILLIAM ROTCH, AND KEEFE, CHARLES S. (ed.). The Georgian period: being photographs and measured drawings of Colonial work with text. N. Y., U. P. C. Book Co., *ca.* 1923. 6v. 454 illus.
First appeared in 1898, New York, American Architect and Buildings News Company. Includes some Early Republican examples.

DETAILS AND MISCELLANEOUS

29 AMERICAN LIBRARY ASSOCIATION. Sources for reproductions of works of art. American library association. Bulletin. 30:287-99. Apr. 1936.
Compiled by A.L.A. visual methods committee. *See also* 56.

30 BARRINGTON, LEWIS. Historic restorations of the Daughters of the revolution. N. Y., R. R. Smith, 1941. illus.

31 BISHOP, JAMES LEANDER. History of American manufacture, from 1608-1860. Philadelphia, Edward Young and Co., 1864. 2v. illus.

32 Brick precedent in American architecture; views and details of early American brickwork. American architect. 149:59-66. July 1936. illus.

33 CAYE, ROGER. Decorative wood-carving in Colonial and Post-Colonial America. Arts and decoration. 11:178-79. Aug. 1919. illus.

34 CORNELIUS, CHARLES OVER. American metalwork and fixed decorations. Architectural record. 51:88-92. Jan. 1922. illus.

35 Decoration of early American interiors. Dutch boy painter. July 1926. p. 115-18. illus.
Includes some color formulas.

36 Detailed charts of architectural styles in America. House beautiful. 77:62-63, Oct. 1935; 77:52-53, Nov. 1935; 77:62-63. Dec. 1935.
Covers 1700–1850.

37 DYER, WALTER ALDEN. Creators of decorative styles. Garden City, N. Y., Doubleday, Page and Co., 1917. 177p. illus.
Sources of early American styles.

38 ———. Comparative study of a group of early American doorways, part 2, porches. White pine series of architectural monographs. v. 7, no. 5. Oct. 1921. 16p. illus.
Covers 1790–1830.

39 ———. Comparative study of a group of early American windows. Monograph series. 16:197-224. 1930. illus.

40 ———. Roofs, the varieties commonly used in the architecture of the American colonies and the early Republic. Pencil points. 13:249-64. Apr. 1932. Monograph series. 18:166-80. illus.

41 (Early American details.) Many isolated photographs and measured drawings have appeared from time to time in various numbers of the *Architectural Forum, Architectural Record, Brickbuilder, Pencil Points*, etc.

42 EBERLEIN, HAROLD DONALDSON. The best use of brickwork. House and garden. 19:85-87, 118-19. Feb. 1911. illus.
Discussion of bond types.

43 FRARY, IHNA THAYER. Early American doorways. Richmond, Va., Garrett and Massie, 1937. 193p. illus.

44 Glossary of architectural and antiquarian terms. House beautiful. 55:676; 56:52, 144, 240, 356, 484, 600; 57:52, 148, 264, 396, 564, 602, 604. June 1924—May 1925. illus.

45 Guide to the material in the National archives. Washington, D. C., Government printing office, 1940. 303p.

46 GUILD, LURELLE VAN ARSDALE. Geography of American antiques. Garden City, N. Y., Doubleday, Page and Co., 1927. 283p. illus.
Includes some material on builders.

47 GUTH, ALEXANDER CARL. (The) H.A.B.S. Pencil points. 15:271-72. June 1934.
Experiences of the architects working for the Historic American Buildings Survey.

48 HALSEY, RICHARD TOWNLEY HAINES, AND CORNELIUS, CHARLES OVER. The American wing. Metropolitan museum of art. Bulletin. 19:251-65. Nov. 1924. illus.

49 ———. Handbook of the American wing. N. Y., Metropolitan museum of art, 1938. 295p. illus.
First edition 1924.

50 HOLLOWAY, EDWARD STRATTON. The practical book of American furniture and decoration—Colonial and Federal. Philadelphia, J. B. Lippincott Co., 1928. 191p. illus.
New edition 1937.

51 (Inventories of Federal, state, county, and city archives, church records, manuscript collections.) *See* Historical Records Survey, Works Progress Administration, for each state.

52 KIMBALL, SIDNEY FISKE. The preservation movement in America. American society of architectural historians. Journal. v. 1, no. 3-4. p. 15-17. July-Oct. 1941.
Considered historically.

53 KOCHER, A. LAWRENCE. Restoration of old buildings. Architectural record. 67:174-75. Feb. 1930. illus.

54 LOCKWOOD, ALICE G. B. Problems and responsibilities of restoration. Old time New England. 28:49-59. Oct. 1937. illus.

55 MERCER, HENRY CHAPMAN. Ancient carpenters' tools—in 8 parts. Old time New England. Part 1, 15:164-97, Apr. 1925; part 2, 16:19-52, July 1925; part 3, 16:75-97, Oct. 1925; part 4, 16:118-37, Jan. 1926; part 5, 16:175-98, Apr. 1926; part 6, 17:63-89, Oct. 1926; part 7, 17:179-91, Apr. 1927; part 8, 18:99-108, Jan. 1928. illus.

56 METROPOLITAN MUSEUM OF ART. Photographs of American architecture, painting, sculpture and decorative arts; a list of photographers and dealers from whom the museum has purchased photographs. N. Y., Metropolitan museum of art, 1937. 28p.

A list of dealers in photographs also appeared in Richard F. Bach, *Books on Colonial Architecture*, part 7—photographs. Architectural record. 42:283–84. Sept. 1917. *See also* 29.

57 NATIONAL PARK SERVICE. Historic American buildings survey: catalogue of the measured drawings and photographs of the survey in the Library of Congress, Mar. 1, 1941. Washington, D. C., Government printing office, 1941. 470p. illus.

58 PETERSON, CHARLES E. Our national archives of historic architecture. The Octagon. July 1936. 4p.

Origin in 1933 of Historic American Buildings Survey.

59 ———. A museum of American architecture. The Octagon. Nov. 1936. 5p.

Concerning a proposed museum in connection with the Jefferson National Expansion Memorial in St. Louis. *See also* 2560.

60 POWYS, A. R. Repair of ancient buildings. N. Y., Dutton Co., 1929. 208p. illus.

(Restored buildings.) For notices of individual buildings restored, see various numbers of the *Museum News* and *New York Times* index.

61 RUSK, WILLIAM SENER. What price progress? Art and archaeology. 33:195-205. 1932.

Covers destruction of old buildings in Boston, New York, and Philadelphia.

62 SONN, ALBERT H. Early American wrought iron. N. Y., Charles Scribner's Sons, 1928. 3v. 320 illus.

63 STAUFFER, DAVID McNEELY. American engravers upon copper and steel. N. Y., Grolier club of the City of New York, 1907. 2v. illus.

Lists views.

64 STOKES, I. N. PHELPS, AND HASKELL, DANIEL C. American historical prints, early views of American cities. . . . N. Y., New York public library, 1932. 327p. illus.

Covers 1497–1891.

65 TRAIN, ARTHUR, JR. The story of everyday things. N. Y., Harper and Bros., 1941. 428p. illus.

Discussion of many items associated with living and architecture.

66 UNITED STATES. LIBRARY OF CONGRESS. Division of manuscripts. List of manuscript collections in the Library of Congress to July 1931, by Curtis Wiswell Garrison. . . .Washington, D. C., Government printing office, 1932.
Reprinted from *Annual Report of American Historical Association,* for 1930, pp. 123–249.

67 ———. Manuscripts in public and private collections in the United States. Washington, D. C., Government printing office, 1924. 98p.

68 UNITED STATES. NATIONAL PARK SERVICE. Popular study series. No. 1, 1941.
Small pamphlets with some material on early architecture.

69 WATERMAN, THOMAS TALBOT. Architecture of the American Indians. American anthropologist. 29:210-30. Apr.-June 1927. illus.
Classifies types.

70 ———. North American Indian dwellings. Annual report of the Smithsonian institution for 1924. Pt. 1. 461-85. illus.
Identifies and locates types. Bibliography.

71 WILLIAMSON, SCOTT GRAHAM. American craftsman. N. Y., Crown publishers, *ca.* 1940. 239p. illus.

72 Wood precedent in American architecture; views and details of early American architecture from Maine and Georgia. American architect. 148:59-66. June 1936. illus.

DOMESTIC

73 ALLEN, EDWARD B. Early American wall paintings, 1710-1850. New Haven, Yale university press, 1926. 110p. illus.

74 American heritage: private homes of historic and antiquarian interest open to public inspection. Antiques. 37:281. June 1940.

75 ARCHITECTS' EMERGENCY COMMITTEE. Great Georgian houses of America. N. Y., Kalkhoff press, 1933-1937. 2v. illus.
W. T. Bottomley, chairman of the committee; R. T. H. Halsey, author of Preface. Vol. 2 published by Charles Scribner's Sons.

76 BOGAN, HELEN DEAN. Old pictorial wall papers. Country life in America. 32:48-50. July 1917. illus.

77 BROOKS, ARTHUR C. The old time house. Art world. 3:63-65. Oct. 1917. illus.

78 BROWN, FRANK CHOUTEAU. Examples of interior doors and doorways from the eighteenth and early nineteenth centuries. Pencil points. 21:245-60. Apr. 1940. Monograph series. 26:113-28. illus.
Ca. 1725—*ca.* 1820.

79 ———. Some examples of period windows with details of their interior treatment. Pencil points. 20:793-808. Dec. 1939. Monograph series. 25:81-96. illus.

Covers 1668–1820.

80 BUGBEE, BURTON ASHFORD. On fireplaces. Antiques. 20:349-53. Dec. 1931. illus.

Colonial and Classic revival.

81 BURTON, E. MILBY. Historic house restoration. Yearbook, Park and recreation service, United States Department of the Interior, National park service, 1941. p. 60-65. illus.

Discussion of historic house museums and illustrations of Tempe Wicke house, near Morristown, N. J.

82 CANDEE, MRS. HELEN CHURCHILL (HUNGERFORD). Decorative styles and periods in the home. N. Y., Frederick A. Stokes and Co., 1906. 298p. illus.

83 COLEMAN, LAURENCE VAIL. Collecting old houses. Scientific monthly. 41: 461-63. Nov. 1935.

84 ———. Historic house museums. Washington, D. C., The American association of museums, 1933. 187p. illus.

Contains sketch of the development of American building types and a directory.

85 CURTIS, E. R. Visit historic houses. Good housekeeping. 109:110-14. July 1939. illus.

86 DESMOND, HARRY WILLIAM, AND CROLY, HERBERT. Stately homes in America from Colonial times to the present day. N. Y., D. Appleton and Co., 1903. 532p. illus.

87 DOW, JOY WHEELER. The American renaissance, a review of domestic architecture. N. Y., William T. Comstock Co., 1904. 182p. illus.

88 EBERLEIN, HAROLD DONALDSON. Early Colonial types and their lessons to present-day house-builders. Arts and decoration. 11:224-25. Sept. 1919.

89 EVENTWORTH, IRVING B. Dependencies of the old-fashioned house. White pine series of architectural monographs. v. 8, no. 2. Apr. 1922. 14p. illus.

Covers 1790–1830.

90 FITZPATRICK, JOHN CLEMENT. Some historic houses: their builders and their places in history. N. Y., The Macmillan Co., 1939. 160p. illus.

91 FOWLER, ROBERT LUDLOW. Historic houses and revolutionary letters. Magazine of American history. 24:81-100. Aug. 1890. illus.

92 FRASER, ESTHER STEVENS. Some Colonial and early American decorative floors. Antiques. 19:296-301. Apr. 1931. illus.

93 GODDARD, PLINY EARLE. Native dwellings of North America. Natural history. 28:191-203. 1928. illus.
   Mostly Southwest and west coast.

94 HALSEY, RICHARD TOWNLEY HAINES. Wall papers and paint in the new
   American wing. Metropolitan museum of art. Bulletin. 19:235-39.
   Oct. 1924. illus.

95 ——— AND TOWER, ELIZABETH. The homes of our ancestors as shown in
   the American wing of the Metropolitan museum of art. N. Y., Doubleday,
   Page and Co., 1925. 320p. illus.
   Later edition, Garden City, N. Y., Garden City Publishing Co., 1937.

96 HEWITT, EDWARD SHEPARD. Mystery of early American doorways. Country
   life in America. 39:35-39. Apr. 1921. illus.
   Colonial and Early Republican.

97 Historic houses. Antiques. 40:38-42. July 1941.
   A list.

   (Houses, historically considered and in terms of preservation and restoration.)
   Much material may be found in the publications of the various state and
   county historical societies. Some titles from these sources are included
   here. County atlases of the late nineteenth century contain lithographed
   illustrations of individual houses. *See also* American scenic and historical
   preservation society: *Annual reports,* 1896-1928, *Bulletin,* 1929———;
   Museum News, 1924———.

98 HUNTER, GEORGE LELAND. Early American wall papers. Good furniture
   magazine. 19:175-79. July 1922. illus.

99 ISHAM, NORMAN MORRISON. Early American houses. Boston, The Walpole
   society, 1928. 61p. illus.

100 KEEFE, CHARLES S. (ed.). The American house. N. Y., U. P. C. Book Co.,
    1922. 24p. illus.

101 KETTELL, RUSSELL HAWES (ed.). Early American rooms, 1650-1858.
    Portland, Me., The Southworth-Anthoensen press, 1936. 200p. illus.

102 KIMBALL, SIDNEY FISKE. Domestic architecture of the American colonies and
    of the early Republic. N. Y., Charles Scribner's Sons, 1922. 314p. illus.

103 LAMB, MARTHA JOANNE READE (NASH) (ed.). The homes of American
    authors. N. Y., D. Appleton and Co., *ca.* 1879. 256p. illus.

104 LATHROP, ELISE L. Historic houses of early America. N. Y., R. M. McBride
    and Co., 1927. 464p. illus.
    Later edition, N. Y., Tudor Publishing Co., 1937.

105 McCLELLAND, NANCY VINCENT. Furnishing the Colonial and Federal house.
    Philadelphia, J. B. Lippincott Co., 1936. 164p. illus.

106 MASON, GEORGE CHAMPLIN. The old house altered. N. Y., G. P. Putnam's
Sons, 1878. 179p. illus.

107 MERCER, HENRY CHAPMAN. The dating of old houses. Bucks county, Pa.,
Bucks county historical society, Oct. 1923. 15p. illus.

Observations based upon notes taken upon an examination of about one hundred and
twenty old houses in Bucks County and Philadelphia, built in the eighteenth and early
nineteenth centuries.

108 ———. The dating of old houses. Old time New England. 14:170-90.
Apr. 1924. illus.

Concerns hardware and paneling.

109 ———. The origin of log houses in the United States. Bucks county historical society. Papers. 5:568-83. 1926. illus.

110 ———. The origin of log houses in the United States. Old time New England. 18:1-20, July 1927. 18:51-63, Oct. 1927. 19:28-43, July 1928.
illus.

Reprinted from 109 with additions.

111 NEWCOMB, REXFORD. Brief history of rural architecture in the United States.
President's conference on home building and home ownership, Washington, D. C., 1932. 7:35-56. 1932.

112 ———. The Colonial and Federal house. Philadelphia, J. B. Lippincott
Co., 1933. 174p. illus.

Reprinted 1938.

113 Nightingale house at Providence, Rhode Island; Dower house, West Chester,
Pa.; Bremo in Virginia; Rosedown, St. Francisville, La. Arts and decoration. 39:6-13. Oct. 1933. illus.

114 PEET, STEPHEN DENISON. Ethnic styles in American architecture. American
antiquarian. 24:19-34, 59-76. Jan. 1902.

115 ———. Houses and house life among the prehistoric races. American antiquarian. 10:333-57. 1888.

116 ——— (ed.). Village life and village architecture. American antiquarian
and oriental journal. 24:239-54. July and Aug. 1902. illus.

American Indian.

117 RAWSON, MRS. MARION NICHOLL. Old house picture book. N. Y., E. P.
Dutton and Co., 1941. 96p. illus.

118 ROBINSON, A. G. Snapshots of cottages, old and new. Architectural record.
36:545-50. Dec. 1914. illus.

119 ROBINSON, ETHEL FAY, AND ROBINSON, THOMAS P. Houses in America.
N. Y., Viking press, 1936. 239p. illus.

120 SCHELL, SHERRILL, AND OTHERS. Old American homes and their stories. Mentor. 11:21-36. June 1923. illus.

121 SHACKLETON, ELIZABETH. Old American houses, the framed house. Saturday evening post. 199:30-31, 46, 48. Mar. 12, 1927. illus.

122 SHERLOCK, CHELSA C. Homes of famous Americans. Des Moines, Ia., Meredith publications, 1926. 2v. illus.

123 SHURTLEFF, HAROLD ROBERT (completed by S. E. Morison). The log cabin myth: a study of the early dwellings of the English colonists in North America. Cambridge, Mass., Harvard university press, 1939. 215p. 33 illus.

> Devoted to proving that log cabin construction did not originate spontaneously in the United States, with special reference to documentary sources of information.

124 WHARTON, ANNE HOLLINGSWORTH. Salons Colonial and Republican. Philadelphia, J. B. Lippincott Co., 1900. 286p. illus.

PUBLIC

125 General government and state capitol buildings of the United States. Richmond, Va., Allen and Ginter, 1890. 13p.

126 GREER, WILLIAM ROYAL. Gems of American architecture. St. Paul, Minn., Brown and Bigelow, 1935. 56p. illus.

> Curiosa.

127 HAMMOND, JOHN MARTIN. Quaint and historic forts of North America. Philadelphia, J. B. Lippincott Co., 1915. 308p. illus.

128 KELLY, JOHN FREDERICK. Public buildings—part 1. Monograph series. 16:309-336. 1930. illus.

> Covers 1724–1820.

129 LATHROP, ELISE L. Early American inns and taverns. N. Y., Tudor Publishing Co., 1935. 365p. illus.

> N. Y., Robert M. McBride and Co., 1926.

(Observatories.) *See* 923.

130 (U. S. public buildings.) *See* U. S. Superintendent of documents, *Catalogue of Public Documents*, for numerous reports.

131 UNITED STATES TREASURY DEPARTMENT. History of public buildings under the control of the Treasury department. Washington, D. C., Government printing office, 1901. 648p. illus.

> Contains photographs and histories of post offices and other Federal buildings in all states.

132 WHITE, RICHARD GRANT. Old public buildings in America. Century magazine. 27:677-88. Mar. 1884. illus.

Religious

133 BACH, RICHARD FRANZ. Church planning in the United States—part 1.
Architectural record. 40:15-29. July 1916. illus.
Further numbers of this series give no reference to early churches.

134 BOURNE, FRANK A. Early American country churches. Architectural record.
45:188. Feb. 1919. illus.

135 DEXTER, HENRY MARTYN. Meeting houses considered historically and sug-
gestively. Boston, J. E. Tilton and Co., 1859. 29p. illus.

136 DOW, JOY WHEELER. American renaissance steeples—in two parts. Architects and builders magazine. Part 1, 6:122-31, Dec. 1904; part 2, 6:
162-72, Jan. 1905. illus.
Ca. 1750—*ca.* 1820.

137 EMBURY, AYMAR II. Early American churches. N. Y., Doubleday, Page and
Co., 1914. 189p. illus.

138 ———. Early American churches—in 11 parts. Architectural record. Part
1, 30:584-96, Dec. 1911, Bruton parish, Bennington, Guilford, and
Augusta; part 2, 31:57-66, Jan. 1912, St. Peter's, Philadelphia, Pa.;
Farmington, Conn.; Christ church, Hartford, Conn.; Old Swede's church,
Wilmington, Del.; part 3, 31:153-61, Feb. 1912, North and Center
churches in New Haven, Conn.; Christ church and Pohick meeting house
near Alexandria, Va.; part 4, 31:256-66, Mar. 1912, Ship meeting house,
Hingham, Mass.; St. Peter's, New Kent county; St. Luke's, Smithfield;
Old meetinghouse, Lancaster, Mass.; part 5, 31:417-24, Apr. 1912, Sag
Harbor, Long Island; Meetinghouse, Springfield, New Jersey; King's
Chapel, Boston, Mass.; St. Michael's, Charleston, S. C.; part 6, 31:547-
56, May 1912, Deerfield; Winston-Salem; Old South, Boston, Mass.;
Old Dutch, Tappan; part 7, 31:629-36, June 1912, Independent Pres-
byterian, Savannah, Ga.; First Presbyterian, Newark, N. J.; Trinity,
Newport, R. I.; Park street, Boston, Mass.; part 8, 32:81-88, July 1912,
St. Paul's, Edenton, N. C.; First Baptist, Providence, R. I.; Congrega-
tional, East Avon, Conn.; Christ church, Philadelphia; part 9, 32:159-68,
Aug. 1912, St. Paul's, St. Mark's, St. John's chapel, City of New York;
Trinity church, Newark, N. J.; part 10, 32:257-66, Sept. 1912, First
church, Springfield, Mass.; First church, Lenox, Mass.; Gloria Dei,
Philadelphia; Monumental church, Richmond, Va.; part 11, 32:453-63,
Nov. 1912, St. Phillip's church, Charleston, S. C.; First Reformed
church, Hackensack, N. J.; North Reformed church, Schvaalenburg,
N. J.; First Reformed church, New Brunswick, N. J. illus.

139 Historic churches of America: their romance and their history. . . . illustrated by etchings, photogravures and other reproductions. . . . with full
letter text by sixteen competent authorities, compiled from the chronicles,
legends and traditions of the most famous churches, meeting houses, mis-

sions and cathedrals in the United States and adjoining countries. Philadelphia, H. L. Everett, 1890. 160p. illus.

Publication in 20 parts extended through the years 1891-94.

140 RINES, EDWARD FRANCIS. Old historic churches of America, their romantic history and their traditions. N. Y., the Macmillan Co., 1936. 373p. illus.

141 SHINN, GEORGE WOLFE. King's handbook of notable Episcopal churches in the United States. Boston, Moses King Corporation, 1889. 286p. illus.

142 UPJOHN, HOBART B. Churches in eight American colonies, differing in elements of design. Monograph series. v. 15, no. 1, 1929. 28p. illus.

Covers 1736–1835 and South Carolina, North Carolina, New York, New Jersey, Connecticut, New Hampshire, Vermont, and Massachusetts.

143 WALLINGTON, MRS. NELLIE (URNER). Historic churches of America. N. Y., Duffield and Co., 1907. 259p. illus.

COLONIAL

GENERAL REFERENCES

144 ALLIS, MARGUERITE. English prelude. N. Y., G. P. Putnam's Sons, 1936. 323p. illus.

145 AMERICAN SOCIETY OF LANDSCAPE ARCHITECTS. Colonial gardens; the landscape architecture of George Washington's time. Washington, D. C., United States George Washington bicentennial commission, 1932. 72p. illus.

146 BANNISTER, WILLIAM P. The American spirit in Colonial architecture. Dutch boy painter. July 1926. p. 102-107. illus.

147 BLACKALL, CLARENCE H. Good and bad Colonial architecture. Architectural review. n. s. 1:1-5. Jan. 1899; 1:13-18. Feb. 1899. illus.

148 BOYD, JOHN TAYLOR, JR. Some examples of Colonial lettering. Architectural record. 40:588-90. Dec. 1916. illus.

149 BROOKS, W. F. Colonial architecture. American institute of architects. Journal. 16:175-79, 224-29. May-June 1928.

150 BUCKLER, RIGGIN, AND OTHERS. Early American architectural details. Brickbuilder, continued as Architectural forum. v. 24-27. Jan. 1915—Nov. 1917. illus. only.
Photographs and measured drawings. Mostly Colonial. New England, Maryland, and Virginia.

151 CAMPBELL, WILLIAM M. Some Colonial lettering. American architect. 122:478-81. Nov. 1922. illus.

152 CEWIN, OLOF Z. So-called Colonial architecture of the United States. American architect and building news. 48:63-65, 75-77, 87-88, 97-99, 107-108, 115-18, 130-31. May 18-June 29, 1895. illus.
Probably Olof Z. Cervin.

153 CHANDLER, JOSEPH EVERETT. Colonial architecture of Maryland, Pennsylvania and Virginia. Boston, Bates, Kimball and Guild Co., 1892. 55p. illus.

154 Characteristic details of the Georgian Colonial style. American architect. 124:557-62. Dec. 19, 1923. illus.

155 Colonial architecture and other early American arts. Pittsburgh, Pa., Carnegie library, 1926. 28p.

156 COONTZ, JOHN LEO. Light-houses of Colonial times. D. A. R. magazine. 62:685-89. Nov. 1928.

157 Dow, George Francis. Old English pattern books of hardware used in the building and cabinet makers' trades. Old time New England. 17:30-41. July 1926. illus.

158 Dyer, Walter Alden. Early American craftsmen: being a series of sketches of the lives of the more important personalities in early development of the industrial arts in America. N. Y., Century Co., 1915. 387p. illus.

159 Eberlein, Harold Donaldson. The architecture of Colonial America. Boston, Little, Brown and Co., 1927. 289p. illus.
First edition 1910.

160 ———. Decorative cast iron in Colonial America. Arts and decoration. 6:373-77. Aug. 1914. illus.

161 ———. Doors and shutters of the Colonial period. House and Garden. 35:20-21, 60. Feb. 1919. illus.

162 ———. Varieties of Colonial architecture. Craftsman. 30:91-94. Apr. 1916.
Reprinted from 159.

163 Eggers, Otto R. Early American architecture. American architect. 118:144, 176, 212, 250, 284, 320, 352, 380, 410, 442, 472, 500, 534, 576, 604, 642, 670, 704, 736, 788, 822, 860. Aug.-Dec. 1920; 119:14, 42, 68, 92, 120, 146, 174, 206, 244, 274, 364, 394, 426, 452, 488, 514, 554, 584, 612, 648. Jan.-June 1921; 120:12, 44, 80, 116, 152, 188, 224, 270, 346, 392, 428, 476. July-Dec. 1921; 121:12, 58. Jan. 1922. illus.
Also issued separately in portfolio by the *American Architect*, 1922.

164 Embury, Aymar II. The beauty of Colonial doorways. Country life in America. 18:647-50. Oct. 1910. illus.

165 Examples of old Colonial. Architectural record. 9:109-114. July 1899. illus.

166 Ewan, N. R. Early brickmaking in the Colonies. Camden, N. J., Camden historical society, 1938.

167 Georgian period; original details of measured drawings. N. Y., U. P. C. Book Co., 1922. 24p. illus.

168 Gilbert, F. Mason. Origin and characteristics of Colonial architecture. Western architect. 14:21-22. Sept. 1909. illus.

169 Griffin, Martin I. J. Bricks from England. American Catholic historical researches. n.s. 5:46-47. Jan. 1909.

170 Higgins, J. F. Colonial details. Architectural forum. 42:335-36. May 1925. illus.

171 Hopkins, Alfred. Fences and fence posts of Colonial times. White pine series of architectural monographs. v. 8, no. 6. Dec. 1922. 16p. illus.

172 HOWELLS, JOHN MEAD. Lost examples of Colonial architecture. N. Y., William Helburn, 1931. 142p. illus.

"Buildings that have disappeared or been so altered as to be denatured; public buildings, semi-public buildings, churches, cottages, country houses, town houses, interiors, details."

173 ISHAM, NORMAN MORRISON. Glossary of Colonial architectural terms. N. Y., Walpole society, 1939. 37p. illus.

174 JACKSON, JOSEPH. American Colonial architecture, its origin and development. Philadelphia, David McKay Co., 1924. 228p. illus.

First printed serially in the magazine, *Building*.

175 JONES, ALVIN LINCOLN. Under Colonial roofs. . . . Boston, Charles B. Webster, 1894. 237p.

176 KIMBALL, SIDNEY FISKE. The study of Colonial architecture. Architectural review. 6:28-29, 37-38, 76. Feb.-May 1918.

177 KOCHER, A. LAWRENCE. Color in early American architecture. Architectural record. 64:278-90. Oct. 1928.

178 LITCHFIELD, ELECTUS D. Colonial fences. Country life in America. 31:61-64. Mar. 1917. illus.

179 MASON, GEORGE CHAMPLIN, JR. Colonial architecture, a preliminary report presented to the annual convention of the American institute of architects. American architect and building news. 10:71-74, Aug. 13, 1881; 10:83-85, Aug. 20, 1881. illus.

180 ———. Environment the basis of Colonial architecture. Philadelphia, printed by the order of the society, 1906. 24p. illus.

Address before the Society of Colonial Wars in the Commonwealth of Pennsylvania.

181 MIDDLETON, G. A. T. English Georgian architecture, the sources of the American Colonial style. Architectural record. 9:97-108. Oct. 1899. illus.

182 NUTTING, WALLACE. Early American hardware. Antiques. 4:78-81. Aug. 1923. illus.

183 POLLEY, G. HENRY. Architecture, interiors and furniture of the American colonies during the eighteenth century. Boston, G. H. Polley and Co., 1914. illus.

184 POPE, JOHN RUSSELL. Some Colonial doorways. Country life in America. 48:48-49. Oct. 1925. illus. only.

184A PRIME, ALFRED COXE (comp.). The arts and crafts in Philadelphia, Maryland and South Carolina, 1721-1785. Boston, The Walpole Society, 1929. 323p. illus.

Advertisements from newspapers. Some architects included.

185 ROSE, CHRISTINA LIVINGSTON. An unknown Colonial type. Country life in
America. 32:67-69. June 1917. illus.

186 ROWE, HENRY W. Reflections gleaned from a Colonial scrapbook. American
architect. 109:202-207. March 1916. illus.

187 SCHUYLER, MONTGOMERY. Education of a Colonial carpenter. Architectural record. 19:227-29. Mar. 1906. illus.
Carpenters as designers, and builders' handbooks.

188 ———. A history of old Colonial architecture. Architectural record. 4:312-
66. Jan.-Mar. 1895. illus.
Includes Early Republican work.

189 SODERHOLTZ, ERIC ELLIS. Colonial architecture and furniture. Boston, G. H.
Polley and Co., 1895. 66p. illus.

190 TELLER, MYRON S. Early Colonial hand forged iron work. Architectural
record. 57:395-416. May 1925. illus.

191 UPJOHN, RICHARD M. Colonial architecture of New York and the New
England states. Proceedings of the third annual convention of the American institute of architects. Nov. 16, 17, 1869. p. 47-51.

192 WALLIS, FRANK EDWIN. American architecture, decoration and furniture of
the eighteenth century. N. Y., Paul Wenzel, 1895. 53p. illus.

193 ———. The case for Colonial: what and why is Colonial architecture.
House and garden. 16:188-92. Dec. 1909. illus.

194 ———. Old Colonial architecture and furniture. Boston, G. H. Polley and
Co., 1888. 66p. illus.

195 WERTZ, SYLVIA STARR, and WERTZ, JOSEPH B. What and why the Palladian
window. Antiques. 27:219-22. June 1935. illus.

DOMESTIC

196 ALLEN, EDWARD B. Tudor houses of Colonial days. International studio.
77:345-48. July 1923. illus.
Covers Bacon's castle, Province house, Boston, and houses near Charleston, South
Carolina.

197 ARCHER, GLEASON L. How the Pilgrims built their houses. Americana.
39:147-55. 1936.

198 BROWN, FRANK CHOUTEAU. Some examples of corner cupboards generally of
early design and construction. Pencil points. 21:795-810. Dec. 1940.
Monograph series. 26:177-92. illus.
Covers 1686–1770, mostly from Massachusetts.

199 CHANDLER, JOSEPH EVERETT. The Colonial house. N. Y., Robert McBride
and Co., 1916. 341p. illus.

200 Cousins, Frank. Footscrapers of a bygone day. Country life in America. 24:58. Oct. 1913. illus.

201 The doorway inside the Colonial house. Country life in America. 31:34-35. Dec. 1916. illus.
Massachusetts and Maryland ca.1800.

202 Dow, Joy Wheeler. Colonial houses of the earliest type. American architect. 115:701-706. May 1918. illus.

203 Drake, Samuel Adams. Our Colonial homes. Boston, Lothrop, Lee and Shepherd, 1894. 211p. illus.

204 Footscrapers from Colonial houses. House and garden. 40:49. Aug. 1921. illus.

205 Glenn, Thomas Allen. Some Colonial mansions and those who lived in them. Philadelphia, H. T. Coates and Co., 1899, 1900. 2v. 503p. illus.

206 Hamlin, A. D. F. The genesis of the American country house. Architectural record. 42:292-99. Oct. 1917.

207 Hammond, John Martin. Colonial mansions of Maryland and Delaware. Philadelphia, J. B. Lippincott Co., 1914. 304p. illus.

208 Harland, Marion (pseud. of Mrs. M. V. Hawes Terhune). More Colonial homesteads and their stories. N. Y., G. P. Putnam's Sons, 1899. 449p. illus.

209 ———. Some Colonial homesteads and their stories. N. Y., G. P. Putnam's Sons, 1897. 511p. illus.

210 Hewitt, Edward Shepard. The mystery of early American doorways. Country life in America. 39:35-39. Apr. 1921.

211 Hollister, Paul Merrick. Famous Colonial houses. Philadelphia, David McKay Co., 1921. 170p. illus.

212 Holtzoper, E. C. Doors and doorways. Country life in America. 6:135-39. June 1904. illus.
Georgian.

213 Houston, Frank. Salvage for town betterment. House and garden. 49:88-89. Jan. 1926. illus.
Philipse manor house, Yonkers, New York; home of Chief Justice Marshall, Richmond, Virginia; Stenton, Germantown, Pennsylvania; Capen house, Topsfield, Massachusetts.

214 McClelland, Ada A. Some D. A. R. homes. D. A. R. magazine. 50:147-57. Mar. 1917.

215 Master detail series; the Georgian Colonial house. Architectural forum. 60:49-64. Jan. 1934. illus.

216 MILLAR, DONALD. Measured drawings of some Colonial and Georgian houses. N. Y., Architectural Book Publishing Co., 1916, 1930. 3v. illus.

217 NASH, GEORGE W. Old chimney cupboards. Architectural record. 41:287-88. Mar. 1917. illus.

218 NORTHEND, MARY HARROD. Colonial homes and their furnishings. Boston, Little, Brown and Co., 1912. 252p. illus.

219 OAKLEY, IMOGENE B. Six historic homesteads. Philadelphia, University of Pennsylvania Press, 1936. 191p. illus.

Moffatt-Ladd house, Portsmouth, New Hampshire; Quincy mansion, Braintree, Massachusetts; Webb house, Wethersfield, Connecticut; Jumel house, New York; Stenton, Philadelphia; Mount Clare, Baltimore.

220 PAINT MANUFACTURERS' ASSOCIATION OF THE UNITED STATES. EDUCATIONAL BUREAU. A photographic study of frame dwellings of Colonial times. Washington, D. C., Judd and Detweiler, 1915. 52 illus.

221 PINDAR, PETER AUGUSTUS (pseud.). Small Colonial houses. Monograph series. v. 17, no. 6. 23p. 1931.

Covers 1730–1803.

222 Preserving old houses. House and garden. 51:106-107, 162, 164. Jan. 1927. illus.

Dyckman house, New York City; Abraham Browne house, Watertown, Massachusetts; Scotch Boardman house, Saugus, Massachusetts; Samuel Fowler house, Danvers, Massachusetts. Comment on restoration by various societies.

223 RILEY, PHILIP, AND COUSINS, FRANK. Landscape wall paper, famous old wall papers in famous old houses. House beautiful. 39:148-49. Apr. 1916. illus.

224 ROBINSON, JANE TELLER. Kitchen of the Colonial house. House and garden. 46:78-79, 90. Aug. 1924. illus.

225 ROBINSON, THOMAS P. The study of Colonial houses. House beautiful. 48:85-88. Aug. 1920. illus.

226 SEWELL, ANNE. Wall papers of Colonial times. American homes and gardens. 11:204-208. June 1914. illus.

227 SYMONDS, R. W. Georgian porticos in an American collection. International studio. 99:15-18. July 1931.

Some English examples.

228 WALLIS, FRANK E. The Colonial renaissance—houses of the middle and southern colonies. White pine series of architectural monographs. v. 2, no. 1. Feb. 1916. 14p. illus.

Covers 1707–1813, in Maryland and Virginia.

RELIGIOUS

229 ALVORD, JAMES CHURCH. Colonial churches of America. Art world. 2:286-89. June 1917.

230 GARDNER, G. R. Some remodeled Colonial churches. American architect and building news. 76:37-38. May 3, 1902. illus.

INTERIORS

231 ACKERMAN, PHYLLIS. Wallpapers in early American homes; engaging facts about the first pictorial wall-coverings in this country. Arts and decoration. 17:100-101, 138, 140. June 1922.
Primarily New England.

232 ALLEN, EDWARD B. Ye old picture wallpapers. House beautiful. 49:369-72, 412. May 1921.

233 BRAZER, ESTHER STEVENS. Early American decorations; a comprehensive treatise. Springfield, Mass., Pond-Ekberg Co., 1940. 273p. illus.
Revealing the technique involved in the art of early American decoration of furniture, walls, tinware, etc.; reference book for the student of early design and restoration.

234 EBERLEIN, HAROLD DONALDSON. What early America had on its walls. International studio. 38:52-56. Sept. 1927.
Pictorial and other decoration.

235 ELWELL, NEWTON W. Colonial furniture and interiors. Boston, G. H. Polley and Co., 1896. 69p. illus.

236 FRENCH, LEIGH, JR. Colonial interiors; photographs and measured drawings of the Colonial and early Federal periods. N. Y., William Helburn, 1923. 125 illus.
This is *Colonial Interiors*, first series. *See also* 258, 1650.

237 HAYWARD, ARTHUR H. Colonial lighting. Boston, B. J. Brimmer and Co., 1923. 168p. illus.
Also, Boston, Little, Brown and Company, 1927.

238 LANGDON, WILLIAM CHAUNCEY. Everyday things in American life (1607-1776). N. Y., Charles Scribner's Sons, 1937. 353p. illus.
Social life and customs. *See also* 270.

239 NUTTING, WALLACE. Early American ironwork. Saugus, Mass., Wallace Nutting, Inc., 1919. 24p. illus.
Fireplace furniture and other hardware.

240 PAUL, M. REA. Decorative painting in Colonial times. Dutch boy painter, July 1926. p. 110-14. illus.

241 ———, AND BOWMAN, K. J. Color in Colonial times. N. Y., Department of research and decoration of the National Lead Co., 111 Broadway, N. Y. C. n.d.

242 TUDOR, EVAN J. Georgian fireplaces and interior wall treatments. Arts and decoration. 34:42-46. Nov. 1930. illus.

Examples from Pennsylvania museum collections.

EARLY REPUBLICAN

GENERAL REFERENCES

243 (American architecture. Contemporary discussion.) North American review.
43:356-84. Oct. 1836.
Review (*sic*) of James Gallier's *The American Builder's General Price Book and Estimator*. Includes discussion of sacred, sepulchral, and domestic architecture in Philadelphia, New York, and Boston. Reprinted in 255A.

244-251 (American architecture. Contemporary discussion.) American magazine of knowledge. 2:528. Aug. 1836; American museum. 8:147. Oct. 1790; American repertory of arts and science. 1:106-14. Mar. 1840; Brother Jonathan. 5:31-33. May 13, 1843, 61-62. May 20, 1843, 91-92, May 27, 1843, 121-22. June 3, 1843, 151-52. June 10, 1843, 181-82. June 17, 1843, 211-12. June 24, 1843, 241-44. July 1, 1843, 271-74. July 8, 1843, 301-303. July 15, 1843, 331-32. July 22, 1843, 421-22. Aug. 12, 1843; Gazette of the United States. v. 5, May 12, 1794. Literary magazine and American register, v. 1, no. 6:405-409. Mar. 1804; New York mirror. 8:110. Oct. 9, 1830; Register of Pennsylvania. 2:271-72. Nov. 8, 1828.

252 (Architecture and democracy. Contemporary discussion.) Harbinger. 8:106. Feb. 3, 1849.

253 CAEMMERER, HANS PAUL. The influence of classical art on the architecture of the United States. Doctoral dissertation, American university, 1938.

254 Church architecture in the United States. Literary world. 3:733, 920-21. Oct. 14, Dec. 9, 1848.

255 CLARK, T. C. Architects and architecture. Christian examiner and religious miscellany. 49:251-77. Sept. 1850.

255A CLEVELAND, HENRY R. A selection from his writings. Boston, The Author, 1844. 384p.
Contains reprint of 243.

256 (College architecture. Contemporary criticism.) Yale literary magazine. 18:240-44. May 1853.

257 CORNELIUS, CHARLES OVER. Some early American doorways. Old time New England. 18:99-108. Jan. 1928. illus.
Doorways owned by the Metropolitan Museum, 1792–*ca.* 1820.

258 EBERLEIN, HAROLD DONALDSON, AND HUBBARD, CORTLANDT VAN DYKE. Colonial interiors, Federal and Greek revival. N. Y., William Helburn, 1938. 84p. illus.
This is *Colonial Interiors*, third series. Covers Delaware, Maryland, New Hampshire, New Jersey, New York, and Pennsylvania. *See also* 236, 1650.

259 Ecclesiastical architecture. Yale literary magazine. 11:65-72. Dec. 1845.

> Difference in structure of houses of worship of different peoples and how these architectural works are somewhat an index of the character of the people who build them.

260 FALLON, JOHN T. Domestic architecture of the early nineteenth century. American architecture. 110:139-44. Sept. 6, 1916.

261 GARDINER, FANNY HALE. The octagon house. Country life in America. 23:79-80. Mar. 1913. illus.

> Orson Squire Fowler houses from several states.

262 GIEDION, SIGFRIED. Space, time and architecture, the growth of a new tradition. Cambridge, Mass., Harvard University press, 1941. 601p. illus.

> Some new material on nineteenth century American architecture.

263 GILLET, LOUIS. L'Architecture aux États-Unis et l'influence française. France-Amérique. 4e année:77-80, 154-57, 240-44, 288-91. Feb., May 1913.

263A (GILMAN, ARTHUR DELEVAN). Architecture in the United States. North American review. 58:436-80. April 1844.

> Critical discussion, primarily of public buildings in Boston, Massachusetts.

264 GREENOUGH, HORATIO. American architecture. N. Y., G. P. Putnam and Co., 1852. 222p.

> In Greenough, Horatio, *Travels, Observations and Experiences of a Yankee Stone-cutter*, pt. 1, by Horace Bender (pseud.), and in the *North American Review* in 1843. *See also* 2773 and *Southern Literary Messenger*. 19:513–17. Aug. 1853; *Democratic Review*. 13:206–10. 1843.

265 HOLLOWAY, EDWARD STRATTON. Interior architecture of the Federal era. House and garden. 52:104-106. Oct. 1927.

266 The introduction of iron buildings. Debow's review. 20:641-42. May 1856.

> On the proposed use of iron as a building material.

267 JACKSON, JOSEPH. The development of American architecture, 1783-1830. Philadelphia, David McKay and Co., 1926. 230p. illus.

268 JARVES, JAMES JACKSON. Art hints. N. Y., Harper and Brothers, 1855. 398p.

> Architecture, sculpture, and painting.

269 ———. The art idea. N. Y., Hurd and Houghton, 1864. 381p.

> Chapters 17, 18 contain comments on American architecture. Other editions 1865–1877. *See* 2773.

270 LANGDON, WILLIAM CHAUNCEY. Everyday things in American life. v. 2 (1776-1876). N. Y., Charles Scribner's Sons, 1941. 398p. illus.

> *See also* 238.

271 MAJOR, HOWARD. Return of cast iron. Country life. 54:69-70. Oct. 1928. illus.

272 METCALF, FRANK J. Octagon houses of Washington and elsewhere. Columbia historical society. Records. 26:91-105. 1924.

273 New article of commerce. New Yorker. 1:381. Sept. 3, 1836.
Houses to be floated from Pennsylvania to Mississippi.

274 Origin of classic place names in central New York. N. Y. state historical association. Journal. 7:155-68. July 1926.

275 PRATT, RICHARD H. From Georgian to Victorian. House and garden. 51:120-21, 142, 146, 196. Apr. 1927. illus.
Includes discussion of Asher Benjamin and Minard Lafever.

276 RANKIN, ROBERT. American architecture. Yale literary magazine. 10:411-14. Aug. 1845.
Townsend prize essay. Short history of the art in the old world and how it is developing in the United States.

277 ROOS, FRANK JOHN, JR. The Egyptian style; notes on our early American taste. Magazine of art. 33:218-23, 255-56. Apr. 1940. illus.

278 RUSK, WILLIAM SENER. Egyptian echoes in American architecture. Americana. 28:295-98. 1934.

279 SWAN, NORMA LIPPINCOTT. Old carved mantel-pieces. Country life in America. 47:50-51. Apr. 1925. illus. only.

280 (THOMPSON, JOHN W.) Cast iron buildings: their construction and advantages. N. Y., J. W. Harrison printer, 1856. 16p. illus.
Refers to an iron building in New York City by James Bogardus.

281 TUTHILL, LOUISA CAROLINE (HUGGINS). History of architecture from the earliest times: its present condition in Europe and the United States. Philadelphia, Lindsay and Balkiston, 1848. 426p. illus.

GREEK REVIVAL

282 BIDDLE, EDWARD. Nicholas Biddle. Numismatic and antiquarian society of Philadelphia. Proceedings. v. 27, 1916.

283 GOODYEAR, W. H. Greek architecture in the United States. Chautauquan. 16:3-11, 131-37, 259-67. 1892. illus.

284 HAMLIN, TALBOT F. The Greek revival in America and some of its critics. Art bulletin. 24:244-58. Sept. 1942.

285 Hints to American architects. National register. 2:209-210. Nov. 30, 1816.
On the nobleness of Grecian architecture, tracing its origin and development.

286 MAJOR, HOWARD. Domestic architecture in the early American Republic—the Greek revival. Philadelphia, J. B. Lippincott Co., 1926. 236p. illus.

287 ———. Greek influence on American homes. Country life in America. 47:41-43. Feb. 1925. illus.

288 ————. The Greek revival: the American national expression. Architectural forum. 40:45-51. Feb. 1924. illus.

289 PRATT, RICHARD H. How the Greek revival began. House and garden. 52:88-89. Aug. 1927. illus.

290 SCHUYLER, MONTGOMERY. The old Greek revival—in four parts. American architect. Part 1, 98:121-26, 128. Oct. 12, 1910; part 2, 98:201-204, 206-208. Dec. 21, 1910; part 3, 99:81-84, 86-87. Mar. 1, 1911; part 4, 99:161-66, 168. May 3, 1911. illus.
Discussion of Latrobe, Mills, Strickland, and others.

GOTHIC AND OTHER REVIVALS

291 ADDISON, AGNES ELEANOR. Romanticism and the Gothic revival. N. Y., R. R. Smith, 1938. 187p. illus.
A study of the rise and decline of the romantic movement in Europe and America and its effect on comptemporary literature and architecture. Issued also as Ph.D. thesis, University of Pennsylvania, 1938.

292 CLARK, KENNNETH. The Gothic revival, an essay in the history of good taste. N. Y., Charles Scribner's Sons, 1929. 308p. illus.
Background for American Gothic.

(Gothic revival buildings, including Italian villas, etc.) *See* Godey's lady's book, Peterson's magazine, and similar publications, *ca.*1845—*ca.*1870. *See also* entries under A. J. Downing, Samuel Sloan, Robert Mills, Richard Upjohn, etc., 1288 and 2773.

293 KIENITZ, JOHN F. The generations of the 1850's, 1860's and 1870's in the fine arts of the United States in relation to parallel phases of American culture. Doctoral dissertation, University of Wisconsin, 1938.

294 Steamboat Gothic. Minneapolis institute. Bulletin. 20:161. Nov. 28, 1931.

NEW ENGLAND

(Connecticut, Maine, Massachusetts, New Hampshire, Rhode Island, Vermont)

GENERAL REFERENCES *(see also* 150)

295 APPLETON, WILLIAM SUMNER. Destruction and preservation of old New England buildings. Art and archaeology. 8:131-84. May-June 1919. illus.

296 ———. The society for the preservation of New England antiquities and its work. American society of architectural historians. Journal. v. 1, no. 3-4. p. 19-20. July-Oct. 1941.

297 BROWN, FRANK CHOUTEAU. Architecture 1620-1750. House and garden. 75:35, 64. June 1939. illus.

298 ———. Architecture 1750-1850. House and garden. 75:40-41. June 1939. illus.

299 ———. Early brickwork in New England. Pencil points. 15:165-80. Apr. 1934. Monograph series. 20:113-28. illus.
Covers 1668–1763 in and around Boston.

300 ———. Some New England paneled room ends from the seventeenth and early eighteenth centuries. Pencil points. 21:379-94. June 1940. Monograph series. 26:129-44. illus.

301 ———. Some interior arched openings found in northeastern Colonial work. Pencil points. 21:651-66. Oct. 1940. Monograph series. 26:161-76. illus.
Covers 1660–1818.

302 BYNE, ARTHUR G. Some century-old doorways in rural New England. Architectural record. 30:574-83. Dec. 1911. illus. only.

303 CHAMBERLAIN, NATHAN HENRY. A paper on New England architecture. Boston, Crosby, Nichols and Co., 1858. 30p.
Read before the New England Historic Genealogical Society, September 4, 1858. Hitchcock suggests that this pamphlet is probably the first separate publication on Colonial architecture.

304 CHAMBERLAIN, SAMUEL. New England doorways. N. Y., Hastings house, 1939. 101p. illus.

305 CORSE, MURRAY PINCHOT. Colonial architecture of New England. Architecture. 47:62-63. Apr. 1923. illus. only.

306 ———. Puritan architecture. Architecture. 45:1-5, 43-46. Jan.-Feb. 1922.

307 Dow, George Francis. Arts and crafts in New England, 1704-75. Topsfield, Mass., Wayside press, 1927. 326p. illus.
Gleanings from Boston newspapers relating to printing, engraving, silversmiths,
pewterers, furniture, pottery, old houses, costumes, trades and occupations, etc.

308 Drake, Samuel Adams. Nooks and corners of the New England Coast.
N. Y., Harper and Brothers, ca.1875. 459p. illus.

309 Federal Writers' Project. Here's New England! Boston, Houghton,
Mifflin Co., 1939. 122p. illus.

310 Forbes, Allen. Towns of New England and old England. N. Y., Tudor
Publishing Co., 1936. illus.

311 Gardner, George Clarence. Massachusetts Bay influence on Connecticut
Valley Colonial. White pine series of architectural monographs. v. 11, no.
1. 1925. 17p. illus.
Covers ca.1700–1800.

312 Graham, Benjamin. Some New England staircases—1670-1770. Pencil
points. 14:445-60. Oct. 1933. Monograph series. 19:65-80. illus.

313 Grandgent, Louis. Colonial doorways. House beautiful. 49:476-77. June
1921; 50:102-103, 200-201. illus.
Unlabeled illustrations.

314 Hamlin, Talbot Faulkner. Variety and harmony. Pencil points. 22:83-
88. Feb. 1941. illus.
Examples from New England.

315 Haskell, Arthur C. Early interior doorways in New England—part 1.
Pencil points. 13:680-94. Oct. 1932. Monograph series. 18:230-44.
illus.
Covers 1652–1768.

316 Hipkiss, Edwin J. Early eighteenth century American interiors. Architectural forum. 38:35-40. Jan. 1923. illus.

317 ———. Interior woodwork in New England during the seventeenth and
eighteenth centuries. White pine series of architectural monographs.
v. 11, no. 2. 1925. 15p. illus.
Mostly Connecticut.

318 Hooper, Marion, and Crane, Charles Edward. Life along the Connecticut River. Brattleboro, Vt., Stephen Daye press, 1939. 120p. illus.

319 Howe, Oliver H. Early town planning in New England. American architect. 118:464-69. Oct. 13, 1920. illus.

320 Howells, John Mead. Architectural heritage of the Merrimack. N. Y.,
Architectural Book Publishing Co., 1941. 248p. illus.

321 KILHAM, WALTER H. Colonial brickwork of New England. Brickbuilder. 10:244-48; 11:3-6, 25-28. Dec. 1901—Feb. 1902. illus.

322 ———. Colonial gateways and fences in New England. House and garden. 7:225-32. Apr. 1905. illus.

323 KINGMAN, RALPH CLARKE. New England Georgian architecture. N. Y., Architectural Book Publishing Co., 1913. illus.

324 LAWRENCE, ROBERT MEANS. New England Colonial life. Cambridge, Mass., Cosmos press, 1927. 276p. illus.

325 NASH, SUSAN HIGGINSON. New England decoration—the development of interior design—1620-1850. House and garden. 75:30-34. June 1939. illus.

(New England.). For miscellaneous titles on New England see various issues of the *New England Quarterly.*

326 (New England number.). House and garden. v. 75. June 1939. illus.
Major articles are included elsewhere. Also includes brief references to particular houses.

327 NICHOLS, ARTHUR HOWARD. The bells of Paul and Joseph W. Revere. Boston, 1911. 40p. illus.
Reprinted from *Historical Collections of Essex Institute,* Salem, Massachusetts.

328 PHILLIPS, J. H. Early American interiors. Architectural review. n. s. 8:105-109, 131-37, 163-70. Apr.-June, 1919. illus.
Colonial, mostly New England.

329 POWELL, LYMAN P. (ed.). Historic towns of New England. N. Y., G. P. Putnam's Sons, 1898. 599p. illus.

330 PRESSEY, PARK. Preserving the landmarks. House beautiful. 36:97-100. Sept. 1914. illus.
Covers 1650–1808.

331 ROBERTS, GEORGE S. Historic towns of Connecticut River valley. Schenectady, N. Y., Robson and Adee, 1906. 494p. illus.

332 ROBINSON, ALBERT GARDNER. Old New England doorways. N. Y., Charles Scribner's Sons, 1919. 21p. illus.

333 SAYLOR, HENRY H. Early American style of New England. House and garden. 67:46-47, 78, 80-81, 92. Apr. 1935. illus.

334 Some old New England doorways, records of the craftsmanship of Colonial days. Craftsman. 22:216-19. May 1912.

335 Synopsis of New England architecture and decoration from 1620-1850. House and garden. 75:24-25. June 1939.

336 WAILES, REX. Notes on some windmills in New England. Old time New England. 21:99-128. Jan. 1931. illus.

336A WARING, JANET. Early American stencils on walls and furniture. N. Y., W. R. Scott, 1937. 148p. illus.

337 WHIPPLE, J. RAYNER. Old New England weather vanes. Old time New England. 31:45-56. Oct. 1940. illus.

DOMESTIC (*see also* 231)

338 ALLEN, EDWARD B. Colonial porticoes of New England. House beautiful. 48:102-103. Aug. 1920. illus.
Marblehead and Salem.

339 ———. Some old New England frescoes. Old time New England. 25:78-84. Jan. 1935. illus.
Weymouth, Massachusetts.

340 BARTLETT, STUART. Garrison houses along the New England frontier. Pencil points. 14:253-68. June 1933. Monograph series. 19:33-48. illus.
Covers 1640–1750.

341 BRIGGS, MARTIN S. Homes of the pilgrim fathers in England and America (1620-1685). London, Oxford university press, 1932. 211p. illus.

342 BROWN, FRANK CHOUTEAU. New England Colonial houses of the early portion of the eighteenth century. White pine series of architectural monographs. v. 1, no. 2. 15p. 1915. illus.

343 ———. Three-story Colonial houses of New England. White pine series of architectural monographs. v. 3, no. 1. 14p. Feb. 1917. illus.
Covers 1760–1809.

344 CHAMBERLAIN, SAMUEL. A small house in the sun; the visage of rural New England. N. Y., Hastings house, 1936. 96p. illus.

345 ———. Beyond New England thresholds. N. Y., Hastings house, 1938. 95p. illus.

346 ———. Open house in New England. Brattleboro, Vt., Stephen Daye press, 1937. 191p. illus.

347 CORNER, JAMES M., AND SODERHOLTZ, ERIC ELLIS. Examples of domestic Colonial architecture in New England. Boston, The Boston architectural club, 1892. 50 illus.
First edition 1891.

348 COUSINS, FRANK. Stairways of old New England. Country life in America. 26:66-67. Oct. 1914. illus.

349 COVELL, ALWYN T. Old Chatham and neighboring dwellings south of the Berkshires. White pine series of architectural monographs. v. 5, no. 5. Oct. 1919. 14p. illus.
New York and Connecticut.

350 CRAWFORD, MARY CAROLINE. The romance of old New England rooftrees. Boston, L. C. Page and Co., 1903. 390p. illus.

351 DERBY, RICHARD B. Early houses of the Connecticut Valley. White pine series of architectural monographs. v. 2, no. 3. June 1916. 14p. illus.
Covers 1660–1800. Frary house and Williams house, Deerfield, Massachusetts. Wheeler house, Orford, New Hampshire (1800), credited to Bulfinch.

352 DOW, GEORGE FRANCIS. Domestic life in New England in the seventeenth century. Topsfield, Mass., Perkins press, 1925. 48p. illus.
A lecture at the opening of the American wing of the Metropolitan Museum of Art.

353 ——. Houses of the first settlers in New England. Antiques. 18:127-30. Aug. 1930. illus.

354 ERSKINE, RALPH C. Architectural sermons in early American homes. Arts and decoration. 18:32-33. Feb. 1923. illus.

355 HIPKISS, EDWIN J.; KELLY, J. FREDERICK; REAGAN, OLIVER; FOSTER, WILLIAM D.; WELSH, LEWIS E. Early American domestic architecture. Architectural forum. 32:53-60. Feb. 1920. Wentworth-Gardner house, Portsmouth, N. H.; 33: 101-108. Sept. 1920. Wellington house near Waltham, Mass.; 33:175-82. Nov. 1920. Warner house near Chester, Conn.; 33:219-26. Dec. 1920. Jessup house, Westport, Conn.; 34:47-54. Feb. 1921. Sir William Johnson house, Fort Johnson, N. Y. illus.

356 Historic houses in New England open to the public. House and garden. 76:65. June 1939.

(Houses, New England.) *Old Time New England* has numerous short notes on New England houses, not listed here.

357 HOWE, LOIS L., AND FULLER, CONSTANCE. Details from old New England houses. N. Y., Architectural book publishing Co., 1913. 52p. illus.

358 HUNTER, WALKER C. Various types of old Colonial knockers found on houses in New England. House beautiful. 39:12. Apr. 1916. illus.

359 LITTLE, ARTHUR. Early New England interiors. . . . Salem, Marblehead, Portsmouth and Kittery. . . . Boston, A. Williams and Co., 1878. 45p. illus.

360 MACDONALD, ALBERT J. Colonial brick houses of New England. Boston, Rogers and Manson Co., 1917. 55p. illus.

361 MIXER, KNOWLTON. Development of the New England homestead. House beautiful. 62:245-46, 393-95. Sept.-Oct. 1927. illus.

362 ———. Old houses of New England. N. Y., the Macmillan Co., 1927. 346p. illus.

363 NORTHEND, MARY HARROD. Historic homes of New England. Boston, Little, Brown and Co., 1914. 274p. illus.

364 ———. Old time latches and knockers. American homes and gardens. 5:466-68. Dec. 1908. illus.

365 ———. Old time wall papers. American homes and gardens. 2:403-405. June 1906. illus.

366 PEABODY, R. S. Georgian houses of New England. American architect and building news. 2:338-39. Oct. 20, 1877; 3:54-55. Feb. 16, 1878. illus.
First article signed, "Georgian."

367 ROBIE, VIRGINIA. A Colonial pilgrimage. House beautiful. 15:78-83, 171-75, 315-17. Jan.-Apr. 1904; 16:13-15. Aug. 1904. illus.
Part 1—Portsmouth, New Hampshire, and Kittery, Maine; part 2—Exeter, New Hampshire.

368 ROBINSON, ALBERT G. Old New England houses. N. Y., Charles Scribner's Sons, 1920. 127p. illus.

369 SANBORN, KATE. Old time wall papers and decorations. House beautiful. 12:304-308. Oct. 1902. illus.

370 SMITH, CHARLES LYMAN. Colonial doorways from a layman's standpoint. American architect. 121:204-209. Mar. 1922. illus.
Primarily Massachusetts.

371 TEMPLE, GRACE LINCOLN. Hunting old-time wall-papers. American magazine of art. 11:381-90. Sept. 1920. illus.

372 WATERMAN, THOMAS TILESTON. Two eighteenth century panelled rooms, Connecticut and Massachusetts. Architecture. 50:pl. 153. Oct. 1924. illus.
East chamber, Parker Tavern, Reading, Massachusetts; North parlour, house at Flanders, Connecticut.

373 WHITEFIELD, EDWIN. The homes of our forefathers, being a selection of the oldest and most interesting buildings, historical houses and noted places in Maine, New Hampshire and Vermont. Reading, Mass., The Author, 1886. 3p. illus.

374 ———. The homes of our forefathers, being a selection of the oldest and most interesting buildings, historical houses and noted places in Rhode Island and Connecticut. Boston, Whitefield and Crocker, 1882. 6p. illus.

375 WILLOUGHBY, CHARLES C. Houses and gardens of the New England Indians. American anthropologist. 8:115-32. illus.
Cites early references.

376 WORTH, HENRY BARNARD. The development of the New England dwelling house. Lynn, Mass., F. S. Whitten, 1911. 24p. illus.

Reprinted from: Lynn Historical Society *Register.* 14:129–52. 1911.

PUBLIC

377 CRAWFORD, MARY CAROLINE. Among old New England inns, being an account of little journeys to various quaint inns and hostelries of Colonial New England. Boston, L. C. Page and Co., 1907. 381p. illus.

378 DEAN, ELDON L. Early college and educational buildings in New England. Pencil points. 15:597-612. Dec. 1934. Monograph series. 20:177-92. illus.

Covers 1744–1829.

379 GREELEY, W. R. Flora of democracy; New England meeting houses and city halls. American architect. 133:217-24. Feb. 1928. illus.

380 NORTHEND, MARY HARROD. We visit old inns. Boston, Small, Maynard and Co., 1925. 176p. illus.

381 PRENTICE, THOMAS MORGAN. Historic taverns in New England. Connecticut magazine. 7:459-72. 1903.

382 RIPLEY, HUBERT G. New England inns and taverns. Pencil points. 13:804-818. Dec. 1932. Monograph series. 18:246-60. illus.

Covers 1686–1797.

383 SCHUYLER, MONTGOMERY. Architecture of American colleges. Part 6. Dartmouth, Williams and Amherst. Architectural record. 28:425-42. Dec. 1910.

384 ———. Architecture of American colleges. Part. 7. Brown, Bowdoin, Trinity, and Wesleyan. Architectural record. 29:144-66. Feb. 1911.

385 WILLOUGHBY, MALCOLM F. Lighthouses of New England. Boston, T. O. Metcalf Co., 1929. 253p. illus.

RELIGIOUS

386 BACON, LEONARD. The genesis of the New England churches. N. Y., Harper and Brothers, 1874. 485p. illus.

387 BACON, MRS. MARY SCHELL (HOKE). Old New England churches and their children. N. Y., Doubleday, Page and Co., 1906. 442p. illus.

388 BELLOWS, ROBERT P. Country meeting houses along the Massachusetts-New Hampshire line. White pine series of architectural monographs. v. 11, no. 5. 1925. 19p. illus.

Covers 1809–1825.

389 CRAWFORD, MARY CAROLINE. The romance of old New England churches. Boston, L. C. Page and Co., 1907. 377p. illus.

390 LATHROP, ELISE. Old New England churches. Rutland, Vt., Tuttle Publishing Co., 1938. 171p. illus.

391 MURCHISON, KENNETH M. The spired meeting house of old New England. Arts and decoration. 48:8-12. Mar. 1938. illus.

392 PLACE, CHARLES A. From meeting house to church in New England—in 4 parts. Old time New England. Part 1, 13:69-77, Oct. 1922; part 2, 13:111-23, Jan. 1923; part 3, 13:149-64, Apr. 1923; part 4, 14:3-20, July 1923. illus.

393 PORTER, NOAH. New England meeting house. New Haven, Conn., Yale university press, 1933. 34p.
Reprint of a paper written in 1882. Published by the Committee on Historical Publications, Tercentenary Commission of the State of Connecticut.

394 ROSS, H. C. Two interesting restorations of old New England churches. Old time New England. 3:2-8. Feb. 1913. illus.
Christ Church, Boston, and Center Church, New Haven.

395 SMITH, CHARLES LYMAN. New England churches of architectural historical interest. American architect. 23:261-66. Mar. 1923. illus.

396 WEIS, FREDERICK LEWIS. Colonial clergy and Colonial churches of New England. Lancaster, Mass., 1936. 280p. illus.
Dates churches.

397 WIGHT, CHARLES ALBERT. Some old time meeting houses of the Connecticut Valley. Chicopee Falls, Mass., The Rich print, 1911. 225p. illus.

398 WILLARD, ASHTON R. Early architecture of New England. Western architect. 17:64-67. July 1911. illus.
Domestic and public.

CONNECTICUT

GENERAL REFERENCES (see also 317, 349, 374, 393)

399 ALLIS, MARGUERITE. Historic Connecticut. N. Y., Grosset and Dunlap Co., 1938. 343p. illus.
Originally published as Connecticut Trilogy. Covers Hartford, Saybrook, and New Haven.

400 BESSELL, WESLEY SHERWOOD. Colonial architecture in Connecticut—in 5 parts. Architectural record. Part 1, 37:360-69, Apr. 1915; part 2, 37:445-52, May 1915; part 3, 37:547-56, June 1915; part 4, 38:672-80, Dec. 1915; part 5, 39:53-64, Jan. 1916. illus.

401 BICKFORD, CLARA EMERSON. The homes of our forefathers. Connecticut
    magazine. 7:493-500; 8:78-84. 1902-1903.

402 CROFUT, FLORENCE S. MARCY. Guide to the history and historic sites of
    Connecticut. New Haven, Conn., Yale university press, 1937. 2v. illus.

403 EBERLEIN, HAROLD DONALDSON. Seventeenth century Connecticut house.
    White pine series of architectural monographs. v. 5, no. 1. Feb. 1919.
    14p. illus.

404 FEDERAL WRITERS' PROJECT. Connecticut: a guide to its roads, lore and
    people. Boston, Houghton Mifflin Co., 1938. 593p. illus.

405 FOSTER, WILLIAM D. River towns of Connecticut. White pine series of
    architectural monographs. v. 9, no. 2. Apr. 1923. 14p. illus.
    Covers Hartford, Wethersfield, and Windsor.

406 ISHAM, NORMAN MORRISON, AND BROWN, ALBERT F. Early Connecticut
    houses; an historical and architectural study. Providence, R. I., Preston
    and Rounds Co., 1900. 303p. illus.

407 KELLY, JOHN FREDERICK. Architectural guide for Connecticut. New Haven,
    Conn., Yale University press, 1935. 44p.
    Published for the Tercentenary Commission of the State of Connecticut.

408 ———. Early Connecticut architecture. N. Y., William Helburn, 1924.
    25 illus.

409 ———. Early Connecticut architecture. Second series. N. Y., William Hel-
    burn, 1931. 23p. illus.

410 ———. Early domestic architecture of Connecticut. New Haven, Conn.,
    Yale University press, 1924. 210p. illus.

411 ———. Early domestic architecture of Connecticut. New Haven, Conn.,
    Yale University press, 1933. 30p.
    Published by the Committee on Historical Publications, Tercentenary Commission of
    the State of Connecticut.

412 ———. Raising Connecticut meeting houses. Old time New England.
    27:3-9. July 1936. illus.

413 ———. Three early Connecticut weather-vanes. Old time New England.
    31:96-99. Apr. 1941. illus.

414 ———; HAMILTON, LORENZO; AND KELLY, HENRY S. Early architecture of
    Connecticut. Architecture. A series of illus., v. 43-49. Jan. 1921—Feb.
    1924.

415 MARLOWE, GEORGE, AND CHAMBERLAIN, SAMUEL. Old Bay paths; their
    villages and byways and their stories. N. Y., Hastings house, 1942. 126p.
    illus.

416 MAY, CHARLES C. The old time mansions of northern Connecticut. Architectural review. 12:175-78, 192. June 1921. illus.

417 NATIONAL SOCIETY OF COLONIAL DAMES OF AMERICA. CONNECTICUT SOCIETY. Connecticut houses. Hartford, Conn., Bulletin of the Connecticut state library, no. 16. 1931. 39p.
List of 655 manuscript histories of historic houses. First published 1916 as No. 7 of the *Bulletin of the Connecticut State Library*.

418 ————. Old houses of Connecticut. New Haven, Conn., Yale University press, 1923. 519p. illus.
Mrs. Anna Bertha Trowbridge, ed.

418A ————. Old inns of Connecticut. Hartford, Conn., Prospect press, 1937. 253p. illus.
Marian Dickinson Terry, ed.

419 Old houses, Connecticut; views. American institute of architects. Journal. 8:113-15. Mar. 1920. illus. only.

420 PINDAR, PETER AUGUSTUS (pseud.). Boston post road. White pine series of architectural monographs. v.6,no.1. Feb. 1920. 14p. illus.

421 ————. Stage coach road from Hartford to Litchfield. White pine series of architectural monographs. v. 9, no. 5. Oct. 1923. 16p. illus.
Covers 1650-1833.

422 SEYMOUR, GEORGE DUDLEY. Researches of an antiquary. Five essays on early American architects. New Haven, Conn., 1928. 32p. illus.
Mentions various architects of Connecticut, including Ithiel Town.

LOCATIONS

Bethany

423 Wheeler-Beecher house, Bethany, Connecticut, built 1805. Architectural forum. 46:193-200. Feb. 1927. illus.

Canterbury

424 DANA, RICHARD H., JR. Old Canterbury on the Quinnebaug. White pine series of architectural monographs. v.9,no.6. Dec. 1923. 16p. illus.
Covers 1732-1815.

Chester (see also 355)

425 FOSTER, THEODORE. Old homes of Chester, Connecticut. West Haven, Conn., O. K. Walker, 1936. 92p. illus.

Clinton

426 CRAMER, MRS. EFFIE STEVENS. Adam Stanton house, Clinton, Conn. Old time New England. 22:88-95. Oct. 1931. illus.

427 WANGNER, ELLEN D. Old Adam Stanton house, Clinton, Conn. Country life in America. 48:70-76. Aug. 1925. illus.
1789.

Darien

428 Domestic setting for antiques. Antiques. 37:75-77. Feb. 1940. illus.
Lt. William Parsons house, 1754.

429 GILLESPIE, H. S. Biography of a Colonial house. Arts and decoration. 20:38-39. Mar. 1924. illus.

430 In the Jeffersonian tradition: Hancock house, Darien. Arts and decoration. 41:36-38. Oct. 1934. illus.

Derby

431 SHELTON, ADA STEWART. Commodore Hull house. D. A. R. magazine. 62:473-75. Aug. 1928.

432 STIVERS, MABEL P. Trueman Gilbert house. Old time New England. 19:75-79. Oct. 1928. illus.

East Haven

433 KELLY, JOHN FREDERICK. Moulthroup house, East Haven, Connecticut. Old time New England. 12:147-52. Apr. 1922.
Seventeenth century.

Easton

434 KELLY, JOHN FREDERICK. Seventeenth century Connecticut log house. Old time New England. 31:29-40. Oct. 1940. illus.
Lt. James Bennett house, 1675–80.

Essex

435 MAGONIGLE, H. VAN BUREN. Essex, a Connecticut river town. White pine series of architectural monographs. v. 6, no. 6. Dec. 1920. 16p. illus.

Fairfield

436 CHILD, FRANK SAMUEL. An historic mansion, being an account of the Thaddeus Burr homestead, Fairfield, Connecticut. 1654-1915. 27p. 1915. illus.
1790.

Farmington

437 Ancestral home of the Whitman family of Farmington, Conn. House beautiful. 45:89. Feb. 1919. illus.
Ca.1660.

438 BESSELL, WESLEY SHERWOOD. Farmington, Connecticut. White pine series of architectural monographs. v. 12, no. 2. 1926. 22p. illus.
Whitman house, Cowles house, and others.

439 BRANDIGEE, ARTHUR L., AND SMITH, EDDY N. Farmington, Connecticut, village of beautiful homes. Farmington, Conn., The Authors, 1906. 213p. illus.

Greenwich

440 TALCOTT, NORMAN. The tavern and the old Post road. Connecticut magazine. 10:647-54. Oct. 1906.
Putnam cottage (1731).

Guilford

441 KELLY, JOHN FREDERICK. Norton house, Guilford, Conn. Old time New England. 14:122-30. Jan. 1924. illus.
1690.

442 ———. Restoration of the Henry Whitfield house, Guilford, Connecticut. Old time New England. 29:75-89. Jan. 1939. illus.
1639–40.

443 New England heritage. House beautiful. 81:24-27. Sept. 1939. illus.
Ebenezer Scranton house, 1720.

444 Old Guilford 1639-1939. House beautiful. 81:14-17. July-Aug. 1939. illus.

445 SNYDER, R. Rescue of a Colonial house, once the old home of L. Beecher at Guilford. American home. 2:7-8. Apr. 1929.

446 STATE HISTORICAL MUSEUM, CONNECTICUT. Historical papers relating to the Henry Whitfield house, Guilford, Connecticut. New Haven, Conn., Tuttle, Morehouse and Taylor press, 1911. 59p. illus.

Hartford (*see also* 384, 399, 405)

447 KELLER, GEORGE. The old City hall, Hartford, Connecticut. American architect. 79:55. Feb. 14, 1903.
Also known as Old State House.

448 MERRITT, ARTHUR H. Hartford state house Staffordshire. Antiques. 33: 312-13. 1938. illus.

449 MUNICIPAL ART SOCIETY, HARTFORD, CONN. Preservation and restoration of the City hall, Hartford, Conn. Hartford, Conn., Municipal Art society, 1906. 16p. illus.
Bulletin 6 of the society publications.

450 (State House. Contemporary description.) Atkinson's casket. No. 8:458. Aug. 1835.

451 TALCOTT, MARY KINGSBURY. Old State house, Hartford, Connecticut. D. A. R. nineteenth annual report. 289-90. 1917.
(1796) Charles Bulfinch, architect.

Lebanon

452 CHAMPE, HOWARD CRULL. Old meeting-house at Lebanon, Conn. Old time New England. 30:82-85. Jan. 1940. illus.

Litchfield (*see also* 487)

453 BULKLEY, ALICE TALCOTT. Historic Litchfield, 1721-1907. Hartford, Conn., Hartford press, 1907. 37p. illus.

A short account of the history of the old houses of Litchfield. Compiled from Kilborn's *History of Litchfield*, Woodruff's *History of the Town of Litchfield*, Kilborn's *History of Litchfield Tradition*.

454 Elton house at Litchfield, Connecticut. Country life in America. 31:43. Nov. 1916. illus.

455 GILLESPIE, HARRIET SISSON. Toll-gate Hill tavern. Country life in America. 48:58-59. Sept. 1925. illus.

1745. Moved from Litchfield to Torrington, Connecticut.

456 PRICE, C. MATLACK. Historic houses of Litchfield, Connecticut. White pine series of architectural monographs. v. 5, no. 3. June 1919. 16p. illus.

Covers 1753–1832.

Middletown (*see* 384)

Milford

457 FEDERAL WRITER'S PROJECT. History of Milford, Connecticut, 1639-1939. Bridgeport, Conn., Braunworth and Co., *ca.* 1939. 204p. illus.

New Canaan

458 GILLESPIE, HARRIETT SISSON. The old Wardwell house, New Canaan, Connecticut. House beautiful. 49:30-31. Jan. 1921.

New Haven (*see also* 394, 399, 422)

459 BROCKWAY, JEAN LAMBERT. John Trumbull as architect at Yale. Antiques. 28:114-15. 1935.

460 DENISON, ROBERT C. The United church on the Green, New Haven, Conn. New Haven, 1915. 16p.

1813–15. David Hoadley, architect.

461 O'DONNELL, THOMAS E. Home of the Greek revivalist, Ithiel Town, at New Haven, Conn. Architectural forum. 49:71-72. June 1928. illus.

462 SCHUYLER, MONTGOMERY. Architecture of American colleges. Pt. 2. Yale. Architectural record. 26:393-416. Dec. 1909. illus.

463 SEYMOUR, GEORGE DUDLEY. Henry Caner, 1680-1731, master carpenter, builder of the first Yale college buildings, 1718, and of the rector's house, 1722. Old time New England. 15:99-124. Jan. 1925. illus.

464 ———. Residence and library of Ithiel Town. New Haven, Conn., 1930.

Reprinted from *New Haven*, p. 546–60.

465 (Yale college. Contemporary description.) Philadelphia Souvenir. 1:32, 249. Feb. 5, 1828. illus.

New London

466 ROGERS, EDNA MINER. New London, Connecticut; homes visited by Washington and Lafayette—stage coaches and taverns. Americana. 16:21-37. Jan. 1922.

467 (New London exchange. Contemporary description.) Merry's museum. 6:143-45. Nov. 1843. illus.

New Preston

468 Cogswell tavern. New Preston, Connecticut. American monthly magazine. 23:360-62. Nov. 1903.
     1760–62.

Noroton

469 RUSSELL, E. H. Yesterday's treasure; Milestone house, Noroton, Connecticut. Country life in America. 59:35-42. Apr. 1931.
     Built 1690 at Stratford, Connecticut; moved to Noroton, 1931.

Norwich

470 PERKINS, MARY E. Old houses of the antient (sic) town of Norwich, 1660-1800. Norwich, Conn., Bulletin Co., 1895. 621p. illus.

Old Lyme

471 SPAULDING, MELVIN PRATT. Old Lyme: Roger Griswold house. Arts and decoration. 49:2-6. Jan. 1939. illus.

Saybrook (see also 399)

472 HOLMAN, MABEL CASSINE. The romance of a Saybrook mansion. Connecticut magazine. 10:46-51. Jan.-Mar. 1906.

Shelton

473 MORSE, C. Z. Commodore Isaac Hull's house at Shelton, Connecticut. Old time New England. 26:65-68. Oct. 1935. illus.

Southington

474 (SKILTON, JOHN DAVIS, AND SKILTON, HENRY ALSTONE). Doctor Henry Skilton house, Southington, Hartford county, Connecticut. (Hartford?) Conn., 1930.

Stonington

475 DAVIS, SARAH M. History of an old Connecticut homestead. American monthly magazine. 41:45-47. Aug. 1912.
     Stanton Davis homestead.

476 Hunting houses; four 19th century houses at Old Mystic and Stonington. House and garden. 67:26-27. June 1935. illus.

477 PENTZ, M. W. Stonington, Connecticut—where the Colonial atmosphere is preserved to a marked degree. Architectural record. 32:230-37. Sept. 1912. illus.

478 WHEELER, GRACE DENISON. The homes of our ancestors in Stonington, Connecticut. Salem, Mass., Newcomb and Gauss, 1903. 286p. illus.

Stratford (see also 469)

479 SULLIVAN, NORINE C. Time passes by this New England town. . . . Arts and decoration. 51:18-21. Dec. 1939. illus.

480 WILCOXSON, WILLIAM H. History of Stratford, Conn. 1639-1939. Stratford, Conn., Stratford tercentenary commission, 1939. 783p. illus.
Numerous illustrations.

Suffield

481 TARN, DAVID E. The town of Suffield, Connecticut. White pine series of architectural monographs. v. 7, no. 6. Dec. 1921. 16p. illus.
Covers 1736–1824.

Wallingford

482 ROYCE, LUCY ATWATER. Nehemiah Royce or Washington elm house, Wallingford, Connecticut. Old time New England. 25:40-49. Oct. 1934. illus.
1672.

Westbury

483 ROBERTSON, T. M. Very early American house; Guinea Hollow farm, Old Westbury. Arts and decorations. 30:80. Mar. 1929. illus.

Westport (see 355)

Wethersfield (see 219, 405)

Windham County

484 DANA, RICHARD H., JR. Old hill towns of Windham county, Connecticut. White pine series of architectural monographs. v. 10, no. 1. Feb. 1924. 16p. illus.
Covers 1808–1835.

Windsor (see also 405)

485 The Ellsworth homestead; Elmwood, the state chapter house of the Connecticut Daughters of the American Revolution. American monthly magazine. 23:353-58. Nov. 1903.
1740.

486 DAUGHTERS OF THE AMERICAN REVOLUTION. CONNECTICUT. A memorial of the opening of the Ellsworth homestead at Windsor, Connecticut, October eighth, nineteen hundred and three under the auspices of the Connecticut Daughters of the American Revolution. New Haven, Conn., Tuttle, Morehouse and Taylor, 1907. 109p. illus.

Woodbury

487 BESSELL, WESLEY S. Old Woodbury and adjacent domestic architecture of Connecticut. White pine series of architectural monographs. v. 2, no. 5. Oct. 1916. 14p. illus.

Jabes Bacon house (1762), Woodbury; Sanford house, Litchfield; Bostwick house, Southbury.

488 KENT, HENRY W. The Glebe-house, Woodbury, Conn. Old time New England. 13:169-73. Apr. 1923. illus.

1745–50.

MAINE

GENERAL REFERENCES (*see also* 373)

489 American home pilgrimages, no. 4.—Maine. American home. 20:8-11, 54-56. Aug. 1938. illus.

Covers 1750–1890.

490 CHAMBERLAIN, SAMUEL. The coast of Maine. N. Y., Hastings house, 1941. 101p. illus.

491 DUNNACK, HENRY E. Maine forts. Augusta, Maine, Charles E. Nash and Son, 1924. 252p. illus.

Covers 1607–1908.

492 FEDERAL WRITERS' PROJECT. Maine: a guide down east. Boston, Houghton Mifflin Co., 1937. 476p. illus.

493 HILL, W. SCOTT. Early Kennebec taverns. Sprague's journal of Maine history. 9:21-23. Jan. 1921.

494 MAINE WRITERS' RESEARCH CLUB (comp.). Historic churches and homes of Maine. Portland, Me., Falmouth book house, 1937. 289p. illus.

495 MITCHELL, GEORGE R. Early architecture of Maine. Architecture. v. 37-38. Jan.-Oct. 1918. illus. only.

496 NASON, MRS. EMMA HUNTINGTON. Old Colonial house in Maine built prior to 1776. Augusta, Me., Kennebec journal, 1908. 106p. illus.

497 ORCHARD, WILLIAM C. Notes on Penobscot houses. American anthropologist. n. s. 11:601-606. 1909. illus.

498 PORTER, FREDERICK HUTCHINSON. A survey of existing Colonial architecture in Maine. Architectural review. 7:29-32, 47-51, 94-96. Aug.-Nov. 1918; 11:13-15, 45-48, 83-88, 119-20, 155-56, 183-86. July-Dec. 1920; 12:41-46, 64, 92, 151-52. Feb.-June 1921. American architect. 120:149-51. Aug. 1921. illus.

499 WALKER, C. HOWARD. Some old houses on the southern coast of Maine. White pine series of architectural monographs. v. 4, no. 2. Apr. 1918. 14p. illus.

LOCATIONS

Aroostoock County

500 ATKINSON, MINNIE. Molunkus house. Sprague's journal of Maine history. 13:82-90. 1925.

Augusta (see also Hallowell)

501 BASSETT, NORMAN L. History of the Blaine mansion. Americana. 15:288-93. July 1921.

502 FEDERAL WRITERS' PROJECT. Augusta-Hallowell on the Kennebec. Augusta, Me., Augusta-Hallowell chamber of commerce. 168p. illus.

503 ———. Maine's Capitol. Augusta, Me., Kennebec print shop, 1938. 44p.
1828–31. Charles Bulfinch, architect.

Bangor

504 CHAPMAN, HARRY J. The first Bangor city hall. Bangor historical society. Proceedings. 1914-15:51-56.

Bar Harbor

505 WASSON, M. Up the road to yesterday; Woodlawn, scene of the Bingham purchase. Country life in America. 58:65-66. May 1930. illus.
1802.

Brunswick (see 384)

Castine

506 STANWOOD, CORDELIA J. Castine, a village by the sea. House beautiful. 48:92-94, 126, 128. Aug. 1920. illus.
Covers 1765–ca. 1820.

Columbia Falls

507 GOLDSMITH, MARGARET O. Ruggles house at Columbia Falls, Maine. Old time New England. 15:68-76. Oct. 1924. illus.

Ellsworth

508 STANWOOD, CORDELIA J. The story of Ellsworth, Maine. House beautiful. 46:373-75. Dec. 1919. illus.

Hallowell (see also Augusta)

509 GOLDSMITH, MARGARET O. Two early homes in Hallowell, Maine. House beautiful. 55:361-64. Apr. 1924. illus.
Vaughan house and Merrick house, ca.1800.

Head Tide

510 Brown, Frank Chouteau. Congregational church at Head Tide, Maine.
Old time New England. 30:94-100. Jan. 1940. illus.
1838.

Kennebunk, including *Kennebunkport*

511 Dow, Joy Wheeler. Old-time dwellings in Kennebunkport. Kennebunk,
The Star print, 1926. 82p. illus.

512 Howe, Florence Thompson. Brick store museum at Kennebunk, Maine.
Antiques. 38:74-75. Aug. 1940. illus.
1825.

Kittery (see also *Portsmouth, N. H.,* and 359, 367)

513 Richardson, H. T. John Bray house in Kittery, Maine. House beautiful.
65:704-712. May 1929. illus.

514 Robie, Virginia. Colonial pilgrimage, no. 3—Sir William Pepperrell (*sic*) and
his staircase. House beautiful. 15:315-17. Apr. 1904. illus.
Sparhawk house, 1742.

Machias

515 Donworth, Grace. Burnham tavern, ancient hostelry at Machias. D. A. R.
magazine. 69:35. 1935.

Matinicus Island

516 Condon, Vesta. An island store one hundred years ago. Old time New
England. 32:52-56. Oct. 1941. illus.

Penobscot Bay Area

517 Loomis, Charles Dana. Port towns of Penobscot Bay. White pine series of
architectural monographs. v. 8, no. 1. Feb. 1922. 14p. illus.

Phippsburg

518 Harriman, A. J. Doorway, Thomas McCobb house, Phippsburg, Maine.
Architecture. v. 51, no. 5. May 1925. illus. only.

Portland

519 Elden, A. Tate house, Stroudwater, Portland, Maine. Old time New England. 26:138-41. Apr. 1936. illus.

520 First Parish Church, Portland, Maine. Architectural review. n. s. 6:67-69.
June 1918. illus.

521 Thompson, Florence Whittlesey. Early churches in Portland. Sprague's
journal of Maine history. 9:81-83. Apr. 1921.

South Berwick

522 Baer, Annie Wentworth. Captain Nathan Lord's house. Granite monthly.
59:201-206. July 1927.

523 Brown, Frank Chouteau. Interior details and furnishings of the Sarah
    Orne Jewett dwelling, built by John Haggins in 1774 at South Berwick,
    Maine. Pencil points. 21:115-30. Feb. 1940. Monograph series. 26:
    97-112. illus.

524 Kingsbury, Edith. Hamilton house; historic landmark, South Berwick.
    House beautiful. 65:782-87, 874, 876. June 1929. illus.
    1770.

525 Shelton, Louise. The garden at Hamilton house. American homes and
    gardens. 6:422-25. Nov. 1909. illus.
    1770.

Thomaston
526 Carleton, Sara H. Knox mansion returns to life. National republic. 20:24.
    Nov. 1932.
    Replica, built 1932, of home of Major General Henry Knox, 1794.

Topsham
527 Harriman, A. J. General McLellan house, Topsham, Maine. Architecture.
    52:150-52. Oct. 1925. illus. only.

528 ———. Doorway of the General Veasie house, Topsham, Maine. Architec-
    ture. v. 51, no. 6. June 1925; v. 52, no. 2. Aug. 1925. illus. only.

Wiscasset
529 Goldsmith, M. O. Some old houses in Wiscasset, Maine. Architectural
    forum. 45:265-72. Nov. 1926. illus.
    Includes a bibliography.

530 Harriman, A. J. Doorway of the Nickels house, Wiscasset, Maine. Architec-
    ture. 51:121-22. Apr. 1925. illus. only.

531 Lowndes, M. Yankee mansion, known in 1790 as the Bunch of Grapes
    tavern, Wiscasset, Maine. House and garden. 77:40. June 1940. illus.

532 Patterson, William D. Wiscasset, Maine. White pine series of architec-
    tural monographs. v. 12, no. 6. 1926. 22p. illus.
    Early Republican.

533 Wiscasset open house. House beautiful. 81:81-83. Nov. 1939. illus.

York County
533A Bourne, Edward Emerson. Garrison houses, York county. Me. hist. soc.
     Collections. 7:107-120. 1876.

York Harbor
534 Vaughan, Dorothy M. Sayward-Barrell house on York River, York Har-
    bor, Maine. Old time New England. 29:15-20. July 1938. illus.
    *Ca.*1717.

MASSACHUSETTS

GENERAL REFERENCES (*see also* 198, 370, 388)

535 BAGG, ERNEST NEWTON. Late eighteenth century architecture in western
Massachusetts. White pine series of architectural monographs. v. 11, no.
4. 1925. 19p. illus.
Covers 1800–*ca.* 1828.

536 BROWN, FRANK CHOUTEAU. Entrance halls and stairways, illustrated by
examples from Massachusetts and central New England. Pencil points.
20:245-60. Apr. 1939. Monograph series. 25:17-32. illus.
Covers 1670–1820.

537 ———. Some Colonial wall cabinets and kitchen dressers, principally from
early Massachusetts settlements. Pencil points. 20:373-88. June 1939.
Monograph series. 25:33-48. illus.
Covers 1650–1786.

538 ———. Some low mantels and fireplace enframements, principally of the
beginning of the nineteenth century. Pencil points. 20:673-88. Oct.
1939. Monograph series. 25:65-80. illus.
Covers 1687–1811 in Massachusetts.

539 BUCKLY, JULIAN. Architecture in Massachusetts during the latter part of
the eighteenth century. White pine series of architectural monographs.
v. 2, no. 2. Apr. 1916. 14p. illus.

540 CHANDLER, JOSEPH EVERETT. Colonial cottages of Massachusetts during the
latter half of the seventeenth century. White pine series of architectural
monographs. v. 1, no. 1. 1915. 13p. illus.

541 CHAMBERLAIN, SAMUEL. Lexington and Concord. N. Y., Hastings house,
1939. 72p. illus.

542 COUSINS, FRANK. Mantel details. Some of the early craftsman's work in
Salem, Danversport and Peabody, Mass., and in Portsmouth, N. H. Country life in America. 30:46-47. May 1916. illus. only.

543 DOW, GEORGE FRANCIS. Building agreements in seventeenth century Massachusetts. Old time New England. 12:135-39. Jan. 1922; 13:28-32.
July 1922; 13:131-34. Jan. 1923.

544 EMBURY, AYMAR II. Houses in southeastern Massachusetts. White pine
series of architectural monographs. v. 14, no. 1. 1928. 19p. illus.
Houses dated 1790 and earlier, in Taunton and Weymouth.

545 FEDERAL WRITERS' PROJECT. Massachusetts: a guide to its places and people.
Boston, Houghton Mifflin Co., 1937. 675p. illus.

546 GARDNER, G. C. Colonial architecture in western Massachusetts. American
architect and building news. Part 1, 45:99-100. Sept. 15, 1894; part 2,
46:89-90. Dec. 1, 1894; part 3, 47:39-41. Jan. 26, 1895. illus.

547 HAMLIN, TALBOT FAULKNER. Americana: spirit of early buildings transcends periods. Pencil points. 19:655-62. Oct. 1938. illus.
Examples from the Massachusetts coast.

548 HOUSE, ALBERT VIRGIL. The lean-to house and the life it sheltered. Danvers historical society. Collections. 11:113-33. 1923.

549 JACKSON, ROBERT TRACY. History of the Oliver, Vassall and Royall houses in Dorchester, Cambridge and Medford. Genealogical magazine. 2:3-17. Jan. 1907.

550 LORING, KATHERINE PEABODY. Earliest summer residents of the north shore and their houses. Essex institute historical collections. 68:193-208. 1932.
Ca.1840.

551 MACKENNAL, ALEXANDER. Homes and haunts of the Pilgrim fathers. Philadelphia, J. B. Lippincott Co., 1899. 200p. illus.
Later editions to 1920.

552 Minor Colonial details—part 1. Some old summer houses from eastern Massachusetts gardens. Architectural review. n.s. 5:169-71. Aug. 1917. illus.

553 MITCHELL, GEORGE R. Early architecture of Massachusetts. Architecture. v. 43. Jan. 1921. illus. only.

554 NEWTON, BENJAMIN H. A group of early Massachusetts vestibules. Pencil points. 15:273-88. June 1934. Monograph series. 20:129-44. illus.
Covers 1670–1796.

555 NORTHEND, MARY HARROD. Group of Colonial doorways. American homes and gardens. 12:52-55. Feb. 1915. illus.
From Salem and Dedham.

556 POOR, ALFRED EASTON. Colonial architecture of Cape Cod, Nantucket and Martha's Vineyard. N. Y., William Helburn, 1932. 147p. illus.

557 SCHUYLER, MONTGOMERY. Architecture of American colleges—part 10. Three women's colleges—Vassar, Wellesley, and Smith. Architectural record. 31:513-37. May 1912. illus.

558 Three old New England houses. Magazine of history. 12:273-76. Nov. 1910.
Covers Fairbanks house, Dedham; Horseshoe (or Coffin) house, Nantucket; Whipple house, Ipswich.

559 WATKINS, WALTER KENDALL. Three contracts for seventeenth century building construction in Massachusetts. Old time New England. 12:27-32. July 1921.
Contracts for houses at Malden and Boston, and King's Chapel, Boston.

560 WHITEFIELD, EDWIN. Homes of our forefathers. . . . in Massachusetts. Dedham, Mass., The Author, 1892. 41p. illus.
First edition 1879.

561 WICKHAM, JENNETTE ADAMS. Historic churches of Massachusetts. American monthly magazine. 39:127-32. Sept. 1911.

LOCATIONS

Amherst (*see also* 383)

562 SEE, ANNA PHILLIPS. The old Strong house, home of Mary Mattoon chapter, Amherst, Mass. D. A. R. magazine. 55:509-514. Sept. 1921.
1744.

Andover

563 DOUGLAS-LITHGOW, R. A. A group of early Colonial houses at Andover, Massachusetts. Massachusetts magazine. 5:3-9. Jan. 1912.

564 HOWES, JENNIE WRIGHT. North Andover homesteads. D. A. R. magazine. 64:623-32. Oct. 1930.

565 LE BOUTILLIER, ADDISON B. Early wooden architecture of Andover, Mass. White pine series of architectural monographs. v. 3, no. 2. Apr. 1917. 14p. illus.
Covers 1667–1824.

Aptucxet (near *Bourne*)

566 LOMBARD, PERCIVAL HALL. Aptucxet trading post, first trading post of Plymouth colony; its restoration on the original foundations. Old time New England. 23:159-74. Apr. 1933. illus.
1627.

Auburn

567 FEDERAL WRITERS' PROJECT. Auburn: 1837-1937. Auburn, Mass., Auburn centennial committee. 63p. illus.

Barnstable

568 GOODELL, EDWIN B., JR. Meeting-house at West Barnstable, Mass. Old time New England. 21:37-42. July 1930. illus.
1719 and later.

569 SHUMWAY, HARRY IRVING. Old tavern of Cape Cod. American cookery. 37:171-75. 1932.
Barnstable Inn.

Berkshire County and the Berkshires

570 COOKE, ROBERT HILLYER. Historic homes and institutions and genealogical and personal memoirs of Berkshire county, Massachusetts. N. Y., Lewis Publishing Co., 1906. 2v. illus.

571 FEDERAL WRITERS' PROJECT. The Berkshire hills. N. Y., Funk and Wagnalls Co., 1939. 368p. illus.

572 RAMSDELL, ROGER WEARNE. Wooden architecture in the Berkshires. White pine series of architectural monographs. v. 10, no. 5. 1924. 16p. illus. Covers 1734–1803.

573 KILHAM, WALTER H. Cabot-Lee-Kilham house, Beverly, Mass. Old time New England. 15:157-63. Apr. 1925. illus. Eighteenth century.

Billerica

574 EGBERT, HANS. Manning manse; an old homestead at North Billerica, Massachusetts. House beautiful. 50:26-29, 66. July 1921. illus.

Boston—General (see also *Brookline, Cambridge, Dorchester, Roxbury,* and 299, 307, 559)

575 BACON, EDWIN M. A guide book. Boston, Ginn and Co., 1903. 190p. illus.

576 Boston brickwork, Colonial era. Brickbuilder. 14:27-33. Feb. 1905. illus.

577 BOSTON. MUSEUM OF FINE ARTS. Museums and some historic houses in Boston and vicinity. Boston, Museum of fine arts, 1934. 16p.

578 BROWN, FRANK CHOUTEAU. Beacon Hill, Boston, Mass. Pencil points. 19: 177-92. Mar. 1938. Monograph series. 24:97-112. illus. Covers 1795–1844.

579 ———. Historic Boston, Massachusetts. Pencil points. 18:287-302. May 1937. Monograph series. 23:1-16. illus. Covers 1713–1826.

580 Buildings and house hardware: gleanings from eighteenth century Boston newspapers. Old time New England. 17:20-29. July 1926. illus.

581 CHAMBERLAIN, SAMUEL. Historic Boston in four seasons. N. Y., Hastings house, 1938. 73p. illus.

582 DRAKE, SAMUEL ADAMS. Old landmarks and historic personages of Boston. Boston, J. R. Osgood and Co., 1873. 484p. illus.

583 (Franklin music warehouse. Contemporary description.) National register. 4:239. Oct. 11, 1817.

584 HERSEY, HORATIO BROOKS. Old west end Boston. Old time New England. 20:162-77. Apr. 1930. illus.

585 MITCHELL, GEORGE R. Boston Colonial series. Architecture. v. 47-48. Mar.-Aug. 1923. illus. only.

586 PORTER, EDWARD G. Rambles in old Boston, New England. Boston, Cupples, Hurd and Co., 1887. 439p. illus.

587 SCHUYLER, MONTGOMERY. Boston, Massachusetts, ancient and modern. Pall Mall magazine. 28:325. 1902.

588 TOLMAN, GEORGE R. Twelve sketches of old Boston buildings. Boston, Heliotype Printing Co., 1882. 12 illus.

589 WINSOR, JUSTIN. Memorial history of Boston. Boston, J. R. Osgood and Co., 1880-81. 4v.
V.4, pp.383-414 refer to architecture.

Boston—Domestic

590 AMORY, MARTHA BABCOCK. Gardiner Greene mansion on Pemberton Hill. Bostonian society. Proceedings. Jan. 15, 1924. p. 21-27.

591 BENTON, JOSIAH HENRY. Story of the old Boston Town house, 1658-1711. Boston, Merrymount press, 1908. 212p. illus.

592 BROWN, JOHN PERKINS, AND RANSOM, ELEANOR. Thomas Creese house, being a description of a typical townhouse of the early eighteenth century and containing a history of the site thereof from the time of Anne Hutchinson to the present day. Boston, J. P. Brown, 1940. illus.
1711.

593 CARRICK, ALICE VAN LEER. The Revolutionary home of Paul Revere. Country life. 39:63-65. Dec. 1920. illus.
*Ca.*1677.

594 CHAMBERLAIN, ALLEN. Beacon Hill, its ancient pastures and early mansions. Boston, Houghton Mifflin Co., 1925. 309p. illus.

595 DOGGETT, SAMUEL BRADLEY. The model of the Bradlee-Doggett house, Hollis street, Boston. Old time New England. 19:174-80. Apr. 1929. illus.

596 DOUGLAS-LITHGOW, R. A. Andrew Oliver house, Dorchester. Massachusetts magazine. 3:57-61. Jan. 1910.

597 ———. Governor Hutchinson's house on Milton Hill. Massachusetts magazine. 3:121-24. Apr. 1910.

598 FLICK, A. C. Old Hancock house. New York state historical association. Quarterly. 7:291-93. Oct. 1926.
A replica has been built at Ticonderoga, N. Y. *See also* 1408, 1409.

599 Harrison Gray Otis house, corner Lynde and Cambridge streets, Boston. Old time New England. 8:7-16. Mar. 1917. illus.
1795.

600 Harrison Gray Otis house. Old time New England. 22:151-61. Apr. 1932. illus.
Account of a loan exhibition. 1795. Attributed to Charles Bulfinch.

601-603 (Houses. Contemporary descriptions.) Southern literary messenger. 5:793-98. Dec. 1839; American magazine of knowledge. 2:80. Oct. 1835; The Parley. Pt. 2:200. 1842.

604 INGRAHAM, F. Visit to the Harrison Gray Otis house. Old time New England. 29:21-31. July 1938. illus.
114 Cambridge St. Same house as 600, 605.

605 In the old Harrison Gray Otis house. House beautiful. 42:246. Oct. 1919. illus.

606 John Singleton Copley's houses on Beacon Hill, Boston; correspondence between Copley and his half-brother, Henry Pelham. Old time New England. 25:85-95. Jan. 1935. illus.

607 (Julien house. Contemporary description.) American magazine of knowledge. 2:81. Oct. 1835.

608 KEYES, H. E. The Crescent that waned; Franklin Crescent, Boston. Antiques. 30:27. July 1936. illus.
1796, by Bulfinch.

609 LAWRENCE, ROBERT MEANS. Old Park street and its vicinity. Boston, Houghton, Mifflin Co., 1922. 172p. illus.

610 LAWRENCE, SARAH B. Some old white doorways. New England magazine. n. s. 44:635-43. July 1911.
Beacon Hill.

611 Parker-Inches-Emery house, 40 Beacon Street, Boston. Old time New England. 4:1-11. Aug. 1913. illus.
1818.

612 RIPLEY, HUBERT G. Boston dry points—part 4. Paul Revere house. Architectural record. 59:388-91. Apr. 1926. illus.

613 ROBINSON, FREDERICK B. Beacon Hill house from Bulfinch designs. International studio. 99:20-23. July 1931. illus.
Louisberg Square. After 1800.

614 STATE STREET TRUST COMPANY. Forty of Boston's historic houses; a brief illustrated description of the residences of historic characters of Boston who have lived in or near the business section. Boston, State street trust co., 1912. 44p. illus.

615 WATERMAN, THOMAS TILESTON. Certain brick houses in Boston from 1700-1776. Old time New England. 23:22-27. July 1932. illus.

616 ———. The Savage house, Dock square, Boston. Old time New England. 17:107-110. Jan. 1927. illus.
1706-1707.

617 WATKINS, WALTER KENDALL. The Hancock house and its builder. Old time New England. 17:3-19. July 1926. illus.

618 WHITEFIELD, EDWIN. Homes of our forefathers in Boston, old England and Boston, New England. Boston, The Author, 1889. 138p. illus.

Boston—Public

619 (Beacon Hill Column. Contemporary description.) American magazine of Knowledge. 2:47. Sept. 1835.

620 Boston's new Old State house. Magazine of history. 13:305-310. June 1911.

621 BROWN, ABRAM ENGLISH. Faneuil Hall and Faneuil Hall market; or Peter Faneuil and his gift. Boston, Lea and Shepherd Co., 1900. 671p. illus.
1742. Addition by Bulfinch 1805.

622 (Bunker Hill monument. Details of the costs.) Niles weekly register. 59: 304. Jan. 9, 1841.

623 (Capitol. Contemporary description.) American magazine of knowledge. 2:68-69. Oct. 1835.

624 DOUGLAS-LITHGOW, R. A. The Province house, Boston. Massachusetts magazine. 3:199-203. July 1910.
Also known as the Peter Sergeant house, 1676. *See also* 196.

625 DRAKE, SAMUEL ADAMS. Old Boston taverns and tavern clubs. Boston, W. A. Butterfield, 1917. 124p. illus.

626 ELIOT, WILLIAM HAVARD. Description of the Tremont house with architectural illustrations. Boston, Gray and Bowen, 1830. 36p. illus.
1828. Isaiah Rogers, architect.

627 (Exchange Coffee house. Contemporary description.) National register. 3:216-17. April 5, 1817; New world. 3:96. Aug. 7, 1841.

628 FOX, THOMAS A. Brief history of the Beacon Hill State house. American architect and building news. 48: 127-29. June 29, 1895.
(1795. Charles Bulfinch, architect.)

629 NORCROSS, FREDERICK WALTER. Ye ancient inns of Boston town. New England magazine. 25:315-25. 1901-1902.

630 READ, CHARLES F. The Old State house, and its predecessor the first Town house. Bostonian society. Proceedings. p. 32-50. 1908.

631 Rededication of the Old State house, Boston, July 11, 1882. Boston, Printed by Order of the Council, 1885. illus.

632 RIPLEY, HUBERT G. Boston dry points—part 2. Faneuil hall. Architectural record. 59:165-69. Jan. 1926. illus.

633 ———. Boston dry points—part 3. The Old Tremont house. Architectural record. 59:287-91. Mar. 1926. illus.

634 ———. Boston dry points—part 5. Copley square. Architectural record. 59:467-71. May 1926. illus.

635 ———. Boston dry points—part 8. Old City hall. Architectural record. 60:363-68. Oct. 1926. illus.
1810.

636 ———. Boston dry points—part 9. Old granary burying grounds. Architectural record. 60:575-79. Dec. 1926. illus.

637 ———. Boston dry points—part 10. The New State house. Architectural record. 61:315-20. Apr. 1927. illus.
Bulfinch front 1798.

638 ———. Boston dry points—part 1. Old State house. Architectural record. 58:542-48. Dec. 1925. illus.

639 ———. Boston dry points—part 3. Old Tremont house. Architectural record. 59:287-91. Mar. 1926. illus.
1840.

640 (Triangular building. Contemporary description.) American magazine of knowledge. 2:80. Oct. 1835. illus.
Used as a customhouse and warehouse.

641 WILLARD, SOLOMON. Plans and sections of the obelisk on Bunker's Hill. . . . Boston, S. N. Dickinson, 1843. 31p. illus.
1824–42. Solomon Willard, architect.

Boston—Religious

642 BOLTON, CHARLES KNOWLES. Christ church, Salem street, Boston, 1723. Boston, The Church, 1912. 49p. illus.
Second edition, 1930. *See also* 394.

643 BROWN, FRANK CHOUTEAU. Early Boston churches. Pencil points. 18:799-814. Dec. 1937. Monograph series. 23:81-96. illus.

644 BROWN, GILBERT PATTEN. The real Old North church; a landmark of the Republic. Granite monthly. 45:159-62. May 1913.
Christ Church (1723).

645 COLE, WILLIAM I. Early churches at the North end, Boston. New England magazine. 26:241-56. 1902. illus.

646 FAGAN, JAMES O. The Old South; or the romance of early New England history. Boston, George H. Ellis Co., 1923. 141p. illus.
Old South Church (1729).

647 FOOTE, HENRY WILDER. Annals of King's chapel, from the Puritan age of New England to the present day. Boston, Little, Brown and Co., 1882-96. 2v. illus.
1749. Peter Harrison, architect. *See also* 559.

648 FRENCH, WILLARD. Paul Revere's Old North church. Architectural record. 19:215-22. Mar. 1906. illus.

649 GREENE, JOHN GARDNER. Charles street Meeting-house, Boston. Old time New England. 30:86-93. Jan. 1940.
1807. Asher Benjamin, architect.

650 LEAHY, WILLIAM AUGUSTINE. Catholic churches of Boston and vicinity and St. John's seminary, Brighton. Boston, McClellan, Hearn and Co., 1892. 43p. illus.

651 Old South meeting house. Stone and Webster. Journal. 46:506-514. Apr. 1930.

652 OLD SOUTH SOCIETY. Our heritage, Old South church, 1669-1919. Norwood, Mass., Plimpton press, 1919.

653 ———. The two hundred and fiftieth anniversary of the founding of the Old South church in Boston. Norwood, Mass., Plimpton press, 1919. 138p. illus.

654 PLACE, CHARLES A. New South church, Boston, Mass. Old time New England. 11:51-53. Oct. 1920. illus.

655 Preservation of Park street church, Boston. Boston, 1903. Pamphlet.
(1809. Peter Banner, architect.)

656 (Trinity church. Contemporary description.) Boston musical gazette. 1:100. Oct. 17, 1838.

Braintree

657 Quincy homestead, Braintree, Mass. Antiquarian. 2:15-17. June 1924. illus.
See also 219.

Brookfield

658 GILLESPIE, HARRIET S. Brookfield tavern restored. House beautiful. 51:44-46. Jan. 1922. illus.
(1771.)

Brookline

659 AMORY, MARGOT. Captain Cook cottage, Brookline, Massachusetts. House beautiful. 62:646-49. Dec. 1927. illus.

660 CANDAGE, RUFUS G. F. Gridley house, Brookline and Jeremy Gridley. Brookline historical society. Publications. no. 1:3-32. 1903.

661 1827 Gothic; home of R. S. Humphrey, a famous one-acre estate in Brookline. House and garden. 73:38-40. May 1938. illus.

662 GODDARD, JULIA. The Goddard house, Warren street, Brookline, built about 1730; its owners and occupants. Brookline historical society. Proceedings, 1903. p.16-34.

663 STEARNS, CHARLES H. The Sewall house. Brookline historical society. Proceedings, 1903. p.35-45.

Cambridge

664 BROWN, FRANK CHOUTEAU. Old Judge Lee house, Cambridge, Mass. Architectural review. 4:77-78. May 1916. illus.

665 BULFINCH, ELLEN SUSAN. The Tudor house at Fresh Pond. Cambridge historical society. Publications. 3:100-109. 1908.

666 CAPEN, OLIVER BRONSON. Country homes of famous Americans. Part 6. Ralph Waldo Emerson. Country life in America. 6:40-43. May 1904. illus.

1828.

667 ———. Country homes of famous Americans. Part 9. Henry Wadsworth Longfellow. Country life in America. 6:346-49, 363. Aug. 1904. illus.

Craigie-Vassall-Longfellow house 1759. *See also* 549.

668 CHAMBERLAIN, SAMUEL. Historic Cambridge in four seasons. N. Y., Hastings house, 1942. 73p. illus.

669 CHANDLER, JOSEPH EVERETT. Judge Joseph Lee house, Cambridge, Mass. House beautiful. 51:108-110. Feb. 1922. illus.

670 COGSWELL, CHARLES N. Cambridge, Massachusetts. Part 1. Pencil points. 18:589-604. Sept. 1937. Monograph series. 23:49-64. illus.

671 ———. Cambridge, Massachusetts. Part 2. Pencil points. 18:665-80. Oct. 1937. Monograph series. 23:65-80. illus.

Covers 1686–1808.

672 CONANT, KENNETH. Group of old Cambridge houses. House beautiful. 53:33-36. Jan. 1923. illus.

673 DANA, HENRY WADSWORTH LONGFELLOW. Chronicles of the Craigie house; the coming of Longfellow. Cambridge historical society. Proceedings. 25:19-60. 1938-39. illus.

Contains an 1815 sketch of the house (1759).

674 DAUGHTERS OF THE AMERICAN REVOLUTION. MASSACHUSETTS. An historic guide to Cambridge, compiled by members of the Hannah Winthrop chapter, National society, Daughters of the American revolution. Cambridge, Mass., 1907. 207p. illus.

675 FRASER, ESTHER STEVENS. Cinderella house; John Hicks house, Cambridge, Mass. Country life in America. 47:70-76. Dec. 1924. illus.

676 ———. John Hicks house. Cambridge historical society. Proceedings. 20:110-24. 1934.

677 ————. John Hicks house, Cambridge, Mass. Old time New England. 22:99-113. Jan. 1932. illus.
1760.

678 ————. Painted decoration in Colonial homes. Cambridge historical society. Proceedings. 31:50-57. 1936.

679 GOZZALDI, MARY ISABELLA. A few old Cambridge houses. Cambridge historical society. Proceedings. 6:17-26. 1912.

680 ————; DANA, ELIZABETH ELLERY; AND POTTINGER, DAVID T. The Vassall house. Cambridge historical society. Proceedings. 21:78-118. 1936.

681 LeBARON, FRANCIS. The Washington-Craigie-Longfellow house. Washington's headquarters and Longfellow's home in Cambridge, Mass. Century. 73:487-98. Feb. 1907.

682 LILLIE, RUPERT B. Gardens and homes of the Loyalists. Cambridge historical society. Proceedings. 26:49-62. 1940.

683 MORISON, SAMUEL ELIOT. Conjectural restoration of the Old college at Harvard. Old time New England. 23:131-58. Apr. 1933. illus.
1638.

684 Painters in the house; Elmwood, home of J. R. Lowell. Mentor. 14:14-16. Aug. 1926. illus.

685 Ruggles mansions built in 1641 and 1764. House beautiful. 48:89. Aug. 1920. illus.
1641 house has been destroyed.

686 RUGGLES, HENRY STODDARD. Ruggles mansion, Cambridge, Massachusetts. N. Y. geneaological and biographical records. 56:101. Apr. 1925.

687 SCHUYLER, MONTGOMERY. Architecture of American colleges. Part 1, Harvard. Architectural record. 26:243-69. Oct. 1909. illus.

688 WHEELWRIGHT, JOHN BROOKS. Valentine-Fuller house, Cambridgeport, Massachusetts. Old time New England. 28:68-71. Oct. 1937.
Ca.1847.

Cape Ann (see also Gloucester)

689 BARTLETT, STUART. Later dwelling architecture of Cape Ann. Part 1. Pencil points. 15:379-94. Aug. 1934. Monograph series. 20:145-60. illus.
Covers 1740–1820, Gloucester and Rockport.

690 ————. Later dwelling architecture of Cape Ann. Part 2. Pencil points. 15:501-516. Oct. 1934. Monograph series. 20:161-76. illus.
Interiors of houses in 689.

691 BREWSTER, DANIEL O. The cottages of Cape Ann—Part 1. Pencil points. 14:535-50. Dec. 1933. Monograph series. 19:81-96. illus.
Covers 1665–1825.

692 BROWN, FRANK CHOUTEAU. Cape Ann: some earlier Colonial dwellings in and about Annisquam, Massachusetts. Pencil points. 14:69-84. Feb. 1933. Monograph series. 19:1-16. illus.
Covers 1650–1715.

693 CHAMBERLAIN, SAMUEL. Gloucester and Cape Ann. N. Y., Hastings house, 1938. 73p. illus.

694 FRANKLIN, M. S. Cottage interiors of Cape Ann. Pencil points. 15:65-80. Jan. 1934. Monograph series. 20:97-112. illus.
Interiors of houses mentioned in 691.

Cape Cod (see also *Barnstable, Yarmouth,* and 556)

695 BANGS, M. R. Cape Cod where houses were built to suit the land. House beautiful. 60:252-58. Sept. 1926. illus.

696 CARRICK, ALICE VAN LEER. Oldest house on Cape Cod. Country life in America. 44:42-45. Sept. 1923. illus.
Dillingham house, Brewster (1660).

697 CHAMBERLAIN, SAMUEL. Cape Cod in the sun. N. Y., Hastings house, 1937. 95p. illus.

698 EARLY, ELEANOR. And this is Cape Cod! Boston, Houghton Mifflin Co., 1936. 223p. illus.

699 EDWARDS, AGNES. Cape Cod—new and old. Boston, Houghton, Mifflin Co., 1918. 239p. illus.

700 READ, EDWARD SEARS. Cape Cod farm and village houses. Architectural forum. 39:7-10. July 1923. illus.

Carlisle

701 WILKINS, MRS. B. P. Century-old houses of Carlisle. Old time New England. 23:44-55. Oct. 1932. illus.

Clinton

702 STONE, CHRISTOPHER C. Old houses in Clinton. Clinton historical society. Papers. 1:39-43. 1912.

Concord (*see also* 541)

703 BARTLETT, GEORGE B. Concord: historic, literary and picturesque. Boston, Lothrop, Lee and Shepard Publishing Co., 1895. 200p. illus.
This is the fifteenth edition.

704 BROWN, FRANK CHOUTEAU. Some records of old Concord, first inland township of Massachusetts. Pencil points. 13:332-46. May 1932. Monograph series. 18:181-96. illus.
Includes Bedford, Groton, Shirley Center.

705 CAPEN, OLIVER BRONSON. Country homes of famous Americans. Part 4. Henry David Thoreau. Country life in America. 5:285-88. Feb. 1904. illus.
Birthplace, Concord, before 1800. Description of Walden Pond hut, ca.1845.

706 FRENCH, ALLEN. Old Concord. Boston, Little, Brown and Co., 1915. 186p. illus.

707 KEYES, JOHN S. Story of an old house. Concord antiquarian society. Publications. no. 5, 1903. 17p. illus.
Smedley-Jones house.

708 LATHROP, M. L. Literary shrine open to visitors; home of three authors, the Wayside, Concord, Massachusetts. Library journal. 58:362. Apr. 15, 1933.

Danvers (see also 542, 823)

709 BROWN, FRANK CHOUTEAU. Danvers (old Salem Village), Massachusetts—Part 1. Pencil points. 19:719-34. Nov. 1938. Monograph series. 24:161-76. illus.
Covers 1648–1812.

710 ———. Danvers (old Salem Village), Massachusetts—Part 2. Pencil points. 19:783-98. Dec. 1938. Monograph series. 24:177-92. illus.
Covers 1670–1809.

711, 712 Contract and expense account for building the Samuel Fowler house, Danversport, 1810. Essex institute. Historical collections. 67:46-48. 1931.
Also appeared in *Old Time New England*. 21:185–87. 1931. *See also* 222.

713 An early East Danvers house. Danvers historical society. Collections. 3:59-63. 1915.
Built 1641 or 1642 by Richard Ingersoll.

714 FALES, WINNIFRED. Lindens, a house with a history. Country life in America. 33:46-49. Mar. 1918. illus.
Before 1754. Moved to Washington, D. C. *New York Times*, Dec. 5, 1937, section 9.

715 HOUSE, ALBERT VIRGIL. Historic cellar holes. Danvers historical society. Collections. 15:87-107. 1927.
Notes on houses.

716 Lindens, built in Danvers, Massachusetts, in 1754, re-erected and furnished in Washington, D. C. in 1938. Antiques. 33:67, 76-79. Feb. 1938. illus.

717 PERLEY, SIDNEY. Nurse house. Essex institute. Historical collections. 62:1-3. Jan. 1926.
Rebecca Nurse house.

718 PHILBRICK, JULIA A. Old Putnam houses in Danvers. Danvers historical society. Collections. 5:70-73. 1917.

719 PRIEST, GEORGE F. Old houses of Salem Village. Danvers historical society. Collections. 3:1-12. 1915.

720 PUTNAM, ALFRED P. Danvers people and their homes. Danvers historical society. Collections. 9:57-64. 1921; 11:50-54. 1923; 11:55-73. 1929.

721 Samuel Fowler house, Danversport, Mass. Old time New England. 3:1-6. Mar. 1912. illus.
1809.

722 TAPLEY, HARRIET S. Old tavern days in Danvers. Danvers historical society. Collections. 8:1-32. 1920.

Dedham (see also 555, 558)

723 APPLETON, WILLIAM SUMNER. Scenic wallpaper from East Dedham, Massachusetts. Old time New England. 22:51-58. Oct. 1931. illus.

724 Oldest frame dwelling in the United States, the Fairbanks house, Dedham, Massachusetts. Mentor. 16:30-31. Apr. 1928. illus.

Deerfield (see also 351)

725 COLEMAN, EMMA L. Frary house, Deerfield, Massachusetts. Old time New England. 23:88-98. Jan. 1933. illus.
1683 and later.

726 HADDON, RAWSON W. Old Deerfield, Massachusetts. White pine series of architectural monographs. v. 6, no. 5. Oct. 1920. 14p. illus.

727 Old Deerfield, containing an appreciation of early New England as evidenced by the now standing seventeenth century houses of Deerfield. Boston, Pinkham press, 1928. 24p. illus.

728 SCALES, JOHN LONGFELLOW. The Longfellow garrison. American monthly magazine. 38:246-51. May 1911.

729 SHELDON, GEORGE, AND SHELDON, J. M. ARMS. The Rev. John Williams house. Deerfield, Mass., 1918. 32p. illus.
(1707.)

730 SHELDON, J. M. ARMS. Old Indian house at Deerfield, Mass., and the effort made in 1847 to save it from destruction. Old time New England. 12:99-108. Jan. 1922. illus.

731 ———. Revolutionary history of a New England homestead; Colonel Joseph Stebbins homestead in Deerfield, Massachusetts. Deerfield, Mass., 1925. 50p. illus.
(Ca.1772.)

732 Three old Deerfield fireplaces, belonging to the latter half of the eighteenth century. Architectural review. 5:113. June 1917. illus.

733 WHITING, MARGARET C. Old-time mural and floor decorations in Deerfield and vicinity. Pocumtuck Valley memorial association. Proceedings. 6:272-81. 1921.

Dennis (see *Yarmouth*)

Dorchester (*see also* 549)

734 STARK, JAMES HENRY. History of the old Blake house, and a brief sketch of the Dorchester historical society. (Dorchester?) Mass., 1907. 13p. illus.

735 STONE, ELMA A. The old Trescott house. Hyde Park historical register. 3:73-76. Apr. 1903.

Duxbury

736 ALDEN, EDWARD SMITH. Alden homestead, Duxbury, Mass. . . . Holyoke, Mass., Alden press. 1932. 64p.

737 BAXTER, SYLVESTER. Alden house at Duxbury, Massachusetts. Architectural record. 49:399-408. May 1921. illus.
1655.

738 HALL, GERTRUDE. Charm of old Duxbury: an historic Massachusetts Bay town and its delightful old and new houses. Indoors and out. 2:161-69. July 1903. illus.

Essex

739 DOW, GEORGE FRANCIS. The Choate house at Essex, Massachusetts, and its recent restoration. Old time New England. 12:6-13. July 1921. illus.
1725.

740 MAGONIGLE, H. VAN BUREN. Essex, a Connecticut river town. White pine series of architectural monographs. v. 6, no. 6. Dec. 1920. 16p. illus.
Houses of the Colonial period.

Framingham

741 First Baptist church, Framingham Centre, Massachusetts. Architectural review. n.s. 6:41-45. May 1918. illus.

Gloucester (see also *Cape Ann*)

742 BROWN, FRANK CHOUTEAU. Interior details and furnishings of the William Haskell dwelling, built before 1650 at West Gloucester, Massachusetts. Pencil points. 20:113-28. Feb. 1930. Monograph series. 25:1-16. illus.

Groveland

743 NORTHEND, MARY HARROD. House with a history. American homes and gardens. 9:128-31. Apr. 1912. illus.
Savony house. Before 1777.

744 POORE, ALFRED. The houses and buildings of Groveland, Massachusetts. Essex institute. Historical collections. 46:193-208, 289-304. July-Oct. 1910; 47:25-40, 133-48, 261-76. Jan.-July 1911.
Compiled in 1854.

Hatfield

745 MILLER, MARGARET. Reminiscences of an old meeting house. Pocumtuck Valley memorial association. Proceedings. 6:95-105. 1921.

Haverhill

746 BACON, EDGAR MAYHEW. Country homes of famous Americans. Part 3. John Greenleaf Whittier. Country life in America. 5:209-13, 256. Jan. 1904. illus.
Birthplace near Haverhill (1668) house at Amesbury.

747 Contract-specifications covering construction of the old Saltonstall house at Haverhill, Mass., executed in 1788. Architectural record. n.s. 6:75. May 1918. illus.

Hingham

748 CORSE, MURRAY P. Old Ship meeting-house in Hingham, Mass. Old time New England. 21:19-30. July 1930. illus.

749 DAUGHTERS OF THE AMERICAN REVOLUTION. MASSACHUSETTS. Hingham; a story of its early settlement and life, its ancient landmarks, its historic sites and buildings. Hingham, Mass., Old Colony chapter, D. A. R., 1911. 123p. illus.

750 RUSSELL, ELIZABETH H. Old Ordinary at Hingham, Massachusetts, an ancient tavern. House beautiful. 58:109-112, 156-57. Aug. 1925. illus.
Before 1700.

751 SHUMWAY, HARRY IRVING. Grandfather among the taverns. American cookery. 39:139-46. 1934.
Old Ordinary.

Ipswich

752 Cap't. Matthew Perkins house, Ipswich, Mass. Old time New England. 15:125-27. Jan. 1925. illus.
Ca.1638.

752A (Houses of Ipswich.) *See* Chronicle report of the 250th anniversary exercises of Ipswich, Mass. Ipswich, 1884. 74p. illus.

753 The Thimbles, Ipswich, Massachusetts. House beautiful. 42:150-51. Aug. 1917. illlus.

754 WATERS, THOMAS FRANKLIN. Early homes of the Puritans, and some old Ipswich houses. Salem, Mass., The Salem Press Co., 1898. 106p. illus.

755 ———. Glimpses of everyday life in old Ipswich. Salem, Ipswich historical society, 1925. 39p. illus.

756 ———. Ipswich in Massachusetts Bay colony. Ipswich, Ipswich historical society, 1905. 2v. illus.
Another edition, 1917.

757 WATERMAN, THOMAS TILESTON. Staircase, Corbett house, Ipswich, Mass. Architecture. v. 50, no. 4, pl. 154. Oct. 1924. illus. only.

758 Whipple house, Ipswich, Mass. Antiquarian. 1:23, 25. Dec. 1923. illus.
(Ca.1640 and later.)

Lancaster

759 BROWN, JOHN P. Notes on the Bulfinch church at Lancaster, Massachusetts. Old time New England. 27:148-51. Apr. 1937. illus.

760 PLACE, CHARLES A. Bulfinch church, Lancaster, Mass. Architectural forum. 34:191-98. June 1921. illus.
(1816) Charles Bulfinch, architect.

761 SAFFORD, MARION FULLER. Historical sketch of the First church of Lancaster. Lancaster, Mass., The Church, 1916. 16p.

Lenox

762 LYNCH, FREDERICK. The church on the Lenox Hilltop and round about it. New England magazine. 23:192-211. Oct. 1900. illus.
Brief discussion of the architecture.

Lexington (see also 541)

763 PIPER, FRED SMITH. Architectural yesterdays in Lexington; a fragmentary account of some of the older buildings and their builders. Lexington historical society. Proceedings. 4:114-26. 1912.

Lowell

764 COOLIDGE, JOHN. Mill and mansion. N. Y., Columbia university press, 1942.
A study of architecture and society, 1820–65.

765 GRIFFIN, SARA SWAN. Old homes and historic byways of Lowell. Lowell historical society. Contributions. 1:451-66. 1913.

766 THOMPSON, ELLEN STRAW. Rediscovering an old house. New England magazine. 37:185-92. Oct. 1907.
Spalding house, 1670.

Lynn

767 HAWKES, NATHAN MORTIMER. Hearths and homes of old Lynne, with studies in local history. Lynn, Mass., Nichols, 1907. 350p. illus.

Malden (see also 559)

768 COREY, DELORAINE PENDRE. The Old Brick. Malden historical society. Register. 6:6-12. 1920.
Brick meeting house, 1803.

769 WATKINS, WALTER KENDALL. Malden's old meeting houses. Malden historical society. Register. 2:33-53. 1912.

Mansfield

770 COPELAND, JENNIE F. Fisher-Richardson house. Old time New England. 21:168-78. Apr. 1931. illus.
1700.

Marblehead (*see also* 338, 359)

771 ALDRICH, WILLIAM TRUMAN. Marblehead, its contribution to eighteenth and early nineteenth century American architecture. White pine series of architectural monographs. v. 4, no. 1. Feb. 1918. 14p. illus.

772 BROWN, FRANK CHOUTEAU. Old Marblehead—part 1. Pencil points. 19: 313-28. May 1938. Monograph series. 24:113-28. illus.
Covers 1683-1750.

773 ———. Old Marblehead, Massachusetts—part 2. Pencil points. 19:455-70. July 1938. Monograph series. 24:129-44. illus.
Covers 1648-1824.

774 ———. Old Marblehead, Massachusetts—part 3. Pencil points. 19:591-606. Sept. 1938. Monograph series. 24:145-60. illus.
Covers 1729-68.

775 CHAMBERLAIN, SAMUEL. Old Marblehead. N. Y., Hastings house. 1940. 72p. illus.

776 FOWLER, SAMUEL PAGE. The King Hooper house and its early occupants. Danvers historical society. Collections. 1:87-89. 1913.
1745. Extracts from a letter from Samuel Page Fowler, May 5, 1875.

777 SPALDING, DEXTER EDWIN. King Hooper mansion, a famous Colonial residence in Marblehead, Massachusetts. House beautiful. 52:106-108. Aug. 1922. illus.

778 WORTHINGTON, FREDERICK WILLIAM. The King Hooper house. American homes and gardens. 11:273-75, 285. Aug. 1914. illus.

Marlborough

779 Contract to build a minister's house at Marlborough, Mass., in 1661. Old time New England. 24:142. Apr. 1934.

Marshfield

780 EATON, WALTER PRICHARD. Winslow house at Marshfield, Mass. House beautiful. 50:184-87, 224-26. Sept. 1921. illus.
1699.

781 ROBINSON, THOMAS P. Historic Winslow house at Marshfield, Mass. Old time New England. 11:107-112. Jan. 1921. illus.

Martha's Vineyard (see also 556)

782 CHAMBERLAIN, SAMUEL. Martha's Vineyard. N. Y., Hastings house, 1941. 73p. illus.

Medford

783 BROOKS, MRS. ALFRED, AND MANN, MOSES W. Colonial houses—old and new. Medford historical society. Register. 15:67-72. July 1912.

784 COOLIDGE, RUTH DAME. The Craddock house, past and future. Medford historical society. Register. 29:37-56. Sept. 1926.
Also known as the Peter Tufts house (1677–80).

785 FULLER, GEORGE S. T. History of the Royall house and its occupants. Medford historical society. Register. 29:1-11. Mar. 1926.
(Before 1697, 1750 and later) *See also* 549.

786 GILL, ELIZA M. At Medford's old civic center. Medford historical society. Register. 25:11-15, 27. Mar.-June 1922.

787 Isaac Royall house on the Plantation, Medford, Massachusetts. American architect and building news. 24:171-72. Oct. 13, 1888. illus.

788 MANN, MOSES W. Dr. Osgood's house. Medford historical society. Register. 23:38-40. June 1920.
1785.

789 ———. Renovation of the Peter Tufts house. Medford historical society. Register. 29:70-75. Dec. 1926.

790 ———. The Tufts family residences. Medford historical society. Register. 18:60-67. July 1915.

791 ———. The Touro house and its owner. Medford historical society. Register. 23:78-83. Dec. 1920.
Before 1822.

792 WILD, HELEN TILDEN (comp.). The building of the Town house. Medford historical society. Register. 9:40-43. Jan. 1906.
Compiled from the town records.

793, 794 ———. The old Royall house. Salem, Mass., Salem Press Co., 1908. 8p. illus.
Reprinted from the *Massachusetts Magazine*, v.1,no.3.

Middlesex County

795 DRAKE, SAMUEL ADAMS. Historical fields and mansions of Middlesex. Boston, James R. Osgood and Co., 1874. 442p. illus.

796 FORBES, HARRIETTE M. Some seventeenth century houses of Middlesex county, Massachusetts. Old time New England. 29:90-105. Jan. 1939. illus.
At Sherborn, Wayland, Lincoln, Stow.

Nantucket (see also 556)

797 CHAMBERLAIN, SAMUEL. Nantucket. N. Y., Hastings house, 1939. 73p. illus.

798 DOUGLAS-LITHGOW, R. A. Jethro Coffin's home, "the oldest house" in Nantucket, 1686-1910. Massachusetts magazine. 4:23-28. Jan. 1911.
See also 558.

799 GARDNER, ARTHUR H. The Big shop. Nantucket historical association. Proceedings. 22:35-43. 1916.
*Ca.*1800.

800 HINCHMAN, LYDIA S. Maria Mitchell house and memorial. Nantucket, Mass. Old time New England. 16:105-117. Jan. 1926. illus.
(1818)

801 HUSBAND, J. Notable restoration; residence of F. H. B. Byrne, Nantucket. House beautiful. 63:421-24. Apr. 1928. illus.

802 ———. 1724; house of E. Tuttle, Nantucket. House beautiful. 61:637-39. May 1927. illus.

803 LINTON, MARY J. More of Nantucket; an early Quaker house. House beautiful. 54:360, 404, 405. Oct. 1923. illus.
*Ca.*1700.

804 MACY, WILLIAM F. Nantucket's oldest house (1686) the Jethro Coffin house, the Horseshoe house. Nantucket, The Inquirer and mirror press, 1929. 35p. illus.

805 MACKAY, HELEN G. Houses of Nantucket, and a bit of its history. House beautiful. 52:220-21, 250-51. Sept. 1922. illus.
Covers 1686–*ca.* 1820.

806 RIPLEY, HUBERT G. The Jethro Coffin house at Sunset Hill, sometimes called the Horseshoe house. American institute of architects. Journal. 16:218-23. June 1928. illus.

807 SCHWEINFURTH, J. A. Early dwellings of Nantucket. White pine series of architectural monographs. v. 3, no. 6. Dec. 1917. 14p. illus.

808 ———. Nantucket revisited. American architect. 110:301-308, 311-13. Nov. 15, 1916. illus.

809 STEVENS, WILLIAM OLIVER. Nantucket, the far-away island. N. Y., Dodd, Mead and Co., 1936. 313p. illus.

New Bedford

810 CRAPO, HENRY HOWLAND. Old buildings in New Bedford. Old Dartmouth historical sketches. 23:17-29. 1909.

811 Dow, Joy WHEELER. A house of the transitional style. Architectural review. n. s. 2:75-77. June 1901. illus.
Bennett house, *ca.*1840.

812 ROSÉ, GRACE NORTON. Past century charm of New Bedford. Architectural record. 33:424-33. May 1913. illus.

813 WORTH, HENRY B. The homesteads at Apponagansett before 1710. Old Dartmouth historical sketches. 25:6-9. 1909.
Near New Bedford.

Newbury

814 BROWN, FRANK CHOUTEAU. Dwellings of Newbury Old Town. Pencil points. 14:169-84. Apr. 1933. Monograph series. 19:17-32. illus.
Covers 1645–97.

815 Ilsley house, Newbury, Mass. Old time New England. 2:10-13. Aug. 1911. illus.
*Ca.*1670.

816 One of the oldest houses in New England, the Spences house, 1651, Newbury, Mass. Country life in America. 30:38-39. June 1916. illus.

817 SPRING, JAMES W. The Coffin house in Newbury, Massachusetts. Old time New England. 20:3-29. July 1929. illus.

Newburyport

818 FISHER, RICHARD ARNOLD. Old houses in and around Newburyport, Massachusetts. White pine series of architectural monographs. v. 3, no. 3. June 1917. 15p. illus.
Covers 1646–1810.

819 HALE, ALBERT. Old Newburyport houses. Boston, W. B. Clarke and Co., 1912. 68p. illus.

820 HUSE, CALEB. The Coffin house, Newburyport, Massachusetts. Old time New England. 27:69-72. Oct. 1936.
Nineteenth century description.

821, 822 MEAD, EDWIN DOAK. The Old South pilgrimage to Newburyport. Boston, 1900. 14p.
Reprinted from the *New England Magazine.* July, 1900.

Northampton (see 557)

Peabody (see also 542)

823 UNDERWOOD, MRS. GEORGE L. The Derby-Osborn farm, Peabody, with its McIntire summer house and barn. Old time New England. 16:55-64. Oct. 1925. illus.
1793–94. Now at Glen Magna Farms, Danvers.

Pelham

824 SEE, ANNA PHILLIPS. Ancient Pelham and the oldest town hall in New England. D. A. R. magazine. 56:286-92. May 1922.
Town hall, 1743.

Pigeon Cove

825 WILLIAMS, THOMAS. Some old houses of Pigeon Cove, Massachusetts. Pencil points. 14:349-64. July 1933. Monograph series. 19:49-64. illus.
Covers 1676–1778.

Plymouth

826 (Allyn house. Contemporary description). American magazine of useful and entertaining knowledge. 3:37. Oct. 1836.

827 BAUM, DWIGHT JAMES. Pilgrimage to Plymouth. Architecture. 44:265-88, 328-33. Sept.-Nov. 1921. illus.

828 Restoring Colonial houses, Plymouth, Massachusetts. Architectural record. 75:530-32. June 1934. illus.

829 STODDARD, FRANCIS R., JR. The old Thomas house at Plymouth. Massachusetts magazine. 3:269-71. Oct. 1910.

830 ———. The old Warren house at Plymouth. Massachusetts magazine. 4:105-109. Apr. 1911.

831 ———. The Winslow house. Massachusetts magazine. 5:102-104. April 1912.

Quincy

832 ADAMS, HENRY II. The Adams mansion. Old time New England. 19:3-17. July 1928. illus.
1731.

833 ———. The birthplace of presidents John and John Quincy Adams, Quincy, Massachusetts. Old time New England. 26:78-99. Jan. 1936. illus.

834 ANNABLE, I. K. Historical notes of the Crombie street Congregational church. Essex institute. Historical collections. 77:204-217. July 1941.

835 COYLE, EDITH WOODBURY. The Quincy homestead. Old time New England. 19:147-58. Apr. 1929. illus.
1706 and earlier.

836 CUSHING, ARTHUR BOARDMAN. The Dorothy Quincy homestead, Quincy, Mass. Massachusetts magazine. 4:96-98. Apr. 1911.

837 NORTHEND, MARY HARROD. Dorothy Quincy house. House and garden. 25:97-101. Feb. 1914. illus.
1623.

838 WHITNEY, FREDERICK AUGUSTUS. Historical sketch of the Old Church, Quincy, Massachusetts. Albany, J. Munsell Co., 1864. 17p.

Reading (see also 372)

839 HOWARD, LOEA PARKER. The Parker tavern; being an account of a most interesting house built by Abraham Bryant in 1694, together with some facts about early owners. Reading, Mass., Reading antiquarian society, 1930. 31p. illus.

Roxbury

840 CORDINGLEY, W. W. Shirley Place, Roxbury, Massachusetts. . . . Old time New England. 12:51-63. Oct. 1921. illus.
(1748.)

840A LANG, WILLIAM BAILEY. Views, with ground plans of the Highland cottages at Roxbury, designed and erected by W. B. Lang. Boston, The Author, 1845. 2p. illus.

Salem (see also 338, 359, 542, 555)

841 BELKNAP, HENRY WYKOFF. The 17th century house. Salem, Mass., Newcomb and Gauss Co., 1930. 8p. illus.
John Ward house, 1684.

842 BRAGDON, CLAUDE FAYETTE. Six houses in Salem. American architect and building news. 39:41-43. Jan. 21, 1893. illus.

843 BROWN, FRANK CHOUTEAU. Salem, Massachusetts. Pencil points. 18:305-320. May 1937. Monograph series. 23:17-32. illus.
Covers 1668–1810. Includes a location map of old buildings.

844 ———. Gardner-White-Pingree house, built in Salem, Massachusetts in 1804 by Samuel McIntire, architect. Pencil points. 21:515-30. Aug. 1940. Monograph series. 26:145-60. illus.

845 CAPEN, OLIVER BRONSON. Country homes of famous Americans. Part 8. Nathaniel Hawthorne. Country life in America. 6:242-45, 282, 283. July 1904. illus.
Old Manse, 1765. Wayside, original house *ca.*1750, many additions.

846 CARRICK, ALICE VAN LEER. House of Seven Gables. Country life in America. 39:45-47. Apr. 1921. illus.
(*Ca.* 1668.)

847 CHAMBERLAIN, SAMUEL. Historic Salem in four seasons. N. Y., Hastings house, 1938. 73p. illus.

848 Contract for building the prison in Salem for the county of Essex, 1764. Essex institute. Historical collections. 68:299-302. 1932.

849 COUSINS, FRANK. Colonial architecture, series 1. Fifty Salem doorways. N. Y., Doubleday, Page and Co., 1912. 50p. illus.

850 COUSINS, FRANK, AND RILEY, PHILIP M. Six old Salem doorways. Architectural record. 42:393-99. Oct. 1917. illus.

851 ———. The Colonial architecture of Salem. Boston, Little, Brown and Co., 1919. 282p. illus.

852 ———. The wood-carver of Salem; Samuel McIntyre, his life and work. Boston, Little, Brown and Co., 1916. 168p. illus.

853 Dow, GEORGE FRANCIS. The Colonial village built at Salem, Massachusetts in the spring of 1930. Old time New England. 22:3-14. July 1931. illus.

854 Dow, JOY WHEELER. Salem enchantment. House beautiful. 12:334-44. Nov. 1922. illus.

855 EMMERTON, CAROLINE O. Chronicles of three old houses. Boston, Thomas Todd Co., 1935. 57p. illus.
House of Seven Gables (ca.1688), Hathaway house (1682), and Retire Beckett house (1655).

856 ESSEX INSTITUTE. Visitor's guide to Salem. Salem, Mass., Essex institute, 1927. 249p. illus.

857 Four doors by Samuel McIntire. House beautiful. 39:75. Feb. 1916. illus.

858 FRANKLIN, M. S. Public buildings—Part 2. Recording the architecture of late Colonial times in Salem, Massachusetts. Pencil points. 13:408-422. June 1932. Monograph series. 18:198-212. illus.
Covers 1782–1828.

859 HUNT, W. H. Old Salem houses. American architect. 119:507-513, 522. Apr. 1921. illus.

860 ———. Samuel McIntyre housewright-architect, Salem, Mass. American architect. 119:415-22, 428. Apr. 1921. illus.

861 KIMBALL, SIDNEY FISKE. The Derby room and its furnishings. Pennsylvania museum. Bulletin. 25:11-17. Apr. 1930. illus.
A room from the Elias Hasket Derby house.

862 ———. Elias Hasket Derby mansion in Salem. Salem, Essex institute. Historical collections. 60:273-92. Oct. 1924.

863 ———. Mr. Samuel McIntire, carver, the architect of Salem. Portland, Me., Southworth-Anthoensen press, 1940. 157p. illus.

864 List of houses built in Salem from 1750-1773. Essex institute. Historical collections. 58:292-96. Oct. 1922.

865 MacDONALD, ALBERT J. Selected interiors of old houses in Salem and vicinity. . . . Boston, Rogers and Manson Co., 1916. 55p. illus.

866 McDONALD, EDITH W. The woodcarver of Salem. Stone and Webster. Journal. 46:53-63. 1930.
Samuel McIntire.

867 MESSER, NELLIE STEARNS. The Ropes memorial at Salem, Massachusetts. Old time New England. 14:146-63. Apr. 1924. illus.
1719.

868 NORTHEND, MARY HARROD. Historic doorways of old Salem. Boston, Houghton Mifflin Co., 1926. 96p. illus.

869 ———. Memories of old Salem. N. Y., Moffat, Yard and Co., 1917. 341p. illus.

870 ———. The old Cook-Oliver house in Salem. American homes and gardens. 11:308-311. Sept. 1914. illus.
1804 by Samuel McIntire.

871 ———. Old fences in Salem and Newburyport. American homes and gardens. 11:48-52. Feb. 1914. illus.

872 ———. Pierce-Nichols house at Salem. American homes and gardens. 12:183-87. June 1915. illus.
1782 by Samuel McIntire.

873 Notes on the Derby houses from the Derby ledgers. Essex institute. Historical collections. 69:90-95. 1933.
Eighteenth century building costs.

874 Old John Ward house, built 1684, now at Essex institute museum yard, Salem, Mass. American architect. 134:10. July 1928. illus.

875 PERLEY, SIDNEY. The court houses in Salem. Essex institute. Historical collections. 47:101-123. Apr. 1911.

876 PHILLIPS, JAMES DUNCAN. Salem in the eighteenth century. Boston, Houghton Mifflin Co., 1937. 533p. illus.

877 ———. Salem in the seventeenth century. Boston, Houghton Mifflin Co., 1933. 426p. illus.

878 PORTER, FREDERICK HUTCHINSON. The Pineapple house, Salem, Mass. Architectural review. n. s. 6:70. Apr. 1918. illus.
In Brown street court. Ca.1740.

879 RILEY, PHILIP M. Inside a McIntire house. Country life in America. 24:52-54. Oct. 1913. illus.

880 ———. In the spirit of old Salem. House beautiful. 39:72-74. Feb. 1916. illus.
Covers 1690–1800.

881 ———, AND COUSINS, FRANK. Windows of old Salem. Country life in America. 28:48-49. Oct. 1915. illus.

882 ROBB, GORDON. Gate and posts, Baldwin-Lyman house, Salem, Mass., built in 1808. Brickbuilder. 24:265-66. Nov. 1915. illus.

883 RYAN, MARGARET. The Assembly house at Salem; built in 1782 and now restored to its former glory. House beautiful. 50:89-92. Aug. 1921. illus.

884 SALEM, MASS., BOARD OF PARK COMMISSIONERS. Colonial village built at Salem, Mass., to commemorate the three hundredth anniversary of the arrival of the Winthrop fleet, June 12, 1630. Salem, 1930. 8p.

885 ———. Guide to Salem, 1630. Salem, 1930. 32p. illus.
Manual for participants and spectators at the pageant of the arrival of Governor Winthrop in the ship Arabella, June, 1930.

886 Selected interiors of old houses in Salem and vicinity. Boston, Rogers and Manson, 1919. 55p. illus.

887 STOW, CHARLES MESSER. Samuel McIntire of Salem. Antiquarian. 12:36-38, 66, 68. Feb. 1929. illus.

888 WATERMAN, THOMAS TILESTON. Staircase, Witch house, Salem, Mass. Architecture. v. 50, no. 4, pl. 155. Oct. 1924. illus. only.

889 WHIPPLE, SHERMAN L., AND WATERS, THOMAS FRANKLIN. Puritan homes. Ipswich historical society. Publications. no. 27. 1929. 99p. illus.

Saugus (see 222)

Shrewsbury

890 General Artemas Ward homestead, Shrewsbury, Mass. Old time New England. 17:147-55. Apr. 1927. illus.
1730.

South Walpole

891 SHUMWAY, HARRY IRVING. Tavern as it used to be. American cookery. 38:139-46. 1933.
Fuller's tavern, 1807.

892 SHURROCKS, ALFRED F. Fuller's tavern, South Walpole, Mass. Old time New England. 18:146-57. Apr. 1928. illus.

893 WHITING, HARRY A. Old Fuller's tavern reopens. Old time New England. 18:158-59. Apr. 1928.

Springfield (see also *West Springfield*)

894 Alexander house—Linden hall, State street, Springfield, Mass. Old time New England. 30:35-40. Oct. 1939. illus.
Designed by Asher Benjamin in 1811.

895 TOBEY, FRANK G. Old State street, its residences and the people who lived in them. Connecticut Valley historical society. Papers. 4:184-202. 1912.

Stockbridge

896 Colonial restoration; so-called Mission house, Stockbridge, Mass. Antiques. 18:216-19. Sept. 1930. illus.
1739.

897 STEELE, F. Mission house; oldest house in Stockbridge. House beautiful
    68:26-33, 54-57. July 1930. illus.

Stotham

898 RIPLEY, HUBERT G. New England village. White pine series of architec-
    tural monographs. v. 6, no. 2. Apr. 1920. illus.
    Covers Cadwallader Simpkins house, Jenks-Greenleaf house, Salmon-White house,
    Podbury-Ives house, and Obadiah Witherspoon house.

Sudbury

899 CARRICK, ALICE VAN LEER. Wayside inn. House beautiful. 65:536-42.
    Apr. 1929. illus.

900 CHAMBERLAIN, SAMUEL. Longfellow's Wayside inn; a camera impression.
    N. Y., Hasting house, 1938. 72p. illus.
    1686 and later.

901 EATON, FLORENCE TAFT. Longfellow's Wayside inn. Landmark. 10:301-
    304. May 1928.

902 Inn where the Tales were told. Mentor. 14:33. Aug. 1926. illus.

903 LAWRENCE, C. A. Longfellow's Wayside inn. Arts and decoration. 6:548-51.
    Oct. 1916. illus.

904 LORING, CHARLES G. Red Horse tavern. Garden and home builder. 43:435-
    43. July 1926. illus.

905 MEAD, LUCIA AMES. How the old Wayside inn came back. Old time New
    England. 22:41-45. July 1931. illus.

906 SEABURY, JOSEPH S. The Wayside inn. House beautiful. 36:32-39. July
    1914. illus.

Taunton (see 544)

Topsfield

907 BESTON, HENRY B. An old world house on a new world lane. House beau-
    tiful. 46:80-81. Aug. 1919. illus.
    Capen house, 1683. *See also* 213.

908 The building of the Congregational meeting house in 1842. Topsfield his-
    torical society. Collections. 20:86-88. 1915.

909 MILLAR, DONALD. Seventeenth century New England house. Architectural
    record. 38:348-61. Sept. 1915. illus.
    Capen house.

910 ———. Seventeenth century New England house. Old time New England.
    11:3-8. July 1920. illus.
    Capen house.

911 PEABODY, CHARLES JOEL. The story of a Peabody house and its neighborhood. Topsfield historical society. Collections. 26:113-20. 1921.
1782.

912 PERLEY, SIDNEY. Topsfield houses and lands. Topsfield historical society. Collections. 29:49-98. 1928.

Uxbridge

913 Well-preserved Colonial home of revolutionary times. House beautiful. 52:560-61. Dec. 1922. illus.

Waltham (see also 355)

914 ORCUTT, P. D. Gore Place, Waltham, Massachusetts, the beginnings of a restoration. American architect. 150:67-74. June 1937.
(Rebuilt between 1799 and 1804. Sometimes credited to Bulfinch.)

Watertown

915 BROWN, FRANK CHOUTEAU. Watertown, Massachusetts. Pencil points. 18: 323-38. May 1937. Monograph series. 23:33-48. illus.
Covers 1663–1806. *See also* 222.

Wayland

916 First Parish church, 1814, Wayland, Massachusetts. Architectural forum. n. s. 6:95. May 1918. illus.

Wellesley (see 557)

Wenham

917 APPLETON, WILLIAM SUMNER. Description of Robert McClaflin's house. Old time New England. 16:157-67. Apr. 1926. illus.
Seventeenth century.

Westborough

917A WESTBOROUGH, MASSACHUSETTS, HISTORICAL SOCIETY. Some old houses in Westborough, Mass., and their occupants. n. p., 1906. 70p. illus.
Some tipped-in photographs.

917B ———. More old houses in Westborough. 1908. illus.

917C ———. Other old houses in Westborough. 1911. illus.

Westfield

918 ISHAM, NORMAN MORRISON. Colonial doorway from the Connecticut Valley. Metropolitan museum of art. Bulletin. 12:32-34. Feb. 1917. illus.

West Springfield

919 (STORROW, HELEN O.?) Storrowton, a New England village. Boston, Mass., Thomas Todd Co., 1930. 25p. illus.
Storrowton comprises a group of houses, 1767–1834, moved to the grounds of the Eastern States Exposition.

Weymouth (see 544)

Wickford

920 CUMMINGS, J. H. An old church and glebe. International studio. 81:293-
96. July 1925. illus.

St. Paul's.

Williamstown (see also 383, 572, 1194)

921 ADRIANCE, VANDERPOEL. New foundations. Williamstown, Mass., 1940.
24p.

Mimeographed. Describes buildings in Williamstown which have been moved to new
sites.

922 GRANT, CHARLES C. Rebuilding of the First Congregational church of Williamstown, Massachusetts. Architectural record. 32:249-57. Oct. 1915.
illus.

923 MILHAM, WILLIS I. Early American observatories. Which was the first
astronomical observatory in America? Williamstown, Massachusetts, Williams College, 1938. 58p. illus.

Describes eleven observatories erected and equipped before 1840. Bibliography.

924 PERRY, ARTHUR LATHAM. Williamstown and Williams College. Williamstown, Mass., 1899. 847p. illus.

925 WATERMAN, THOMAS TILESTON. The President's house, Williams College,
Mass. American architect. 130:269-80. Oct. 1926. illus.

Wollaston

926 Colonial Josiah Quincy homestead, Wollaston. Old time New England.
28:85-89. Jan. 1938.

Worcester

927 Contracts to build the Stephen Salisbury mansion in Worcester, Massachusetts
in 1772, and a store house in 1790. Old time New England. 20:178-85.
Apr. 1930.

928 (Court house and prison, 1732. Description.) Worcester magazine and historical journal. 2:204. July 1826.

929 CRANE, ELLERY BICKNELL (ed.). Historic homes and institutions and
genealogical and personal memoirs of Worcester county, Massachusetts,
with a history of the Worcester society of antiquity. N. Y., Lewis Publishing Co., 1907. 4v. illus.

930 CUTLER, W. WALDO. Isaiah Thomas house, Worcester, Massachusetts. Old
time New England. 18:133-40. Jan. 1928. illus.

1782.

931 FORBES, MRS. HARRIETTE M. Elias Carter, architect, of Worcester, Massachusetts. Old time New England. 11:58-71. Oct. 1920. illus.

932 ———. The Salisbury mansion, Worcester, Massachusetts. Old time New
England. 20:99-111. Jan. 1930. illus.

1772.

933 ISHAM, NORMAN MORRISON. The Stephen Salisbury house in Worcester and its restoration. Old time New England. 20:111-20. Jan. 1930. illus.

934 The passing of the Baldwin house. Worcester magazine. 6:80-86. Sept. 1903.

935 WAITE, EMMA F. Old-time taverns of Worcester. Worcester society of antiquities. Proceedings. 19:70-82. 1903.

936 WHEELER, HENRY M. A New England house one hundred years ago. Worcester society of antiquities. Proceedings. 19:358-94. 1903.

937 WORCESTER BANK AND TRUST COMPANY. Some historic houses of Worcester; a brief account of the houses and taverns that fill a prominent part in the history of Worcester. . . . Worcester, Mass., 1919. 71p. illus.

Yarmouthport

938 HOWES, THOMAS PRINCE. Ancient houses. Yarmouthport, Mass., C. W. Swift, 1911. 6p.
Covers Yarmouth and Dennis.

NEW HAMPSHIRE

GENERAL REFERENCES (*see also* 258, 373, 388)

939 BAER, ANNIE WENTWORTH. Ricker inn. New Hampshire. 61:160-68. Apr. 1929.
Late eighteenth and early nineteenth century.

940 COLBY, FREDERICK MYRON. Granite state rooftrees. Granite state magazine. 1:13-17. Jan. 1906.

941 ———. Old rooftrees of New Hampshire. Magazine of history. 4:160-65. Sept. 1906; 6:276-80. Nov. 1907.

942 FEDERAL WRITERS' PROJECT. Hands that built New Hampshire. Brattleboro, Vt., Stephen Daye press, 1940. 288p. illus.
Some material on architects and builders.

943 ———. New Hampshire: a guide to the granite state. Boston, Houghton Mifflin Co., 1938. 559p. illus.

944 FERGUSON, A. E. Early dwellings in New Hampshire. White pine series of architectural monographs. v. 12, no. 5. 1926. 19p. illus.
Colonial.

945 SPEARE, EVA A. Colonial meeting-houses of New Hampshire compared with their contemporaries in New England. Littleton, N. H., Courier Printing Co., 1938. 238p. illus.
Published under auspices of Daughters of Colonial Wars, State of New Hampshire.

946 STANIELS, EVA F. T. Historic inns. Granite monthly. 44:17-20. Jan. 1912.

947 WOOD, HELEN M. Historic churches of New Hampshire. American monthly
magazine. 38:300-301. June 1911.

948 WOOD, JAMES A. New Hampshire homes. Concord, N. H., The Author,
1895.

LOCATIONS

Allentown

949 DOWST, JOHN. The old Allentown meeting house. Granite monthly. 44:5-
11. Jan. 1912.
(1815.)

Amherst

950 HOWE, LOIS LILLEY. Colonel Robert Means house at Amherst, New Hampshire. White pine series of architectural monographs. v. 13, no. 5. 1927.
19p. illus.
*Ca.*1775.

Boscawen

951 VAUGHAN, DOROTHY M. Old Bonney tavern, Boscawen, New Hampshire.
Old time New England. 31:57-61. Jan. 1941. illus.
1787.

Dover

952 FLANDERS, LOUIS W. Garrisons of ancient Dover, New Hampshire. Old
time New England. 17:51-62. Oct. 1926. illus.

953 STEVENS, LYDIA A. The Varney-Ham house. Granite state magazine. 3:233-
39. June 1907.
On Garrison Hill (1694).

Dunbarton

954 CORSE, MURRAY PINCHOT. Stark mansion, Dunbarton, New Hampshire.
Architecture. 47:123. Apr. 1923. illus.

Durham

955 Bunker Garrison house, Durham, New Hampshire. Old time New England.
1:1-7. Feb. 1911. illus.
*Ca.*1694.

Exeter (*see also* 367)

956 JENKINS, FREDERICK WARREN. The old Garrison house of Exeter. Granite
monthly. 34:386-90. May 1903.
(Between 1650 and 1658.)

957 NORTHEND, MARY HARROD. Ladd-Gilman house, Exeter, New Hampshire. American homes and gardens. 11:409-413. Dec. 1914. illus.
1721.

958 ROBIE, VIRGINIA. Colonial pilgrimage—part 4. House in Governor's land. House beautiful. 16:13-15. Aug. 1904. illus.
Gilman house, before 1747.

959 ROGERS, GEORGE B. The Gilman house. Exeter, N. H., News-Letter press, 1906. 32p. illus.

Fitzwilliam

960 SHUMWAY, HARRY IRVING. Two taverns and a village green. American cookery. 40:203-209. 1935.

Hanover (see 383)

Haverhill

961 GREER, LOIS GOODWIN. General Montgomery house at Haverhill, New Hampshire. House beautiful. 57:48-49, 74, 76-78. Jan. 1925. illus.

Jaffrey

962 BRADFORD, L. M. The historic Baker house. Americana. 7:833-34. Sept. 1912.
Colonial.

Keene

963 SHUMWAY, HARRY IRVING. Old tavern of New Hampshire. American cookery. 37:251-55, 302-304. 1932.
Sawyer Tavern.

Middleton

964 ALLEN, EDWARD B. Frescoed walls of the Meeting house at Middleton, New Hampshire. Old time New England. 20:129-33. Jan. 1930. illus.

New Castle

965 WINGATE, KATHERINE H. G. The historic church of New Castle, New Hampshire. D. A. R. magazine. 50:309-317. May 1917.
Congregational Church.

New Lisbon

966 CHANDLER, JOSEPHINE CRAVEN. Cobleigh tavern, Gunthwaite, now New Lisbon, New Hampshire. Old time New England. 24:38-45. Oct. 1933. illus.

Orford (see 351)

Peterboro

967 NORTHEND, MARY HARROD. Remodeling of an old tavern in Peterboro, New Hampshire. House beautiful. 48:110-13. Aug. 1920. illus.
Wilson Tavern, Colonial.

Portsmouth (*see also* 359, 367)

968 BREWSTER, CHARLES WARREN. Rambles about Portsmouth—first series. 2d ed. Portsmouth, N. H., L. H. Brewster, 1873. 381p.

First edition. Sketches of persons, localities, and incidents of two centuries: principally from tradition and unpublished documents. Portsmouth, N. H., C. W. Brewster and Son, 1859–69. 2v.

969 CHAMBERLAIN, SAMUEL. Portsmouth, New Hampshire. N. Y., Hastings house, 1940. 73p. illus.

970 CORNELIUS, CHARLES OVER. Wentworth-Gardner house. Metropolitan museum of art. Bulletin. 14:24-31. Feb. 1919. illus.

See also 355.

971 DENORMANDIE, JAMES. Three old churches. Boston, G. H. Ellis, 1912. 7p. illus.

Reprinted from *The Portsmouth Book*.

972 FISHER, ROBERT. Houses in old Portsmouth. International studio. 80:478-81. Mar. 1925.

973 HOWELLS, JOHN MEAD. Architectural heritage of the Piscataqua; houses and gardens of the Portsmouth district of Maine and New Hampshire. N. Y., Architectural Book Publishing Co., 1938. 217p. illus.

Bibliographical note on pages xvii-xx, books on architecture and the allied crafts used in America prior to 1830. Another list in 2589.

974 LITCHFIELD, ELECTUS D. Portsmouth, New Hampshire, an early American metropolis. White pine series of architectural monographs. v. 7, no. 1. Feb. 1921. 14p. illus.

Covers 1720–89.

975 MOSES, J. M. John Mason's three great houses. Granite monthly. 50:116-19.

On the Piscataqua river.

976 NORTHEND, MARY HARROD. Historic Wentworth house. American homes and gardens. 5:106-109. Mar. 1908. illus.

1750.

977 ———. Jacob Wendell house. American homes and gardens. 11:200-203. June 1924.

1789.

978 ORCUTT, PHILIP DANA. Moffatt-Ladd house, its garden and its period, 1763. Portsmouth, New Hampshire society of Colonial dames of America, 1935. 48p. illus.

See also 219.

979 Portsmouth, Colonial metropolis. House and garden. 7:33. June 1940. illus.

980 ROBIE, VIRGINIA. Colonial pilgrimage—part 1. Bit of old Portsmouth. House beautiful. 15:77-83. Jan. 1904. illus.

Warner house, 1718; Langdon house, 1780.

981 ———. Colonial pilgrimage—part 2. An old mansion by the sea. House beautiful. 15:171-75. Feb. 1904. illus.

Benning Wentworth house, 1750.

982 STURGIS, RICHARD CLIPSTON. Architecture of Portsmouth. Boston, G. H. Ellis, 1912. 20p. illus.

Reprinted from *The Portsmouth Book.*

983 Wentworth-Gardner house, Mechanic street, Portsmouth, New Hampshire. Old time New England. 30:34. July 1939. illus.

1760.

Salmon Falls

984 BAER, ANNIE WENTWORTH. Colonel John Wentworth and his Salmon Falls house. Granite monthly. 59:103-111. Apr. 1927.

985 BROWN, FRANK CHOUTEAU. Interior details and furnishings of the Colonel Paul Wentworth mansion, built in 1701 at Salmon Falls, New Hampshire, and removed to Dover, Massachusetts, in 1937. Pencil points. 20:509-524. Aug. 1939. Monograph series. 25:49-64. illus.

986 ———. Oldest remaining Wentworth mansion. Old time New England. 19:51-66. Oct. 1928. illus.

1701.

987 CHANDLER, J. C. Paul Wentworth house, the house that made history. Good housekeeping. 97:76-77. Dec. 1933. illus.

Warner

988 COLBY, FREDERICK MYRON. Granite state rooftrees. Historic houses of Warner. Granite state magazine. 1:177-81. 2:75-80. Apr., Aug. 1906.

Weare

989 TAYLER, WILLIAM WALLACE. Captain Samuel Philbrick house, Weare, New Hampshire. Dearborn, Mich. 31 numbered leaves. 1933.

RHODE ISLAND

GENERAL REFERENCES (*see also* 374)

990 DOWNING, ANTOINETTE FORRESTER. Early homes of Rhode Island. Richmond, Va., Garrett and Massie, 1937. 408p. illus.

991 FEDERAL WRITERS' PROJECT. Rhode Island; a guide to the smallest state. Boston, Houghton Mifflin Co., 1937. 500p. illus.

992 FOWLER, A. N. Rhode Island mill towns. Pencil points. 17:271-86. May 1936. Monograph series. 22:17-32. illus.

Covers 1809-1835.

993 Hitchcock, Henry-Russell, Jr. Rhode Island architecture. Providence, Rhode Island museum press, 1939. 69p. illus.

994 Isham, Norman Morrison, and Brown, Albert F. Early Rhode Island houses, an historical and architectural study. Providence, Preston and Rounds, 1895. 100p. illus.
Covers 1701–1830.

995 Jenks, Grover L. Dwellings in northeastern Rhode Island and the Smithfields. Pencil points. 16:317-32. June 1935. Monograph series. 21:33-48.
Covers 1701–1825.

996 Laswell, George D. Corners and characters of Rhode Island. Providence, R. I., The Oxford press, 1924. illus.

997 Miller, William D. Early houses of the King's Province in the Narragansett country. Wakefield, R. I., Privately printed, 1941. 33p. illus.

998 National Society of Colonial Dames. Old houses in the south colony of Rhode Island—part 1. Providence, 1932. 63p. illus.

999 Rhode Island Historical Society. Report of the Committee on marking historical sites in Rhode Island, made to the general assembly at its January session, 1913. Providence, R. I., E. L. Freeman Co., 1914. 183p. illus.
Governor Bull house, Newport; house and home-lot of Roger Williams, Providence; Fort Independence; Reynolds house, Bristol; General Nathanael Greene house, Cumberland.

1000 Two centuries of architecture in Rhode Island. Architectural forum. 71: sup. 16-17. Aug. 1939. illus.

Locations

Blackstone Valley

1001 Brown, Frank Chouteau. Rhode Island houses along the Blackstone river valley. Pencil points. 16:197-212. Apr. 1935. Monograph series. 21:17-32. illus.
Covers 1684–1790.

Bristol (see also 999)

1002 Burleigh, William J. Houses of Bristol, Rhode Island—part 1. Pencil points. 17:335-49. June 1936. Monograph series. 22:33-48. illus.
Covers late seventeenth and early eighteenth centuries.

1003 ———. Houses of Bristol, Rhode Island—part 2. Pencil points. 17:447-62. Aug. 1936. Monograph series. 22:49-64. illus.
Covers eighteenth and early nineteenth centuries.

1004 Dow, Joy Wheeler. Bristol renaissance. White pine series of architectural monographs. v. 3, no. 5. Oct. 1917. 14p. illus.
Classic revival houses; DeWitt-Colt, DeWolf-Myddleton, Parker-Borden, and Cabot-Church houses.

1005 ———. Doorways of the Bristol renaissance. Architectural review. n. s. 3: 28-30. Mar. 1901. illus.

1006 MINER, LILIAN BURLEIGH. Old homes of Bristol, Rhode Island. House beautiful. 46:218-20. Oct. 1919. illus.

1007 ———. Old treasures of Bristol, Rhode Isand. House beautiful. 47:42-44. Jan. 1920. illus.

Centerdale

1008 CADY, JOHN H. The Thomas Clemence house. Rhode Island historical society. Collections. 34:65-77. July 1941. illus.
Ca.1680.

Coventry

1009 GENERAL NATHANAEL GREENE HOMESTEAD ASSOCIATION. Home of General Nathanael Greene at Coventry, Rhode Island. Coventry, R. I., General Nathanael Greene homestead association, 1925. 61p. illus.

East Greenwich

1010 PRESTON, HOWARD W. General Varnum house. Rhode Island historical society. Collections. 20:115-20. Oct. 1927.
(1773.)

Lincoln

1011 GARDNER, HENRY W. Some early single room houses of Lincoln, Rhode Island. Pencil points. 16:93-108. Feb. 1935. Monograph series. v. 21, no. 1. illus.
Covers 1687–1700.

Little Compton

1012 HALDEN, JOHN C. Little Compton and Tiverton Four Corners. Pencil points. 17:707-722. Dec. 1936. Monograph series. 22:81-96. illus.
Covers 1684–1745.

Narragansett

1013 HANSCOM, R. M. Colonial homes nearly two centuries old; Captain Gardiner place, Narragansett, Rhode Island. Arts and decoration. 34:76. Nov. 1930. illus.

1014 UPDIKE, WILKINS. History of the Episcopal church in Narragansett, Rhode Island, including a history of other Episcopal churches in the state, by Wilkins Updike. With a transcript of the Narragansett parish register, from 1718-1774; an appendix containing a reprint of a work entitled: America dissected, by Reverend James MacSparran, D.D., and copies of other old papers; (portraits and views of historic places). Boston, D. B. Updike, 1907. 3v. illus.

Newport (*see also* 999)

1015, 1016 ALLEN, F. J. The ruined mill, or round church of the Norsemen, at
Newport, Rhode Island, U. S. A., compared with the round church at
Cambridge and others in Europe. Cambridge, England, 1921. 16p. illus.
Reprinted from the Cambridge antiquarian society. *Communications.* 22:91–107.
1921.

1017 CLARK, KENNETH. Newport, an early American seaport. White pine series
of architectural monographs. v. 8, no. 3. June 1922. 16p. illus.
Colonial houses.

1018 COVELL, ELIZABETH BENTLEY (GREENE). Historic houses of old Newport.
Country life in America. 43:64-66. Feb. 1923. illus.

1019 ———. Historic types of Newport houses. Newport, R. I., Newport historical society. Bulletin no. 48. 1924. 13p.

1020 ———. The old Robinson house, one of the landmarks of Newport, Rhode
Island. House beautiful. 58:382. Oct. 1925. illus.

1021 COVELL, WILLIAM KING. Newport, Rhode Island, houses before and after.
Old time New England. 25:128-35; 28:1-3. Apr. 1935. July 1937.
illus.
Photographs of sites after demolition of early houses.

1022 GALE, MRS. MARIE J. Some old Newport houses. Newport, Rhode Island,
Newport historical society. 25p.
Newport Historical Society, bulletin 36.

1023 ISHAM, NORMAN MORRISON. Colony house at Newport, Rhode Island. Old
time New England. 8:3-20. Dec. 1917. illus.
1738–39.

1024 ———. The old Brick market or old City hall, Newport, Rhode Island.
Old time New England. 6:2-11. Jan. 1916. illus.
(1761. Peter Harrison, architect.)

1025 ———. Trinity church in Newport, Rhode Island, a history of the fabric.
Boston, D. B. Updike, 1936. 111p. illus.
1725.

1026 KING, DAVID. Historical sketch of the Redwood library and athenaeum in
Newport, Rhode Island. Providence, R. I., Providence Press Co., 1876.
12p.
(1750.) Earlier edition(?), Boston, John Wilson and Sons, 1860. 53p. Peter Harrison, architect.

1027 MACDONALD, WILLIAM. The old State house at Newport. Newport historical
society. Bulletin 11. 11p. 1914.
Also known as the Old Colony House, 1739.

1028 MASON, GEORGE CHAMPLIN. Annals of the Redwood library and athenaeum. Newport, R. I., published by the Redwood Library, 1891. 528p. illus.

1029 ———. Annals of Trinity church, Newport, Rhode Island. Newport, R. I., George H. Carr, 1890. illus.
1725.

1030 ———. Reminiscences of Newport. Newport, R. I., C. E. Hammett, Jr., 1884. 407p. illus.

1031 Maudsley-Gardner-Watson-Pitman house. Old time New England. 28:79-84. Jan. 1938. illus.
Eighteenth century.

1032 MEANS, PHILIP AINSWORTH. Newport tower. N. Y., Henry Holt and Co., 1942. 365p. illus.

1033 POWEL, MARY EDITH. A few words about some old buildings in Newport. Newport, R. I., Newport historical society, 1925. 36p. illus.
Newport Historical Society, bulletin 55.

1034 SHELTON, F. H. More light on the old mill at Newport. Newport, R. I., Newport historical society, 1917. 24p. illus.
Newport Historical Society, bulletin 21.

1035 STEVENS, MAUD LYMAN. Antiquities of Newport, Rhode Island. Old time New England. 21:51-59. Oct. 1931. illus.
Better known buildings.

1036 ———. A history of the Vernon house in Newport, Rhode Island. Newport, R. I., The Charity organization society, 1915. 58p. illus.
1758.

1037 ———. The old Hazard house. Newport, R. I., Newport historical society, 1920.
Newport Historical Society, bulletin 33.

1038 ———. Wanton-Lyman-Hazard house, Newport, Rhode Island. Old time New England. 18:21-34. July 1927. illus.
(After 1675.)

1039 TERRY, RODERICK (ed.). History of the Old colony house at Newport as recorded by early and modern writers. Newport historical society. Bulletin. 63:1-36. Oct. 1927.

North Smithfield
1040 FRANKLIN, M. S. Houses and villages of North Smithfield, Rhode Island. Pencil points. 16:431-46. Aug. 1935. Monograph series. 21:49-64. illus.
Covers 1714–1836.

Providence (*see also* 384, 999)

1041 BROWN, FRANK CHOUTEAU. Providence, Rhode Island, Georgian mansion, the house founded by John Brown, esq., 1786. Pencil points. 17:97-112. Feb. 1936. Monograph series. 22:1-16. illus.

1786. Joseph Brown, architect.

1042 CHAPIN, HOWARD M. The lands and houses of the first settlers of Providence. Rhode Island historical society. Collections. 12:1-8. Jan. 1919.

1043 ISHAM, NORMAN MORRISON. The house of Roger Williams. Rhode Island historical society. Collections. 18:33-39. Apr. 1925.

1044 ———. Providence and its Colonial houses. White pine series of architectural monographs. v. 4, no. 3. June 1918. 15p. illus.

Covers 1700–1820.

1045 ———. Meeting-house of the First Baptist church in Providence, a history of the fabric. Providence, R. I., Akerman-Standard Co., 1925. 33p. illus.

Dedicated May 28, 1775. Joseph Brown, architect.

1046 MERCHANTS NATIONAL BANK OF PROVIDENCE. Old Providence; a collection of facts and traditions relating to various buildings and sites of historic interest in Providence. Providence, R. I., 1918. 65p. illus.

1047 MINER, LILIAN BURLEIGH. Through the streets of old Providence. House beautiful. 44:152-54, 170. Aug. 1918. illus.

1048 Nightingale house at Providence. Arts and decoration. 39:6-7. Oct. 1933. illus.

1792. Attributed to Caleb Ormsbee. *See also* 113.

1049, 1050 PRESTON, HOWARD WILLIS. Notes on old Providence. The old County house in Providence. Providence, R. I., Preston and Rounds, 1918. 8p.

Reprinted from Rhode Island Historical Society. *Collections.* v.11. April 1918.

1051 Providence is rich in Federal mansions. House and garden. 77:28-29. June 1940. illus.

Tiverton (see also *Little Compton*)

1052 MACKAY, H. G. Winnisemet farm; Nathaniel Briggs house, near Tiverton, Rhode Island. House beautiful. 53:632-33. June 1923.

1053 PARKER, RODERICK H. Tiverton, Rhode Island and some of its early dwellings. Pencil points. 17:575-89. Oct. 1936. Monograph series. 22:65-80. illus.

Covers *ca.*1700–1818.

Warren

1054 RUSSELL, J. FENIMORE. Some old houses of Warren, Rhode Island—in two parts. Pencil points. 16:539-54, 635-50. Oct., Dec. 1935. Monograph series. 21:65-80, 81-96. illus.

Part 1 covers 1820–25; part 2 covers 1789–1820.

Warwick

1055 WELLMAN, RITA. Governor Greene house in Rhode Island. International studio. 99:25-26. July 1931. illus.

1680 and later.

Wickford

1056 UPDIKE, DANIEL BERKELEY. Restoration of a Colonial altarpiece. Old time New England. 22:188-92. Apr. 1932. illus.

In St. Paul's Church, 1707.

1057 WHITE, HUNTER C. Wickford and its old houses. Providence, R. I., Reynolds press, 1936. 35p.

VERMONT

GENERAL REFERENCES (*see also* 373)

1058 CHAPPELL, GEORGE S. Colonial architecture in Vermont. White pine series of architectural monographs. v. 4, no. 6. Dec. 1918. 14p. illus.

1059 CONGDON, HERBERT WHEATON. Old Vermont houses. Brattleboro, Vt., Stephen Daye press, 1940. 190p. illus.

Popular sketch from earliest buildings up to 1850. Includes courthouses, taverns, and churches. Review, *House and Garden*, 77:67. June 1941.

1060 CRANE, CHARLES EDWARD. Let me show you Vermont. N. Y., A. A. Knopf, 1937. 347p. illus.

1061 FEDERAL WRITERS' PROJECT. Vermont: a guide to the Green mountain state. Boston, Houghton Mifflin Co., 1937. 392p. illus.

1062 FORBES, P. P. American home pilgrimages—part 10, Vermont. American home. 26:38, 40-43. June 1941. illus.

1063 SWARTWOUT, EGERTON. Some old time churches of Vermont. White pine series of architectural monographs. v. 13, no. 6. 1927. 20p. illus.

Covers 1787–1821.

LOCATIONS

Bennington

1064 BAYHAN, RICHARD S. (ed.). Historical sketch of buildings now or once located in the village on the hill at Bennington, Vermont, formerly known as Bennington Center, and now called Old Bennington. Cleveland, Ohio, Central Publishing Co., 1930. 50p. illus.

1065 BOOTH, VINCENT RAVI. Restoration of the old First Church of Bennington, Vermont. Old time New England. 30:72-81. Jan. 1940. illus.

1805. Attributed to Asher Benjamin.

1066 CLARK, CAMERON. Houses of Bennington, Vermont and vicinity—used as a study of Colonial textures. White pine series of architectural monographs. v. 8, no. 5. Oct. 1922. 16p. illus.

1067 Colonial craftsman's home; Georgian mansion near Bennington built in 1795 by Judge Lyman Norton, still occupied by his descendants. House and garden. 75:68-69. June 1939. illus.

1068 Historic Bennington. House beautiful. 82:22-24. July-Aug. 1940. illus.

1069 SERBE, MILTON J. Old Bennington's historic church. D. A. R. magazine. 67:77-80. 1933.

Brandon

1070 SHUMWAY, HARRY IRVING. Direct from the quarry. House beautiful. 46: 78-79. Aug. 1919. illus.
    Early nineteenth century houses.

Cavendish

1071 GAY, LEON S. Dwellings from the hills. Vermonter. 39:225-31. 1934.

Concord

1072 WALTER, MABEL HALL. Judge Hibbard house, Concord, Vermont. Old time New England. 24:93-96. Jan. 1934. illus.
    *Ca.*1814.

Lyndon

1073 WALTER, MABEL HALL. Cahoon house, Lyndon, Vermont. Old time New England. 26:106-119. Jan. 1939. illus.

Newbury

1074 MUNSELL, L. Town house neighborhood, Newbury, Vermont. Old time New England. 32:57-62. Oct. 1941. illus.

Newfane

1075 CUDWORTH, ADDISON E. Geneaology of the Windham county court house. Vermont historical society. Proceedings. 1923, 1924, and 1925. p. 220-28.

Norwich

1076 WHITE, PHILIP AYLWIN, AND JOHNSON, DANA DOANE. Early houses of Norwich, Vermont. Hanover, N. H., Dartmouth college, 1938. 51p. illus.

Rockingham (near Bellows Falls)

1077 DESMOND, H. W. A forgotten Colonial church. Architectural record. 14:94-106. Aug. 1903. illus.

1078 HAYES, LYMAN SIMPSON, AND HAYES, WILLIAM DANFORTH. The old Rockingham meeting house, erected 1787 and the first church in Rockingham, Vermont, 1773-1840. Bellows Falls, Vt., the P. H. Gobie press, 1915. 102p. illus.

Shaftsbury

1079 GALE, DAVID C. The old Joshua Monroe mansion. Old time New England.
31:74-80. Jan. 1941. illus.
1798–1812. Now known as the Iron Kettle Farm.

Waterford

1080 WALTER, MABEL HALL. Pike-Streeter tavern, Waterford, Vermont. Old
time New England. 22:15-22. July 1931. illus.
1800.

West Newbury

1081 WELLS, FREDERIC P. Union meeting house at West Newberry. . . . Vermonter. 39:36-43. 1934.
1833.

Weston

1082 BOOTHBY, R. E. Farrar-Mansur house. Vermonter. 39:175-76. 1934.

MIDDLE ATLANTIC STATES

(Delaware, New Jersey, New York, and Pennsylvania)

GENERAL REFERENCES

1083 ALLBEE, BURTON HIRAM. Ancient Dutch houses in America; historic structures left by the Hollanders. Journal of American history. 3:286-92. 1908.

1084 BAILEY, ROSALIE FELLOWS. Pre-revolutionary Dutch houses and families in northern New Jersey and southern New York. N. Y., Morrow and Co., 1936. 612p. illus.

1085 EMBURY, AYMAR II. The Dutch Colonial house, its origins, design, modern plan and construction. N. Y., McBride, Nast and Co., 1913. 108p. illus.

1086 ———. Dutch Colonial type of house. House and garden. 17:46-49. Feb. 1910. illus.
Suggesting adaptations of the style.

1086A HAYES, JOHN RUSSELL. Old meeting-houses. Philadelphia, The Biddle press, 1909. 44p. illus.
Second edition, 1911, 74p. illus., titled *Old Quaker Meeting-Houses.*

1087 HIGGINS, HENRY. Some interesting old Dutch houses. House beautiful. 45:35-37, 52. Jan. 1919. illus.
In New Jersey, New York, and Pennsylvania.

1088 NASH, GEORGE W. Some early American hardware, Dutch Colonial examples. Architectural record. 34:329-33. Oct. 1913. illus.

1089 PENNYPACKER, ISAAC R. The Dutch on the Delaware. American mercury. 2:345-50. 1924.

1090 ROGERS, MRS. HENRY WADE. Dutch Colonial farmhouses. House beautiful. 16:15-17. Oct. 1904. illus.
Covers examples in New Jersey and New York.

1091 SCHUYLER, MONTGOMERY. Dutch origins of American architecture. Architectural record. 4:313-66. April-June 1895. illus.

1092 SCOTT, W. W. Dutch buildings, customs, habits . . . Americana. 16:368-79. Oct. 1922.

1093 SLOCUM, S. E. Early Dutch Colonial architecture. American architect. 105:1-10, 12. Jan. 7, 1914. illus.

1094 WALLACE, PHILIP B., AND DUNN, WILLIAM ALLEN. Colonial churches and meeting-houses, Pennsylvania, New Jersey and Delaware. N. Y., Architectural Book Publishing Co., 1931. 313p. illus.

This is v. 3, *Colonial Architecture in Old Philadelphia* series (sic).

1095 WARD, CHRISTOPHER LONGSTRETH. The Dutch and Swedes on the Delaware, 1609-1664. Philadelphia, University of Pennsylvania press, 1930. 393p. illus.

1096 ———. New Sweden on the Delaware. Philadelphia, University of Pennsylvania press, 1938. 160p. illus.

The substance of this book, with alterations, has been taken from 1095.

1097 WERTENBAKER, THOMAS JEFFERSON. The founding of the American civilization: the middle colonies. N. Y., Charles Scribner's sons, 1938. illus.

Documented sketch describing the origin and use of the horizontal log cabin among the eighteenth century German colonists of Pennsylvania, p.298–307.

1098 WISE, HERBERT CLIFTON, AND BEIDLEMAN, FERDINAND H. Colonial architecture for those about to build: being the best examples, domestic, municipal and institutional, in Pennsylvania, New Jersey and Delaware with observations of the local building art of the eighteenth century. Philadelphia, J. B. Lippincott Co., 1913. 270p. illus.

DELAWARE

(See also 207, 258, 1094, 1098, 1636)

1099 BENNETT, GEORGE FLETCHER. Early architecture of Delaware. Wilmington, Delaware, Historical press, 1932. 213p. illus.

1100 CORKRAN, L. C. Peter Marsh, two centuries, and our heritage; The Homestead, Rehoboth Neck, Sussex county. American home. 12:132-35. Aug. 1934. illus.

1101 FEDERAL WRITERS' PROJECT. Delaware; a guide to the first state. N. Y., Viking press, 1938. 550p. illus.

1102 ———. New Castle on the Delaware. Wilmington, Del., W. N. Cann, 1937. 142p. illus.

1103 FOSTER, WILLIAM D. New Castle, Delaware, an eighteenth century town. White pine series of architectural monographs. v. 12, no. 1. 1926. 19p. illus.

1104 Historic American buildings; Old Swedes, Holy Trinity church, Wilmington, Delaware. Architectural forum. 61:445-52. Dec. 1934. illus.

1105 Master detail series: historic American buildings: Amstel, Van Dyke and Chancellor Kensey Johns houses, New Castle. Architectural forum. 65:125-32. Aug. 1936.

1106 MOORE, MRS. FRANCIS HARDY. The removal and restoration of the old First Presbyterian church of Wilmington, Delaware. Presbyterian historical society. Journal. 10:208-216. June 1920.

1107 Old buildings in New Castle, Delaware. American architect. 148:49-56. Feb. 1936. illus.

1108 WATERSTON, ELIZABETH. Churches in Delaware during the revolution, with a brief account of their settlement and growth. Wilmington, Del., Historical society of Delaware, 1925. 117p. illus.

1109 WISE, HERBERT CLIFTON. George Read II house, at New Castle, Delaware. White pine series of architectural monographs. v. 11, no. 6. 1925. 21p. illus.

1791–1801.

NEW JERSEY

GENERAL REFERENCES (*see also* 258, 1094, 1098)

1110 BLACK, WILLIAM NELSON. Colonial buildings in New Jersey. Architectural record. 3:245-62. Jan.-Mar. 1894. illus.

1111 BLAUVELT, HIRAM. Some Jersey Dutch Colonial hardware. New Jersey historical society. Proceedings. 13:30-38. July 1928.

1112 BOYD, JOHN T., JR. Some early Dutch houses in New Jersey—in three parts. Architectural record. Part 1, 36:31-48, July 1914; part 2, 36:148-58, Aug. 1914; part 3, 36:220-30. Sept. 1914. illus.

1113 COLEMAN, OLIVER. Dutch byways in New Jersey. House and garden. 8:1-8. July 1905. illus.

1114 ELLIS, ROWLAND C. Colonial Dutch houses in New Jersey. Newark, N. J., Carteret book club, 1933. 60p. illus.
Twenty wood engravings.

1115 EMBURY, AYMAR II. Three old Dutch roads and the houses along them. Country life in America. 16:591-94, 656, 658, 660, 662. Oct. 1909. illus.
Ca.1750—ca.1850. Between Jersey City and the Ramapo Mountains.

1116 FEDERAL WRITERS' PROJECT. New Jersey: a guide to its present and past. N. Y., Viking press, 1939. 750p. illus.

1117 ———. New Jersey: a profile in pictures. N. Y., M. Barrows and Co., 1939. 59p. illus.

1118 ———. Stories of New Jersey, its significant places, people and activities. N. Y., M. Barrows and Co., 1938. illus.

1119 ———. Swedes and Finns in New Jersey. Bayonne, N. J., Jersey Printing Co., 1938. 165p. illus.

1120 Grosvenor, Jewett A. Wooden architecture of the lower Delaware valley. White pine series of architectural monographs. v. 6, no. 3. June 1920. 14p. illus.
Covers 1740–1813.

1121 Micklewright, Albert E. Early architecture of New Jersey. Series of measured drawings. Architecture. v. 35-37. Jan. 1917—May 1918. illus. only.

1122 Mills, Weymer Jay. Historic houses of New Jersey. Philadelphia, J. B. Lippincott Co., 1903. 348p. illus.

1123 Perry, Matilda Hardendorf. Historic churches of New Jersey. American monthly magazine. 41:129-31. Sept. 1912.

1124 Society of Colonial Wars. New Jersey. Historic roadsides. Princeton, N. J., 1928. 115p. illus.
Location map and bibliography.

1125 Wendehack, Clifford C. Early Dutch houses of northern New Jersey. White pine series. v. 11, no. 3. 1925. 19p. illus.
Covers 1670–1837.

1126 W.P.A. architectural survey: New Jersey's architectural growth to 1860. Architect and engineer. 135:70-71. Oct. 1938. illus.

Locations

Allentown

1127 Boyd, John Taylor, Jr. House of John Imlay, esq., an eighteenth century dwelling, Allentown, New Jersey. Monograph series. v. 15, no. 3. 1929. 21p. illus.
Ca.1790.

Bergen County

1128 Blauvelt, H. Migration of an ancestral home; New Jersey Dutch Colonial house. House and garden. 52:112-13, 162, 164, 166, 202. Nov. 1927. illus.
Demarest house. Ca.1750.

1129 Old Dutch houses in Bergen county. New Jersey historical society. Proceedings. 9:273-75. July 1924.

Bound Brook

1130 Goldsmith, Margaret O. Pre-revolutionary farmhouse. House beautiful. 54:610-12. Dec. 1923.
Built before 1722. Staats farm, Bound Brook, New Jersey.

Burlington County

1131 Mills, Robert. A model jail of the olden time. Designs for a debtors' gaol, and work-house for felons for Burlington county, state of New Jersey. N. Y., Russell Sage foundation, 1928. 2p. illus.

Camden

1132 BOYER, CHARLES S. The old houses in Camden, New Jersey . . . Camden, N. J., The Author, 1920. 15p. illus.

Annals of Camden, no. 1.

Dunellen

1133 FEDERAL WRITERS' PROJECT. The story of Dunellen. Dunellen, N. J., Art color printing co., 1937. 111p. illus.

Elizabeth

1134 DIX, WARREN R. Old houses of Elizabethtown; the Belcher mansion, 1046 East Jersey street, Elizabeth. Union county historical society. Proceedings. 8:68-82. 1923.

(Before 1742.)

1135 ———. Old houses of Elizabethtown; the Governor Belcher mansion. New Jersey historical society. Proceedings. 8:169-85. 1923.

1136 ———. Old houses of Elizabethtown; part 2, the Hetfield house. New Jersey historical society. Proceedings. 13:298-302. 1928.

Heathfield or Hetfield house was acquired by Matthias Heathfield (Hetfield, Hattfield), December 5, 1673.

1137 FIELD, MRS. EDWARD M. Historical Elizabeth—two famous mansions. New Jersey historical society. Proceedings. 13:393-99. Oct. 1928.

General Winfield Scott mansion (destroyed) and Elias Boudinot mansion (*ca.*1752).

1138 HUTCHINSON, ELMER T. The old Wheat Sheaf inn. New Jersey historical society. Proceedings. n.s. 5:246-48. Oct. 1920.

1730.

1139 LAMB, MRS. MARTHA L. House of Elias Boudinot and Governor Livingston. Magazine of American history. 21:361-80. May 1889. illus.

Governor Livingston home is Liberty hall. Both pre-revolutionary.

Flemington

1140, 1141 DEATS, HIRAM EDMUND. Dedication of the restored Fleming house. Flemington, N. J., H. E. Deats, 1928. 8p. illus.

Reprinted from the *Hunterdon County Democrat* of June 21, 1928. (1756)

Greenwich

1142 ANDREWS, BESSIE AYERS. Colonial and old houses at Greenwich, N. Y. Vineland, N. J., G. E. Smith, printer, 1907. 87p. illus.

Hackensack

1143 PEARMAN, JOSEPH BERNARD. An old homestead of Colonial New Jersey. American homes and gardens. 10:267-70, 300. Aug. 1913. illus.

Brinckerhoff house.

Jersey City

1144 GRUNDY, J. OWEN. Prior's mill; a revolutionary landmark. New Jersey historical society. Proceedings. 16:174-79. 1931.
1760.

Matawan

1145 FEDERAL WRITERS' PROJECT. Matawan, 1686-1936. Matawan, N. J., Matawan journal, *ca.* 1936. 95p. illus.

Middleton

1146 Ancient dwellings restored; Marlpit hall, Middleton. Antiques. 30:30. July 1936. illus.
*Ca.*1680.

Middlesex County

1147 FEDERAL WRITERS' PROJECT. Monroe township, Middlesex county, New Jersey, 1838-1938. New Brunswick, N. J., 1938. 140p. illus.

Monmouth County

1148 ELDRIDGE, SARAH E. "Old Tennent" historic church, Monmouth county, New Jersey. American monthly magazine. 39:240-42. Nov. 1911.
The first Presbyterian church of the county of Monmouth.

Morristown (see also 81)

1149 Early continental structures being rebuilt at Morristown national historical park. Pencil points. 15:sup.15-16. Apr. 1934. illus.

1150 HOFFMAN, PHILIP H. (comp.). History of the Arnold tavern, Morristown, N. J. Morristown, N. J., Chronicle press, 1903. 28p. illus.
Views of historic buildings.

1151 Morristown national historical park. Washington, D. C., United States Government printing office, 1940. 16p. illus.

1152 VOGT, GRACE J. Schuyler-Hamilton house, Morristown, N. J. D.A.R. magazine. 59:569-73. Sept. 1925.

1153 Washington's headquarters at Morristown, New Jersey. Antiques. 36:245. Nov. 1939. illus.
*Ca.*1772.

Mount Holly

1154 WOOLMAN, FENIMORE C. The Burlington county courthouse at Mount Holly, New Jersey. White pine series of architectural monographs. v. 12, no. 3. 1926. 19p. illus.
1796.

Newark

1155 FARRAND, WILSON. A brief history of the Newark academy, 1774-1792-1916. Contribution to the celebration of the 250th anniversary of the founding of Newark, May 1916. Newark, N. J., Baker printing co., 1916. 20p. illus.

New Brunswick

1156 ATKINSON, JOSEPHINE. Buccleuch, historic homestead of New Brunswick. D.A.R. magazine. 61:179-86. Mar. 1927.
1729.

1157 ATKINSON, MARY J. The old taverns of New Brunswick. Somerset county historical quarterly. 3:9-18. Jan. 1914.

1158 BENEDICT, WILLIAM H. Early taverns in New Brunswick. New Jersey historical society. Proceedings. n.s.3:129-46. July 1918.

Perth Amboy

1159 MILLER, GEORGE J. Westminster—story of a Colonial house. New Jersey historical society. Proceedings. 15:465-84. Oct. 1930.
1764.

Princeton

1160 CLEMENT, JOHN. Coxe Hall. New Jersey historical society. Proceedings. 3rd ser. 9:27-37. Jan. 1914.

1161 FEDERAL WRITERS' PROJECTS. Old Princeton's neighbors. Princeton, N. J., Graphic arts press, ca. 1939. 96p. illus.
Covers Cedar Grove, Jugtown, Princeton Basin, Penn's Neck, Dutch Neck, Grover's Mills, Aqueduct, Kingston.

1162 GAUSS, KATHERINE. Historic house in Princeton, New Jersey. House beautiful. 66:632, 634, 636, 638. Nov. 1929. illus.
1756. Home of the Dean of the Faculty of Princeton University, formerly the President's home.

1163 ———. Two hundred years of Morven I record. House beautiful. 62:50-51, 87-90. July 1927. illus.
Richard Stockton house, 1701.

1164 SCHUYLER, MONTGOMERY. The architecture of American colleges—part 3. Princeton. Architectural record. 27:129-60. Feb. 1910.

Salem County

1165 EBERLEIN, HAROLD DONALDSON. Early brick houses of Salem county, New Jersey. American architecture and architectural review. 120:139-48. Aug. 1921. illus.

1166 SICKLER, JOSEPH S. Old houses of Salem county. Salem, N. J., Sunbeam Publishing Co., 1934. 56p. illus.

Somerset County

1167 HANSEN, ANDREW. The Van Harlingen homestead—seat of Queen's college in 1780. Somerset county historical quarterly. 6:173-76. July 1917.

Trenton

1168 GODFREY, CHARLES E. Dutch trading post, Trenton, New Jersey. Trenton historic society, 1919. 8p. illus.

1169 Mappa house, Trenton, N. J. American architect. 104:61-68. Aug. 13, 1913. illus.

1170 (State house. Description of the building.) Gazette of United States. 4:139. Sept. 29, 1792.

Troy Hills

1171 HOWELL, CATHERINE S. The Howell homestead of Troy Hills. New Jersey historical society. Proceedings. n. s. 6:152-56. July 1921.

NEW YORK

GENERAL REFERENCES (*see also* 258, 349)

1172 American home pilgrimages—part 7. Eastern New York, Manhattan and Long Island. American home. 22:68, 70, 72, 75, 77, 78, 104-109, 112, 113. June 1939. illus.

1173 ANDREWS, EDWARD DEMING. Communal architecture of the Shakers. Magazine of art. 30:710-15. Dec. 1937.
Mostly New Lebanon and Watervliet.

1174 BETTS, BENJAMIN F. Early architecture of western New York. Architecture. v. 33-34. Jan.-Nov. 1916. illus., with two pages of text.

1175 FEDERAL WRITERS' PROJECT. New York: a guide to the empire state. N. Y., Oxford university press, 1940. 800p. illus.

1176 KING, DOROTHY. Old mantels. House beautiful. 47:406-407. May 1920. illus.

1177 Master detail series: historic American buildings; Jan Breese house, East Greenbush; house at Russia; Beverwyck, W. P. Van Rensselaer house, Rensselaer. Architectural forum. 63:39-50. July 1935. illus.

1178 SCHUYLER, MONTGOMERY. The architecture of American colleges, part 9. Union, Hamilton, Hobart, Cornell, and Syracuse. Architectural record. 30:549-73. Dec. 1911. illus.

1179 STOTZ, CHARLES M. Early architecture of central New York. Architecture. v. 48, 50. Nov. 1923—Aug. 1924. illus. only.

1180 ———. Early architecture of western New York. Architecture. 1. 47. May 1923. illus. only.

1181 TALLMAN, CARL C. Colonial architecture of central New York. Architectural review. 6:73-74. May 1918. illus. only.

1182 ———. Early wood-built houses of central New York. White pine series of architectural monographs. v. 4, no. 5. Oct. 1918. 14p. illus.
Covers 1800–1838 in Finger Lakes region.

LOCATIONS

Albany (*see also* 1177)

1183 (Brick theatre. Contemporary description.) Minerva. 1:279. Dec. 7, 1822.

1184 CUTLER, C. B. Albany Academy—in two parts. Architectural record. Part 1, 39:132-43. Feb. 1916; Part 2, 39:247-64. Mar. 1916. illus.

1185 DYKEMAN, JOHN L. Doorways, Albany, New York. Architecture. v. 38, no. 6. Dec. 1918. illus. only.

1186 ———. Lancaster school, Albany, New York. Architecture. 36:245-46. Dec. 1917.
1816, now Albany Medical College.

1187 ———. New York state national bank, Philip Hooker, architect, 1803. Architecture. 34:271-72, pl. 191-92. Dec. 1916. illus.

1188 ———. Stonework, door and window heads, Albany, New York. Architecture. v. 38, no. 6. Dec. 1918. illus. only.

1189 ———. Three Hooker churches. Architecture. 39:123-25. May 1919. illus.
Some scattered plates adjacent to this article and in v.40.

1190 ———. Three Albany doorways. Architecture. 35:71-72. Apr. 1917. illus. only.

1191 FEDERAL WRITERS' PROJECT. Albany—past and present. Albany, 1938. 28p. illus.

1192 LAMB, MRS. MARTHA L. The Van Rensselaer manor. Magazine of American history. 11:1-32. Jan. 1884. illus.

1193 Opening of the Schuyler mansion at Albany, New York, Oct. 17, 1917. American scenic and historic preservation society. Annual report. 23:607-624. 1918.

1194 RALSTON, R. Van Rensselaer manor house, Albany. Metropolitan museum. Bulletin. 26:sup. 4-9. Dec. 1931.
Moved to Williamstown, Massachusetts.

1195 REYNOLDS, MARIUS T. Colonial buildings of Rensselaerwyck. Architectural record. 4:415-38. Apr., June 1895. illus.

1196 SCHUYLER, GEORGINA. The Schuyler mansion at Albany, New York, residence of Major-General Philip Schuyler, 1762-1804. American scenic and historic preservation society. Reports. 17:603-640. 1912.

1197 The Spirit of '76. The Schuyler mansion at Albany, residence of Major-General Philip Schuyler, 1762-1804. N. Y., The DeVinne press, 1911. 43p. illus.

Auburn

1198 First Presbyterian church, Auburn, N. Y. Architectural review. n. s. 6:74-75. May 1918. illus.
1817.

1199 BONTA, EDWIN. Along the Seneca turnpike: introducing a distinct type of Post-Colonial house. Architectural record. 40:505-515. Dec. 1916. illus.

Aurora

1200 BETTS, BENJAMIN F. Colonial lodge building at Aurora, New York. Architectural review. 5:172, pl. 49-54. Aug. 1917. illus.

Bronxville

1201 BURNETT, BERTRAND G. Masterston homestead—Bronxville. Westchester county historical society. Bulletin. 7:65-69. 1931.

Brownville

1202 FAIRBANKS, J. House of a distinguished pioneer, built by J. Brown in Brownville, New York. House beautiful. 64:534. Nov. 1928. illus.
1811.

Buffalo

1203 Buffalo's architecture in review. Art news. 38:8-9, 17. Jan. 20, 1940.
Review of an exhibition.

1204 City's architecture from 1816 to 1940; photographs. Architectural review. 87:147. Apr. 1940.

1205 (Eagle street theatre. Contemporary description.) New York mirror. 13:121. Oct. 17, 1835.

Cazenovia

1206 Lorenzo, and the Meadows. House and garden. 78:14-15. Aug. 1940. illus.
(1807)

Chautauqua County

1207 STARR, SYLVIA, AND WERTZ, JOSEPH B. Architecture that came from Athens. House and garden. 64:49-51. July 1933. illus.
Examples from Ashville, Panama, Chautauqua, and Westfield.

Cooperstown

1208 WHITING, FRANK P. Cooperstown in the days of our forefathers. White pine series of architectural monographs. v. 9, no. 3. June 1923. 16p. illus.
Covers 1790–1831.

Cutchogue

1209 BROWN, FRANK CHOUTEAU. The old house at Cutchogue, Long Island. Old time New England. 31:10-21. July 1940. illus.
Horton-Wickham-Landon house, 1649.

1210 Old house, built 1649, Cutchogue, Long Island. Antiques. 32:294-95. June 1941. illus.

Dobbs Ferry

1211 CHAMBERS, WALTER B. Messmore Kendall residence at Dobbs Ferry. Westchester county historical society. Bulletin. 7:49-58. 1931.

1212 GILLESPIE, HARRIET SISSON. Restoration of Washington's headquarters at Dobbs Ferry, the Philip VanBrugh Livingston manor. House beautiful. 53:254-56, 284-85. Mar. 1923. illus.
(*Ca.*1700)

Dutchess County (see also *Rhinebeck*)

1213 FEDERAL WRITERS' PROJECT. Dutchess county. Philadelphia, William Penn association of Philadelphia, 1937. 166p. illus.

1214 HASTINGS, HELEN M. Some landmarks of Dutchess county. Architectural record. 45:476-80. May 1919. illus.

1215 NEWLIN, LILIAN WASHBURN. An old homestead on the Hudson. House beautiful. 36:73-76. Aug. 1914. illus.
Mount Gulian, 1740 and later. Near Fishkill Landing.

1216 REYNOLDS, HELEN WILKINSON. Dutchess county doorways. . . . N. Y., W. F. Payson Co., 1931. 280p. illus.
Covers 1730–1830.

1217 SPURLING, GENEVIEVE BROWN. Old Brown homestead in The Orchard. Dutchess county historical society. Year book 54-57.
1753, near Rhinebeck.

East Avon

1218 FULTON, G., JR. Taintor homestead, East Avon, N. Y., built in 1812. Architectural forum. 45:249-56. Oct. 1926. illus.

Easthampton

1219 GILLESPIE, HARRIET SISSON. John Howard Payne homestead. Country life in America. 26:69-72. Oct. 1914. illus.

1220 KAUFFMAN, ELIZABETH, AND KAUFFMAN, CYRUS. John Howard Payne homestead, the shrine of homes—home, sweet home. House beautiful. 54:16-19, 68-70. July 1923. illus.
*Ca.*1666.

1221 SINGLETON, ESTHER. Home, sweet home. . . . Antiquarian. 3:5-8, 26. Nov. 1924. illus.

Esopus (see *Ulster County*)

Fayetteville

1222 GILLESPIE, HARRIET SISSON. Restoration in an old coach town, Fayetteville, New York. Arts and decoration. 35:70. Sept. 1931. illus.

Fort Johnson (*see* 355)

Genesee Valley

1223 BRAGDON, CLAUDE FAYETTE. Colonial architecture in the Genesee Valley. American architect. 43:141-42; 45:26-27; 46:11-12. 1894. illus.
These volumes also contain scattered measured drawings on this subject.

1224 ———. Colonial architecture in the Genesee Valley. Rochester historical society publishing fund series. 2:251-60. 1923.

Geneva (*see also* 1178)

1225 ROSE, CHRISTINA LIVINGSTON. Main street, Geneva, New York. House beautiful. 39:98-99. Feb. 1916. illus.
*Ca.*1820.

1226 SMITH, WARREN HUNTING. An elegant but salubrious village, a portrait of Geneva, New York. Geneva, N. Y., W. F. Humphrey, 1931. 146p. illus.

Haverstraw

1227 BLAUVELT, H. Treason house; the Smith house at West Haverstraw, New York. Mentor. 16:35-37. July 1928. illus.

Hempstead

1228 BINSSE, HARRY LORIN. Rock Hall, an American manorial estate. Antiquarian. 16:34-38, 70. 1931.
Covers 1732–1806.

Hudson Valley (*see also* town and county names)

1229 CARMER, CARL LAMSON. The Hudson. N. Y., Farrar and Rinehart, 1939. 434p. illus.
Rivers of America series. Material on A. J. Downing.

1230 EBERLEIN, HAROLD DONALDSON. Manors and historic homes of the Hudson Valley. Philadelphia, J. B. Lippincott Co., 1924. 328p. illus.

1231 ———. Old houses of the Hudson Valley. Country life in America. 47:45-47, 68-70. Oct., Nov. 1924. illus.

1232 GOODWIN, MRS. MAUD WILDER. Dutch and English on the Hudson, a chronicle of Colonial New York. New Haven, Conn., Yale university press, 1919. 243p. illus.
Other editions 1920, 1921. Vol. 7 of *Chronicles of America* series.

1233 REYNOLDS, HELEN WILKINSON. Dutch houses in the Hudson Valley before 1776. N. Y., Payson and Clarke, 1929. 467p. illus.

1234 (TURNER, A. A.) Villas on the Hudson. . . . N. Y., D. Appleton and Co., 1860. 3p. 52 illus.
Author from 2773.

1235 WHITTEMORE, HENRY. Homes on the Hudson; historical, descriptive. N. Y., Artotype Publishing Co. 1p. 43 illus.
Hitchcock suggests that this book probably appeared in London in 1858–59.

1236 WILSTACH, PAUL. Hudson River landings. Indianapolis, Ind., Bobbs-Merrill Co., 1933. 311p. illus.

Hurley (see *Ulster County*)

Irvington

1237 MAXWELL, PERRITON. Sunnyside, a home and a shrine. American homes and gardens. 5:396-99. Oct. 1908. illus.
1650 and *ca.*1830–1840. Home of Washington Irving.

Ithaca (see also 1178)

1238 (The Clinton house. Contemporary description.) Atkinson's casket. 2:85-86. Feb. 1832.

Jefferson County

1239 DEKAY, CHARLES. Old houses of Jefferson county. Architectural record. 20:103-115. Aug. 1906. illus.

Katonah

1240 Second transformation of an eighteenth century residence. House and garden. 59:99-101. Apr. 1931. illus.

Kingston (see *Ulster County*)

Lewis County

1241 ALLEN, KATHERINE. Old stone house of Lewis county, New York. D. A. R. magazine. 57:663-74. Nov. 1923.
Built in late eighteenth century for Hezekiah M. Tallcott.

Long Island including *Staten Island* (see also *Cutchogue, Easthampton, Hempstead, Oyster Bay*, and 1172)

1242 BORSIG, TET. Long Island studies. Pencil points. 22:267-74. Apr. 1941. illus.

1243 Conservation of a relic of Colonial days: house of E. N. Wicht, Douglaston, Long Island, N. Y. American architect. 126:285-92. Sept. 1924. illus.

1244 CUSHING, CHARLES P. Ben Franklin answers Lord Howe. Mentor. 17:1-6. July 1929.
Conference house, Staten Island. Before 1700. Also known as Billopp house.

1245 DOUBLEDAY, RUSSELL. Long Island. N. Y., Doubleday, Doran and Co., 1939. 80p. illus.

1246 EBERLEIN, HAROLD DONALDSON. Manor houses and historic homes of Long Island and Staten Island. Philadelphia, J. B. Lippincott, 1928. 318p. illus.

1247 Eight old Long Island houses. American institute of architects. Journal. 12:110-17. Mar. 1924. illus. only.

1248 FANNING, RALPH. Some post-Colonial remains on Long Island. American architect. 110:367-71. Dec. 1916. illus.

1249 GILLESPIE, HARRIET SISSON. Historic Dutch houses upon Staten Island. Country life in America. 31:74-75. Apr. 1917. illus.

1250 Historic Billopp house on Staten Island, now to be included in a new park. Americana. 10:961-67. Nov. 1915.

Before 1688. Reprints from the *News Letter*, March 14, 1903, and the *New York Times*, September 7, 1913. This *News Letter* is probably the one published at St. George, Staten Island.

1251 HUNTINGTON HISTORICAL SOCIETY. Long Island's domestic architecture: old churches, mills; special exhibition. . . . Huntington, N. Y., Huntington historical society, 1920. 8p. illus.

1252 ISHAM, NORMAN MORRISON. An example of Colonial panelling, Woodbury, Long Island. Metropolitan museum of art. Bulletin. 6:112-16. May 1911. illus.

1253 MACOSKEY, ARTHUR R. (ed.). Long Island gazetteer, a guide to historic places. Brooklyn, N. Y., Eagle library, 1939. 144p. illus.

1254 MORAN, WILLIAM EDGAR. Settlements on the eastern end of Long Island. White pine series of architectural monographs. v. 5, no. 2. Apr. 1919. 14p. illus.

Covers 1660–1800.

1255 VAN ANDA, G. H. Old Long Island houses. American institute of architects. Journal. 11:355-63. Sept. 1923; 12:110-17. Feb. 1924; 9:161-68. May 1921. illus. only.

1256 WAILES, REX. Windmills of eastern Long Island. Newcomen society. Transactions. 15:117-51. 1936.

Seventeenth to nineteenth centuries.

Ludlowville

1257 TALLMAN, CARL C. Doorway, Miller house at Ludlowville, New York. Architecture. v. 40, no. 2, pl. 128, 129. Aug. 1919. illus. only.

Mohawk Valley

1258 CROUSE, NELLIS M. Forts and block houses in the Mohawk Valley. New York state historical association. Proceedings. 14:75-90. 1915.

Colonial.

1259 FREY, S. L. An old Mohawk Valley house. Magazine of American history. 8:337-45. May 1882.

1260 (Mohawk Valley architecture.) House and garden. v. 78. Aug. 1940. illus. Includes Cazenovia and Syracuse.

Newburgh

1261 BARCLAY, DAVID. Old houses and historic places in the vicinity of Newburgh, N. Y. Newburgh, N. Y., Journal print, 1909. 211p. illus. Newburgh Bay and the Highlands Historical Society publication 15.

1262 WEED, RAPHAEL A. Some Newburgh doorways and their owners. Newburgh historical society publication 26. 11p.

New Paltz (see *Ulster County*)

New York City—General References (see also *Long Island*)

1263 ANDREWS, WILLIAM LORING. New Amsterdam, New Orange, New York; a chronologically arranged account of engraved views of the city from the first picture published in 1651 until the year 1800. N. Y., Dodd, Mead and Co., 1897. 142p. illus.

1264 (Architecture in New York.) Putnam's monthly magazine. 1:121-36, 353-68, 763-86; 2:1-16, 233-48; 3:10-15, 141-52, 233-48. 1853, 1854. illus. Many types of buildings: Colonial, Classic Revival, and contemporary.

1265 BANK OF MANHATTAN COMPANY, NEW YORK. Historic buildings now standing in New York, which were erected prior to eighteen hundred. N. Y., Bank of Manhattan Co., 1914. 45p.

1266 BLUNT, EDMUND MARCH. Blunt's stranger's guide to the city of New York. N. Y., 1817. illus. Description of public buildings, dwelling houses, etc. Variant editions by Andrew T. Goodrich in 1818 and 1825.

1267 BOLTON, REGINALD PELHAM. Bolton priory at Pelham manor. Westchester county historical society. Bulletin. 6:54-58. July 1930. 1838.

1268 ———. Washington Heights, Manhattan: its eventful past. N. Y., Dyckman institute, 1924. 366p. illus.

1269 Bourne's views in . . . . New York. N. Y., 1831. 35 illus. Public buildings, most of which have been destroyed.

1270 BROWN, HENRY COLLINS. Glimpses of old New York. N. Y., H. C. Brown, 1917. illus.

1271 Check list of engraved views of the city of New York in the New York Public Library. New York public library. Bulletin. 5:222-26. 1901.

1272 CITY HISTORY CLUB OF NEW YORK. Landmarks of New York; an historical guide to the metropolis. N. Y., The city history club of New York, 1923. 261p. illus.

Published in 1909 and 1913 under title: *Historical Guide to the City of New York.*

1273 DiMARIANO, JOHN. Some doorways of older New York. Architectural record. 45:169-75. Feb. 1919. illus. only.

1274 ———. Some drawings of older New York. Architectural record. 48:159-65. Aug. 1920. illus. only.

1275 FAY, THEODORE SEDGWICK. Views in New York and its environs. . . . N. Y., Peabody and Co., 1831. 58p. illus.

Drawings by A. J. Davis, J. H. Dakin, and others.

1276 FEDERAL WRITERS' PROJECT. New York city guide: a comprehensive guide to the five boroughs of the metropolis—Manhattan, Brooklyn, the Bronx, Queens and Richmond. N. Y., Random house, 1939. 708p. illus.

Historic houses indexed and illustrated.

1277 ———. New York panorama: a comprehensive view of the metropolis. N. Y., Random house, 1938. 526p. illus.

Some mention, but no illustrations of historic houses.

1278 FRANCIS, C. S. Francis' new guide to the cities of New York and Brooklyn, and the vicinity. N. Y., 1853. illus.

1279 GERARD, JAMES W. Old Dutch streets of New York, under the Dutch. N. Y., D. Taylor, printer, 1874. 65p.

A paper read before the New York Historical Society, June 2, 1874.

1280 GOTTESMAN, RITA. Discarded heritage; New York architecture. Antiques. 33:248-49. May 1938. illus.

*Ca.*1650.

1281 HADDON, RAWSON WOODMAN. Varick street, which is in Greenwich Village, Manhattan, a narrative and some pen drawings. Architectural record. 35:49-57. Jan. 1914. illus.

1282 Jones and Newman's pictorial directory of New York, exhibiting a continued series of colored elevations, of all dwellings, stores and public buildings fronting on the principal streets. In 4 parts. N. Y., 1848. illus.

1283 LAMB, MRS. MARTHA L. The golden age of Colonial New York. Magazine of American history. 24:1-30. July 1890. illus.

1284 ———. Historic houses and landmarks. Magazine of American history. 21:1-23. Jan. 1889; 22:177-207. Mar. 1889. illus.

1285 LEVY, FLORENCE N. Art in New York: a guide to things worth seeing. N. Y., Municipal art society, 1935. 134p. illus.

1286 MOTT, HOPPER STRIKER. The New York of yesterday. N. Y., G. P. Putnam's sons, 1908. 597p. illus.

1287 MYER, JOHN. Gothic revival in New York. Museum of the city of New York. Bulletin. 3:50-56. Apr. 1940. illus.

1288 New York Gothic. Pencil points. v. 22. July 1940.
Exhibition at the Museum of the city of New York.

1289 Old buildings of New York city, with some notes regarding their origin and occupants. N. Y., Brentano and Co., 1907. 179p. illus.

1290 Old New York—1940. House beautiful. 82:26-29. June 1940. illus.

1291 (PASKO, W. W.) Index to engravings in Valentine's Manual. Old New York. 1:25, 105, 165. Aug. 1889.

1292 Shifting New York scene. Antiques. 39:304-305. June 1941. illus.
Review of an exhibition at New York Historical Society—New York as the artist knew it from 1626 to 1940.

1293 Some suburbs of New York. Lippincott's magazine. 8:9-23, 113-25. July-Aug. 1884. illus.
New Jersey, Westchester, and Long Island.

1294 STEVENS, JOHN AUSTIN, JR. Colonial New York. N. Y., J. F. Trow and Co., 1867. 172p.
Covers 1768–84.

1295 STOKES, ISAAC NEWTON PHELPS. Iconography of Manhattan Island. N. Y., R. H. Dodd, 1915-28. 6v. illus.
Covers 1489–1909. Compiled from original sources and illustrated by photo-intaglio reproductions of important maps, plans, views, and documents in various collections.

1296 WALLACE, W. H. Views and prints of old New York. . . . 1633-1878. Journal of American history. 17:149-68. 1923.

1297 WALLIS, F. A. New Amsterdam and its hinterland. Architectural forum. 50:473-81. Apr. 1929. illus.

New York City—Domestic (*see also* 219, 222, 1172)

1298 ADAMS, H. M. Old New York in the new. Good housekeeping. 74:26-27. Mar. 1922.
Covers Dykeman house, Poole house, and others.

1299 BERTON, G. Hamilton Grange today. Mentor. 17:36-37. July 1939. illus.
1802 by John McComb.

1300 BOLTON, REGINALD PELHAM. Washington's headquarters. New York. A sketch of the history of the Morris mansion (or Jumel mansion) in the city of New York, used by Washington as his headquarters in 1776. New York, American scenic and historic preservation society, 1903. 40p. illus.

1301 (Crystal palace, New York World's Fair, 1853. Drawings of this and other buildings for the same fair, proposed but not executed.) American architect. 147:33. Oct. 1935. illus.

1302 DEAN, BASHFORD, AND WELCH, ALEXANDER McMILLAN. The Dyckman house. American scenic and historic preservation society. Reports. 22: 459-84. 1917.

1303 ———. Dyckman house, built about 1783, restored and presented to the city of New York in 1916. N. Y., The Gillis press, 1916. 47p. illus.

1304 DECKER, H. K. Saving the Audubon home. Bird lore. 34:100-102. Jan. 1932.
Minnie's Land, occupied by Audubon in 1852.

1305 DITMAS, CHARLES ANDREWS. Historic homesteads of Kings county. Brooklyn N. Y., The Author, 1909. 120p. illus.

1306 (Dutch houses. Contemporary descriptions.) New York mirror. 10:241-43. Feb. 2, 1833; 12:153. Nov. 15, 1834.

1307 ELDREDGE, ALICE. The old Jumel mansion. Americana. 4:986-90. Dec. 1909.

1308 EMBURY, AYMAR II. Farmhouses of New Netherlands. White pine series of architectural monographs. v. 1, no. 3. Dec. 1915. 14p. illus.
Covers 1656–1825.

1309 FOWLER, LEMUEL HOADLEY. Some forgotten farmhouses on Manhattan Island. White pine series of architectural monographs. v. 9, no. 1. Feb. 1923. 14p. illus.
Covers Jumel and Dyckman houses.

1310 FRASER, GEORGIA. The stone house at Gowanus, scene of the battle of Long Island; Stirling's headquarters, Cornwallis' redoubt, occupied by Washington; Colonial residence of Dutch architecture; built by Nicholas Vechte, 1699. N. Y., Witter and Kintner, 1909. 161p. illus.
In Prospect Park, Brooklyn.

1311 HADDON, RAWSON WOODMAN. Roger Morris house, or Jumel mansion. New York city—in two parts. Architectural record. Part 1, 42:47-62. July 1917; part 2, 42:127-39. Aug. 1917. illus.
(Ca.1765)

1312 HOLLISTER, P. My pilgrimage to the Jumel mansion. Country life in America. 42:58-60. Oct. 1922. illus.

1313 Jumel mansion. Literary digest. 115:27-28. Apr. 29, 1933. illus.

1314 (E. W. King house. Contemporary description.) Atkinson's casket 10:457. Oct. 1831.
At Rodman's Neck, Pelham.

1315 MOSES, LIONEL. Some houses of old New York. Art world. 3:437-39. Feb. 1918. illus.

1316 PELLETREAU, WILLIAM S. Early New York houses. N. Y., Francis P. Harper, 1900. 243p. illus.

1317 ———. Historic homes and institutions and genealogical and family history of New York. N. Y., Lewis Publishing Co., 1907. 4v. illus.

1318 PINTARD, MRS. The Walton mansion house, Pearl st. . . . New York mirror. 9:289. Mar. 17, 1832. illus.

1319 PUMPELLY, JOSIAH COLLINS. The old Morris house, afterwards the Jumel mansion; its history and traditions. New York genealogical and biographical society. Publications. 34:80-89. Apr. 1903.

1320 ———. Washington headquarters. Americana. 6:351-60. Apr. 1911.
Morris-Jumel house.

1321 ROSS, WILLIAM. Street houses of the city of New York. Architectural record. 9:53-56. 1899.
Written in 1834.

1322 SHELTON, WILLIAM HENRY. The Jumel mansion. Art world. 2:245-50. June 1917. illus.

1323 ———. The Jumel mansion, being a full history of the house on Harlem Heights, built by Roger Morris before the revolution. Boston, Houghton Mifflin Co., 1916. 257p. illus.

1324 ———. Wall paper in the Jumel mansion. Architectural record. 43:189-90. Feb. 1918. illus.

1325 STAPLEY, MILDRED. The last Dutch farmhouses in New York city. Architectural record. 32:22-36. July 1912. illus.

1326 STOCKTON, HELEN HAMILTON. Motoring to three manors. Americana. 16:335-46. Oct. 1922.
Covers Claverāck house, Oak Hill, and the Van Cortland house.

1327 STODOLA, GILBERT I. Electric lighting of an old Colonial house: Jane Teller mansion. House beautiful. 51:309-311, 356. Apr. 1922.

1328 (Stuyvesant mansion. Contemporary description.) New York mirror. 9:201. Dec. 31, 1831. illus.

1329 (Washington's residence, Cherry street. Contemporary description.) New pictorial family magazine. 2:69-72. 1845.

New York City—Public

1330 ANDREWS, WILLIAM LORING. The iconography of the Battery and Castle garden. N. Y., C. Scribner's Sons, 1901. 43p. illus.

1331 (Astor House. Contemporary description.) American magazine of knowledge. 2:260. Feb. 1836.
(1834–39. Isaiah Rogers, architect. Also known as Park Hotel)

1332 BAYLES, WILLIAM HARRISON. Old taverns of New York. Journal of American history. 18:19-30, 115-30, 211-29, 317-22. 1924; 23:113-34, 153-97, 217-45. 1929; 24:150-67, 220-47. 1930; 25:117-35, 205-27. 1931; 27:83-99, 187-201. 1933.

1333 ———. Old taverns of New York. N. Y., Frank Allaben Genealogical Co., 1915. 489p. illus.

> Dutch taverns, the Coffee house, the Black Horse, Merchant's coffee house, tavern signs, the King's Arms, Hampden hall, the Province Arms, Fraunces' tavern, the Tontine coffee house, the City hotel, the Shakespeare tavern, road houses.

1334 Bill for the Croton reservoir. New York public library. Bulletin. 31:155-58. Mar. 1927.

> The Egyptian reservoir that stood on the site of the present library building, erected 1838–42. James Renwick, architect. Description of the Croton aqueduct. *New Yorker.* 10:9. Sept. 19, 1840.

1335 (Bowery theatre. Contemporary description.) Atkinson's casket. 6:265. June 1829.

1336-1339 (Custom house. Contemporary descriptions.) New world. 1:270. Sept. 26, 1840; Atkinson's casket. 1:12. Jan. 1831; Niles weekly register. 46:385. Aug. 2, 1834; Monthly chronicle. 3:320-26. July 1842.

> Also known as the Sub-treasury. 1834–41. Ithiel Town and Alexander J. Davis, architects.

1340 DePEYSTER, FREDERIC. History of the Tontine building, founded 1792, demolished in May, 1855. N. Y., 1855. illus.

> Reprinted from Valentine's *Manual* for 1852, with additions.

1341 DROWNE, HENRY RUSSELL. Sketch of Fraunces' tavern and those connected with its history. N. Y., 1925. 35p. illus.

> First edition 1919, 23p.

1342 (Federal hall. Contemporary description.) Columbia magazine. 3:473. Aug. 1789.

1343 (Holt's hotel. Contemporary description.) Atkinson's casket. 8:361. Aug. 1833. illus.

1344 KENNION, JOHN W. Architects' and builders' guide. N. Y., Fitzpatrick and Hunter, 1868. 108p. illus.

> Subtitle: "An elaborate description of all the public, commercial, philanthropic, literary and ecclesiastical buildings already constructed, and about to be erected next spring in New York and its environs, with their cost respectively, and the names of the architects and builders."

1345 McQUADE, WALTER. Measured drawings of New York city hall. Architecture. v. 35-36. Jan.-July 1917. illus. only.

1346, 1347 (Masonic hall. Contemporary descriptions.) Ladies' companion. 6: 255. Apr. 1837; American magazine of knowledge. 1:109-110. Nov. 1834.

> Gothic, 1825.

1348 MAY, CHARLES C. The New York city hall—in three parts. Architectural record. Part 1, 39:299-319. Apr. 1916; part 2, 39:474-90. May 1916; part 3, 39:513-35. June 1916. illus.
Completed 1811. Joseph F. Mangin and John McComb, Jr., architects.

1349-1353 (Merchants' exchange. Contemporary description.) Ladies' companion. 6:255. Apr. 1837; Atkinson's casket. 1:12. Jan. 1831; New Yorker. 4:734. Feb. 3, 1838; Broadway journal. 1:76. Feb. 1, 1845; American penny magazine. 1:536. Sept. 27, 1845.
First Merchants' Exchange completed May, 1827, burned 1835. Some of these references are critical as well as descriptive and include discussions of other buildings.

1354 MOTT, HOPPER STRIKER. Cato's tavern. Americana. 11:123-31. Apr. 1916.
Located on Boston post road about four miles north of the City hall.

1355 ———. Dyde's taverns. . . . Americana. 11:416-26. Oct. 1916.

1356 ———. The windmills of Manhattan; the story of the original industry on this island. Americana. 9:551-67. July 1914.

1357 NEW YORK HISTORICAL SOCIETY. Report on the preservation of the aquarium (Castle garden) by a committee of the society's trustees. New York historical society. Quarterly bulletin. 25:48-50. Apr. 1941. illus.
Before 1812. Destroyed 1941.

1358 Original plans of the City hall, New York. American architect. 23:43-46. Feb. 5, 1908. illus.
Drawn in 1802. John McComb, Jr., architect.

1359 PIERCE, MRS. MELUSINA FAY. Landmark of Fraunces' tavern. N. Y., American scenic and historic society, 1901. 44p. illus.

1360 (Public buildings. Contemporary descriptions.) New York mirror. 7:89-90. Sept. 26, 1829. illus.

1361 ROSS, WILLIAM. Descriptive account of the improvements lately made at the Custom house, New York. Architectural record. 9:57-64. 1899. illus.
The Sub-treasury, Wall street. Written in 1835.

1362 SCHUYLER, MONTGOMERY. The architecture of American colleges—part 4. New York city colleges. Architectural record. 27:443-69. June 1910. illus.

1363 ———. The New York city hall. Architectural record. 23:387-90. May 1908. illus.

1364 ———. The restoration of Fraunces' tavern. Architectural record. 24:444-48. Dec. 1908. illus.

1365 (United States branch bank. Contemporary description.) Atkinson's casket. 1:12. Jan. 1831. illus.
1822–24. Also known as the Assay office. Facade moved from 15 Wall Street to the American wing of the Metropolitan Museum of Art. Martin Thompson, architect.

1366 WHITING, M. A. Federal hall. Stone and Webster journal. 48:454-60. 1931.
Covers 1699–1813.

1367 WILDE, EDWARD SEYMOUR. New York city hall. Century. 27:865-72. Apr.
1884. illus.
Issued as a reprint, 1893.

New York City—Religious

1368 (B. W.) New York and Brooklyn churches. . . . N. Y.(?), Nelson and
Phillips, 1874. 128p. illus.

1369 BRUMBAUGH, C. E. B. Some New York churches during the revolution.
American monthly magazine. 40:1-6. Jan. 1912.

1370 CLARKE, NELL RAY. Old Trinity, New York. Landmark. 6:37-40. Jan.
1924.
(Completed 1846. Richard Upjohn, architect.)

1371 DISOSWAY, GABRIEL POILLON. Earliest churches of New York and its vicinity.
N. Y., J. G. Gregory, 1865. 416p. illus.

1372 HADDON, RAWSON WOODMAN. St. John's chapel, Varick street, New York
city. Architectural record. 35:389-403. May 1914. illus.
1807. John McComb, architect.

1373 HALL, EDWARD HAGAMAN. The first Presbyterian church of New York.
American scenic and historic preservation society. Reports. 22:567-667.
1917.

1374 (St. George's church, Stuyvesant square.) Literary world. 3:853-54. Nov.
25, 1848.
1847.

1375 (St. John's chapel. Contemporary description.) Christian journal and literary
register. 11:145-47. May 1827.

1376 St. John's chapel, New York. Architectural record. 27:125-26. Jan. 1910.
illus.

1377, 1378 (St. Thomas' church. Contemporary descriptions.) Monthly reposi-
tory and library of entertaining knowledge. 4:357-58. Mar. 1834;
American penny magazine. 2:600. Oct. 24, 1846.
(Early structure destroyed 1905.)

1379 SCHUYLER, MONTGOMERY. Trinity's architecture. Architectural record.
25:411-25. June 1909. illus.
Includes other New York churches.

1380 STEWART, WILLIAM RHINELANDER. Grace church and old New York. N.
Y., E. P. Dutton Co., 1924. 542p. illus.
(1846. James Renwick, architect.)

1381 WINGATE, CHARLES F. Saint Paul's chapel in New York city. American scenic and historic preservation society. Reports. 22:435-58. 1917.
(Begun 1764. James McBean, architect.)

Orange County

1382 MOFFATT, ALMET S. Old churches of Orange county, New York. Washingtonville, N. Y., 1927. 32p.

Oyster Bay

1383 CARRICK, ALICE VAN LEER. Historic Raynham hall. Country life. 48:68-70. June 1925. illus.
1740.

Owego

1384 TROWBRIDGE, ALEXANDER B. Greek revival in Owego and nearby New York towns, some suggested antidotes. White pine series of architectural monographs. v. 7, no. 3. June 1921. 16p. illus.

Pawling

1385 STEARNS, AMANDA AKIN. Ancient homes and early days of Quaker Hill. Quaker Hill, N. Y., Akin hall association, 1913. 44p. illus.

Poughkeepsie (see 557)

Rensselaerville

1386 KELLER, WILLIAM A. Rensselaerville, an old village of the Helderbergs. White pine series of architectural monographs. v. 10, no. 4. 1924. 16p. illus.
Early nineteenth century.

Rhinebeck

1387 PAULMIER, HILAH. The oldest hotel in America. D. A. R. magazine. 52:91-92. Feb. 1918.
(Is it?)

Rochester

1388 FAIRCHILD, HERMAN LEROY, AND WARNER, J. FOSTER. Building stones of Rochester; nature's contribution to local edifices. Rochester historical society. Publication. 12:131-56. 1933.

1389 FEDERAL WRITERS' PROJECT. Rochester and Monroe county. Rochester, N. Y., Scrantom's publishers, 1937. 440p. illus.

1390 FOREMAN, EDWARD H. First families of Rochester and their dwellings. Rochester historical society. Publication fund series. 4:353-56. 1925.

Rockland County

1391 BLAUVELT, GEORGE A. Suffern's tavern. New York state historical association. Journal. 6:136-40. Apr. 1925.

1392 GILLESPIE, HARRIET SISSON. A typical old Dutch farmhouse. American homes and gardens. 12:76-80. Mar. 1915. illus.
1758.

Rosendale (see *Ulster County*)

Sackett's Harbor

1393 BRAGDON, CLAUDE FAYETTE. Colonial work in Sackett's Harbor. American architect and building news. 34:9-10. Oct. 1891. illus.

1394 DE KAY, CHARLES. Old houses in Jefferson county. Architectural record. 20:103-115. Aug. 1916. illus.
Early Republican.

Saugerties

1395 RONY, LILA RUSSELL JAMES. Echoes of two centuries, Saugerties: a quaint village of yesterday. House beautiful. 52:332-33, 380, 382. Oct. 1922. illus.

Scarsdale

1396 GILLESPIE, HARRIET SISSON. Wayside, an old homestead in Scarsdale, New York—*ca.* 1725. House beautiful. 54:144-45, 186. Aug. 1923. illus.

Schenectady (see also 1178)

1397 Historic house regains its youth; Governor Yates house, Schenectady, New York. House and garden. 65:55-57. May 1934. illus.

1398 HUNGERFORD, EDWARD. Gentleman of the North; Constable Hall in the Black River Valley country. House beautiful. 63:757, 800-802. June 1928.
1819.

1399 LARRABEE, H. A. Joseph Jacques Ramée and America's first unified college plan. N. Y., (The American society of the French legion of honor), 1934. 7p. illus.
Franco-American pamphlet series, no. 1. Union College.

Scotia

1400 BUTTON, H. V. Glen-Sanders house at Scotia, New York. House beautiful. 48:24-25. July 1920. illus.

1401 SHAFER, DON CAMERON. A treasure house of Colonial days. American homes and gardens. 11:123-25. Apr. 1914. illus.
Glen-Sanders near Schenectady (1713–66).

Sennett

1402 TALLMAN, CARL C. Doorway, Soule house, Sennett, New York. Architecture. v. 39, no. 4, pl. 62. Apr. 1919. illus. only.

Skaneateles

1403 TALLMAN, CARL C. Doorway, Barber house, Skaneateles, New York. Architecture. v. 40, no. 2, pl. 130. Aug. 1919. illus. only.

1404 ———. Measured drawings of the Austin house, Skaneateles, New York. Architecture. v. 39, no. 4. Apr. 1919. illus. only.

Staten Island (see *Long Island*)

Syracuse (*see* 1178, 1260)

Tappan

1405 BLAUVELT, H. The old stone house where Major Andre was imprisoned. Mentor. 16:33-35. Feb. 1928. illus.
1755.

Tarrytown

1406 BACON, EDGAR MAYHEW. Country homes of famous Americans. Part 1. Washington Irving. Country life in America. 4:406-410. illus.

1407 Historical piece hunted; Philipse Castle to be restored. Library journal 65:497. June 1, 1940.
1638.

Ticonderoga (*see also* 598)

1408 BOSSOM, ALFRED C. The restoration of Fort Ticonderoga. American scenic and historic preservation society. Reports. 18:610-18. 1923.

1409 TOWER, ELIZABETH A. John Hancock house. Ticonderoga, N. Y., New York state historical association, 1926. illus.
Replica of the original Hancock house on Beacon Hill, Boston, Massachusetts.

Troy

1410 (St. Paul's church. Contemporary description.) Monthly repository and library of entertaining knowledge. 2:49-50. July 1831.

1411 SHAFER, CARL SCHURZ. A landmark on the Hudson. American homes and gardens. 12:15. Jan. 1915. illus.
Lansing house, 1771.

Ulster County

1412 EBERLEIN, HAROLD DONALDSON. Hurley town, a New Netherland suburb. American suburbs. p. 264-67. May 1911. illus.

1413 GILLESPIE, HARRIET SISSON. Early Dutch architecture in the Hudson Valley; Brykill manor near Kingston. Arts and decoration. 35:28-29. June 1931. illus.
1736 and later.

1414 HAASBROUCK, G. B. D. Old stone houses of Esopus. Ulster county historical society. Proceedings for 1934-35, p. 15-28. 1935.

1415 The Hardenbergh house at Rosendale, Olde Ulster. 5:51-54. Feb. 1909.

1416 HASTINGS, HELEN M. Old stone houses of Esopus. Architectural record. 49:91-95. Jan. 1921. illus.

1417 KEEFE, CHARLES S. Development of the American doorway. American architect. 113:818-23. June 19, 1918. illus.
Examples from Kingston.

1418 KING, DOROTHY. Dutch Colonial houses in Kingston, New York. House beautiful. 47:36-37. Jan. 1920. illus.

1419 LEGALLIENNE, RICHARD. Old Kingston. Harper's magazine. 23:917-26. Nov. 1911. illus.

1420 MACKENSIE, ALAN. Old stone houses of Rosendale. Ulster county historical society. Proceedings. 1930-31:30-37. 1931.
Particularly Jacob Rutsen house.

1421 MILLAR, DONALD. Quaint Dutch survival, Jean Hasbrouck house, New Paltz, New York. Architectural record. 59:229-32. Mar. 1926. illus.
Near Poughkeepsie (1712).

1422 NASH, GEORGE W. The old stone church at Hurley. Olde Ulster. 8:171-79. June 1912.

1423 ———. The old stone school house at Hurley. Olde Ulster. 8:198-204. July 1912.

1424 NASH, WILLIS G. Some historic houses in Marbletown. Ulster county historical society. Proceedings for 1935-36. p. 34-39. 1936.

1425 The old stone church at Warwarsing. Olde Ulster. 3:114-19. Apr. 1907.

1426 PENNINGTON, DOROTHY KING. Dutch Colonial houses in Kingston, New York. House beautiful. 47:36-37. Jan. 1920. illus.

Westchester County (see also *Bronxville, Irvington, Scarsdale, Tarrytown, White Plains, Yonkers*)

1427 STONE, SUSANNE. Some historic houses of Westchester county. New York state historical association. Proceedings. 9:292-98. 1910.

1428 WEEKS, LYMAN HORACE. The Rochambeau house. Americana. 5:961-63. Sept.-Oct. 1910.

1429 WHITE, STEPHEN F. Some old churches of Westchester county. Westchester county magazine. 3:3-5. May 1909.

West Point

1430 (West Point. Contemporary description.) Ladies' companion. July 1844. illus.

White Plains

1431 BOLTON, REGINALD PELHAM. The Hammond house. 21p. 1927.

1432 SMITH, WILSON CAREY. The Miller house; Washington's headquarters at White Plains, N. Y. Magazine of American history. 7:108-118. Aug. 1881. illus.

Yonkers

1433 BOLTON, REGINALD PELHAM, AND MORGAN, H. SEACORD. Philipse manor hall, Yonkers. Westchester county historical society. Bulletin. 9:4-7. 1933.
(1682 and later.)

1434 GLOAG, JOHN. In old New York; Philipse manor hall, Yonkers. Country life, London. 88:460-61. Nov. 23, 1940. illus.

1435 HALL, EDWARD HAGAMAN. Philipse manor hall, Yonkers, New York, the site, the building and its occupants. N. Y., American scenic and historic preservation society, 1912. 255p. illus.

1436 The story of Philipse manor. Catholic world. 130:568-75. Feb. 1930.

1437 TORREY, RAYMOND H. Philipse manor hall, Yonkers. Scenic and historic America. 4:3-28. 1935.

PENNSYLVANIA

GENERAL REFERENCES (*see also* 153, 258, 1094, 1098)

1438 ALLEN, GEORGE H. Some European origins of early Pennsylvania architecture. American journal of archaeology. 40:126. Jan. 1936.
Abstract of a paper submitted to the thirty-seventh general meeting of the Archaeological Institute of America, 1935.

1439 American home pilgrimages—part 9. Western Pennsylvania. American home. 24:38, 40-41. Oct. 1940. illus.

1440 ARCHAMBAULT, A. MARGARETTA (ed.). A guide book of art, architecture, and historic interests in Pennsylvania. Philadelphia, John C. Winston Co., 1924. 509p. illus.

1441 Architectural overtones: Pennsylvania barns; photographs. American architect. 151:43-50. Sept. 1937. illus.

1442 BINING, ARTHUR CECIL. Pennsylvania iron manufacture in the eighteenth century. Harrisburg, 1938. 227p. illus.

1443 BRUMBAUGH, G. EDWIN. Colonial architecture of the Pennsylvania Germans. Lancaster, Pa., Pennsylvania German society, 1933. 60p. illus.
Originally delivered as an address before the forty-first annual meeting of the Pennsylvania German Society at Reading, October 23, 1931. Includes notes on log construction.

1444 COMINGS, MARION. Pioneer architecture of western Pennsylvania. Carnegie magazine. 11:305-308. Mar. 1938. illus.

1445 EMBURY, AYMAR II. Pennsylvania farmhouses, examples of rural dwellings of a hundred years ago. Architectural record. 30:475-85. Nov. 1911. illus.

1446 FEDERAL WRITERS' PROJECT. Pennsylvania: a guide to the keystone state. N. Y., Oxford university press, 1940. 660p. illus.

1447 ———. Harmony society in Pennsylvania. Philadelphia, William Penn association of Philadelphia, 1937. 38p. illus.

1448 ———. Pennsylvania cavalcade. Philadelphia, University of Pennsylvania press, 1942. 462p. illus.

1449 FEGLEY, H. WINSLOW. Among some of the older mills in eastern Pennsylvania. Norristown, Pa., Pennsylvania German society, 1930. 76p. illus.

1450 HARPSTER, JOHN W. Eighteenth century inns and taverns of western Pennsylvania. Western Pennsylvania historical magazine. 19:5-16. 1936.

1451 ISRAEL, CORA M. Historic churches of Pennsylvania. American monthly magazine. 41:10-16. July 1912.

1452 KOCHER, A. LAWRENCE. Early architecture of Pennsylvania—in 14 parts. Architectural record. Part 1, 48:513-30; part 2, 49:31-47; part 3, 49:135-55; part 4, 49:233-48; part 5, 49:310-30; part 6, 49:409-422; part 7, 49:519-35; part 8, 50:27-43; part 9, 50:147-57; part 10, 50:214-26; part 11, 50:398-406; part 12, 51:507-520; part 13, 52:121-32; part 14, 52:434-44. Dec. 1920—Nov. 1922. illus.

1453 LEARNED, MARION DEXTER. The German barn in America. Philadelphia, University of Pennsylvania. Bulletin. 15th ser. no. 3, pt. 5. p. 338-49.

1454 Master detail series. Early architecture of western Pennsylvania; Meason house and Johnston house. Architectural forum. 66:229-36. Mar. 1937. illus.

1455 Master detail series. The Pennsylvania farm house. Architectural forum. 60:369-84. May 1923. illus.

1456 Penn-land. House beautiful. 82:76-77. May 1940. illus.
Covers *ca*.1790-1800, Pennsylvania, New Jersey, and Maryland.

1457 PRICE, B. LLEWELLYN. Early stonework of eastern Pennsylvania. House beautiful. 67:58-59, 95-97. Jan. 1930. illus.
Covers Bull house, Warwick, and Chew mansion, Germantown.

1458 RAYMOND, ELEANOR. Early domestic architecture of Pennsylvania. N. Y., William Helburn, 1931. 158p. illus.

1459 ROSENBERGER, JESSE LEONARD. In Pennsylvania-German land, 1928-1929. Chicago, University of Chicago press, 1929. 90p. illus.

1460, 1461 SACHSE, JULIUS FRIEDRICH. The wayside inns on the Lancaster roadside between Philadelphia and Lancaster. Lancaster, Pa., New Era Printing Co., 1912. 77p. illus.
Reprint from Pennsylvania-German society. *Proceedings*. v. 21.

1462 SCHUYLER, MONTGOMERY. Architecture of American colleges. Part 5. University of Pennsylvania, Girard, Haverford, Lehigh and Bryn Mawr colleges. Architectural record. 28:183-212. Sept. 1910. illus.

1463 STARRETT, C. V. American home pilgrimage—part 9. Western Pennsylvania. American home. 24:38, 40-41. Oct. 1940. illus.

1464 STOTZ, CHARLES MORSE. Early architecture of western Pennsylvania, an exhibition of drawings and photographs. Carnegie magazine. 9:239-43. Jan. 1936. illus.

1465 ———. Early architecture of western Pennsylvania. N. Y., Published by William Helburn for the Buhl foundation, Pittsburgh, 1936. 290p. illus.
A record of building before 1860, based upon the western Pennsylvania architectural survey, a project of the Pittsburgh chapter of the American Institute of Architects.

1466 ———. Old architecture of Pennsylvania. Architecture. 49:79. Mar. 1924. illus. only.

1467 WHARTON, ANNE HOLLINGSWORTH. In old Pennsylvania towns. Philadelphia, J. B. Lippincott, 1920. 352p. illus.

LOCATIONS

Berks County

1468 ESHELMAN, JOHN E. Society of Friends and their meeting houses in Berks county. Berks county historical review. 1:34-40. 1936.
1718–1800.

1469 KENNEDY, DEAN. Century old farmhouses, Oley Valley, Berks county, Pennsylvania. Pencil points. 13:540-54. Aug. 1932. Monograph series. 18:214-228. illus.
Covers 1733–1800.

Bethlehem

1470 (REICHEL, WILLIAM CORNELIUS.) Old Sun inn at Bethlehem, Pa., 1758. . . . Doylestown, Pa., W. W. H. Davis, printer, 1876. 48p. illus.

1471 SNYDER, KARL H. Moravian architecture of Bethlehem, Pennsylvania. White pine series of architectural monographs. v. 13, no. 4. 1927. 19p. illus.
Covers 1745–1803.

Bristol

1472 MAULE, JOHN C. Friends' old meeting house in Bristol, Pennsylvania. Bucks county historical society. Papers. 4:92-96. 1917.

Carlisle

1473 Dickinson college. Portfolio. v. 5. 1811.
Old West, 1804. Benjamin Latrobe, architect.

1474 Sponsler, George C., Jr. Mantel in Blaine house, Carlisle, Pa., built about 1780. American architect. 128:491-92. Dec. 1925. illus. only.

Bucks County (*see also* town names and 107, 108)

1475 Bucks County Historical Society. Collection of papers read before the Bucks county historical society. Doylestown, Pa., The Society, 1926. 769p. illus.

> Covers: homes of George Taylor, Norse mills of Colonial times in Pennsylvania, octagonal school houses, early courthouses of Bucks County, old Heath mill and its early owners, origin of log houses in the United States (Henry Mercer), Neshaminy Presbyterian church.

1476 Old stone houses in Bucks county: exterior views. American architect. 149: 43-50. Oct. 1936. illus.

1477 Paxson, Henry D. Log houses of Bucks county. Bucks county historical society. Papers. 4:204-209. 1917.

1478 Smith, James Kellum. Bucks county Colonial. House and garden. 69:21-23, 74. Jan. 1936. illus.

1479 Watson, Henry Winfield. The Growden mansion. Bucks county historical society. Collections. 2:251-56. 1909.

Chester

1480 Brazer, Clarence Wilson. Colonial court house, Chester, Pennsylvania. Architectural record. 60:527-32. Dec. 1926. illus.
(1724)

1481 Dower house, West Chester, Pennsylvania. Arts and decoration. 38:8-9. Oct. 1933. illus.

1482 Delaware County Historical Society. Bicentennial celebration of the erection in 1724 of the old Colonial court house, Chester, Pennsylvania. Chester, Pa., Chester times, 1924. 24p. illus.

1483 Harvey, Evangeline Lukena. Old Washington inn. Friends' historical association. Bulletin. 21:84-86. 1932.
(1747)

1484 Prescott, Charlotte. Great American patriot; Mordecai Hayes house on the Brandywine River. Better homes and gardens. 19:28-29, 90-91. June 1941. illus.
1770 and later.

Daylesford

1485 Copeland, J. L. Blue Ball inn, Daylesford, Pennsylvania. House beautiful. 65:712-20. May 1929. illus.

Ephrata

1486 Brumbaugh, Martin Grove. Outline for historical romance—history of the Ephrata society in the eighteenth century, Pennsylvania. Norristown, Pa., Pennsylvania German society, 1930. 12p. illus.

1487 JAYNE, HORACE H. F. The Cloisters at Ephrata. American magazine of art. 29:594-98, 620-22. Sept. 1936. illus.
(Ca.1740)

1488 PUGH, ANNA ELOISE. The old cloister at Ephrata, Pennsylvania. D. A. R. magazine. 51:146-49. Sept. 1917.

Erie

1489 FEDERAL WRITERS' PROJECT. Erie; a guide to the city and county. Philadelphia, William Penn association of Philadelphia, 1938. 134p. illus.

Fort Washington

1490 ZIEGLER, C. A. The Highlands, Skippack pike, above Fort Washington, Pa. Architectural review. n. s. 23:1-2. Jan. 1918. illus.
1796.

Germantown (see *Philadelphia*)

Greene County

1491 PARRY, MARY SAMMONS. Greene county forts and block-houses. D. A. R. magazine. 59:234-36. Apr. 1925.

Harrisburg

1492 Description of the state capitol of Pennsylvania, now building at Harrisburg. Analectic magazine. n. s. v. 2. July 1820.

Haverford (*see* 1462)

Kennett Square

1493 MERRICK, H. S. Homestead of the 18th century: Longwood, Kennett square. Arts and decoration. 38:8-12. Jan. 1933. illus.

Lancaster

1494 BYRNE, JACOB HILL. Typical old Lancaster buildings and architecture. Lancaster county historical society. Papers. 26:138-43. June 1922.

1495 Four early American mantels. Architectural record. 34:225-31. Sept. 1913. illus.
Diller house.

1496 HENSEL, WILLIAM UHLER. The passing of an old landmark. Lancaster county historical society. Papers. 18:251-74. Dec. 4, 1914.
Shippen house.

1497 ———. The Shippen house. Lancaster county historical society. Papers. 14:125-43. 1910.
Destroyed.

1498 KOCHER, ALFRED LAWRENCE. The early architecture of Lancaster county, Pennsylvania. Lancaster county historical society. Papers. 24:91-106. 1920.
Colonial.

1499 LANDIS, D. B. Lancaster houses of 150 years ago. Lancaster county historical society. Papers. 26:136-37. June 1922.

Lehigh Valley

1500 ROBERTS, CHARLES R. Historic buildings of the Lehigh Valley. Pennsylvania-German. 8:72-73, 169-70, 598, 599. Feb., Apr., Dec. 1907.

Ligonier

1501 SIPE, CHESTER HALE. Fort Ligonier and its times: a history of the first English fort west of the Allegheny Mountains and an account of many thrilling, tragic, romantic, important but little known Colonial and revolutionary events in the region where the winning of the west began. Harrisburg, Pa., The Telegraph press, 1932. 699p. illus.
Based primarily on Pennsylvania archives and Colonial records (laid out in 1816).

Merion

1502 BARKER, CHARLES R. Colonial taverns of Lower Merion. Pennsylvania magazine of history. 52:205-228. July 1928.

1503 ———. Old mills of Mill Creek, Lower Merion. Pennsylvania magazine of history. 50:1-22. Jan. 1926.

Northampton County

1504 FEDERAL WRITERS' PROJECT. Northampton county guide. Bethlehem, Pa., Times Publishing Co., *ca.* 1939. 246p. illus.

Philadelphia—General References (including *Germantown*) (*see also* 184A)

1505 BARTON, GEORGE. Little journeys around old Philadelphia. Philadelphia, The Peter Reilly Co., 1925. 325p. illus.
Historic churches and houses.

1506 CARPENTERS' COMPANY OF THE CITY AND COUNTY OF PHILADELPHIA. Recording the celebration of the two-hundredth anniversary of the Carpenters' company of the city and county of Philadelphia, Pa., and the one-hundred-fiftieth anniversary of the first meeting of the First Continental congress, September 25, 1924. Philadelphia, Carpenters' company of the city and county of Philadelphia, 1925. 114p. illus.

1507 CARRICK, ALICE VANLEER. Farm that came back: Todmorden farm. Country life in America. 47:38-41. Nov. 1924.
1790, near Philadelphia.

1508-1510 (Chestnut street and Arch street. Descriptions of the buildings.) The Ariel. 2:94. Oct. 4, 1828; 5:384. Mar. 17, 1832; Atkinson's casket. 12:553-54. Dec. 1828; Hazard's register of Pennsylvania. 10:94. Aug. 11, 1832.

1511 COUSINS, FRANK, AND RILEY, PHILIP M. Colonial architecture of Philadelphia. Boston, Little, Brown and Co., 1920. 248p. illus.

1512 DAVIS, LEICESTER K. Early architecture of Germantown. House beautiful. 68:253-55, 274. Sept. 1930.

1513 EBERLEIN, HAROLD DONALDSON. Three types of Georgian architecture—the evolution of the style in Philadelphia—in two parts. Architectural record. Part 1, 34:56-77, July 1913; part 2, 37:159-76, Feb. 1915. illus.

1514 ——, AND HUBBARD, CORTLANDT VAN DYKE. Portrait of a Colonial city; Philadelphia, 1670-1838. Philadelphia, J. B. Lippincott Co., 1939. 580p. illus.

1515 ELLIOTT, HUGER. Architecture in Philadelphia and a coming chance. Architectural record. 23:295-309. Apr. 1908. illus.

1516 FARIS, JOHN T. Old roads out of Philadelphia. Philadelphia, J. B. Lippincott Co., 1917. 327p. illus.

1517 ——. Romance of old Philadelphia. Philadelphia, J. B. Lippincott Co., 1918. 336p. illus.

1518 FEDERAL WRITERS' PROJECT. Philadelphia: a guide to the nation's birthplace. Philadelphia, William Penn association of Philadelphia, 1937. 704p. illus.

1519 FITZ-GIBBON, COSTEN. Architectural Philadelphia—yesterday and today. Architectural record. 34:20-45. July 1913. illus.

1520 GILLINGHAM, HAROLD E. Some early brickmakers of Philadelphia. Philadelphia magazine of history. 53:1-27. Jan. 1929.

1521 GOFORTH, WILLIAM DAVENPORT, AND McAULEY, WILLIAM J. Old Colonial architectural details in and around Philadelphia. N. Y., William Helburn, 1890. 2p. 50pl.

1522 GRAY, WILLIAM F. Philadelphia's architecture. Philadelphia, The City history society of Philadelphia, 1915. 376p. illus.
Publication no. 12 of the Society.

1523 HAMLIN, TALBOT FAULKNER. Some Greek revival architects of Philadelphia. Pennsylvania magazine of history and biography. 65:121-44. Apr. 1941. illus.

1524 JACKSON, JOSEPH. Early Philadelphia architects and engineers. Philadelphia, Privately printed, 1923. 285p. illus.
This work originally appeared serially in the magazine *Building* during the years 1922–23.

1525 ——. Encyclopaedia of Philadelphia. Harrisburg, Pa., The National historical association, 1931-33. 4v. illus.

1526 LIPPINCOTT, HORACE MATHER. Early Philadelphia: its people, life and progress. Philadelphia, J. B. Lippincott Co., 1917. 339p. illus.

1527 (Metal house. Description.) Godey's lady's book. 52:299. Apr. 1856.
Illustration and description of this section of L. Johnson's foundry in Philadelphia.

1528, 1529 (New buildings. Contemporary descriptions.) Ariel. 4:190. Mar. 19,
1831; Niles' weekly register. 37:39. Sept. 12, 1829; 47:280-81. Dec.
27, 1834.

1530 Old doorways, Philadelphia, Pa. Architecture. v. 39, no. 3. Mar. 1919.
illus. only.

1531 PENN MUTUAL LIFE INSURANCE COMPANY. Independence square neighborhood. Philadelphia, Penn Mutual Life Insurance Co., 1926. 155p. illus.
Historical notes on Independence and Washington squares, lower Chestnut Street, and
the insurance district along Walnut Street.

1532 PULLINGER, HERBERT. Old Germantown. Philadelphia, David McKay Co.,
1926. 57p. illus.

1533 ———. Philadelphia, past and present. Boston, L. Phillips, 1915, 2p. 25
illus.

1534 SALOMONSKY, VERNA COOK. Old hardware from Philadelphia and Annapolis.
Architectural record. 48:169-73. Aug. 1920. illus.

1535 SIMS, JOSEPH PATTERSON, AND WILLING, CHARLES. Old Philadelphia Colonial
details. N. Y., Architectural Book Publishing Co., 1914. 55 illus.

1536 WALLACE, PHILIP B., AND DUNN, A. G. Colonial ironwork in old Philadelphia; the craftsmanship of the early days of the Republic. N. Y., Architectural Book Publishing Co., 1930. 157p. illus.

1537 WATSON, JOHN FANNING. Annals of Philadelphia and Pennsylvania in the
olden time. Philadelphia, E. S. Stuart, 1898. 3v. illus.
First edition, 1830.

1538 ———. Historic tales of olden time concerning Philadelphia and Pennsylvania. Philadelphia, E. Littell and Thomas Holden, 1833. 316p. illus.

1539 WEINY, DANIEL W. Early architecture of Germantown, Pa., ca.1768.
Architecture. v. 46, no. 6. Dec. 1922. illus. only.

1540 WESTCOTT, THOMPSON. Historic mansions and buildings of Philadelphia,
with some notice of their owners and occupants. Philadelphia, Porter
and Coates, 1877. 528p. illus.

1541 ZIEGLER, CARL A. Carpenters' company, organized in Philadelphia in 1724.
American architect. 126:313-18. Oct. 8, 1924. illus.

1542 ———. Early American cornices of Philadelphia. American architect.
126:1-10. July 2, 1924. illus.

1543 ———. Fort Mifflin. American architect. 121:47-50. Jan. 18, 1922.
illus.
Ca.1812.

Philadelphia—Domestic (*see also* 213, 219, 1457)

1544 BACON, EDGAR MAYHEW. Country homes of famous Americans, part 2. The home of John Bartram. Country life in America. 5:27-30, 72, 73. illus. *Ca.*1731.

1545 BROWNBACK, G. E. Heivert Papen and the Papen house of Germantown, Pennsylvania. Penn Germania. n.s. 1:78-80. Feb. 1912.

1546 CLAY, E. B. Reliving the days of Washington; Colonial mansions in Fairmount park. Ladies' home journal. 49:14-15. June 1932. illus.

1547 (Colonnade row. Contemporary description.) Atkinson's casket. 11:505. Nov. 1832. illus.

1548 DOWNS, JOSEPH. An eighteenth century Philadelphia mansion. Antiquarian. 16:26-30, 66. May 1931.
Woodford (before 1730).

1549 ———. Cedar Grove, built 1721-1725 retains its original furnishings. Good housekeeping. 94:60-61, 255. May 1932. illus.
Was at Frankford, now in Fairmount Park.

1550 ———. Mount Pleasant, an old Philadelphia house of 1761. Good housekeeping. 94:58-59. Feb. 1932. illus.

1551 ———. Strawberry mansion, 1728—an historic house of Philadelphia. Good housekeeping. 94:54-58. Jan. 1932.

1552 ———. Woodford—a Colonial house of 1734-56. Good housekeeping. 95:54-55. Oct. 1932. illus.

1553 EASTWICK, MRS. ANDREW M. Bartram hall. Philadelphia city historical society. Publications. 2:209-213. 1930.
1851. Not the John Bartram house, 1731.

1554 EBERLEIN, HAROLD DONALDSON. Colonial seats in Fairmount Park, Philadelphia. American homes and gardens. 12:255-60. Aug. 1915. illus.

1555 ———. Restored Quaker farmhouse. House and garden. 42:56-57. Oct. 1922.
Netherfield, in Huntington Valley, 1700 and 1800. Near Philadelphia.

1556 ———, AND LIPPINCOTT, HORACE MATHER. Colonial homes of Philadelphia and its neighborhood. Philadelphia, J. B. Lippincott Co., 1912. 365p. illus.

1557 GILLINGHAM, MRS. H. E. House beautiful of long ago; Mount Pleasant in Fairmount Park, Philadelphia. House beautiful. 60:46-47. July 1926. illus.

1558 HINDERMYER, GILBERT. Wyck, an old house and garden at Germantown, Philadelphia. House and garden. 2:545-59. Nov. 1902. illus.

1559 HOLLOWAY, EDWARD STRATTON. Pennsylvania Colonial homestead, Walnut
Grove farm. House beautiful. 48:379-81, 416. Nov. 1920. illus.
Eighteenth century, near Philadelphia.

1560 HORNOR, W. M., JR. Mount Pleasant, 1761. American institute of architects. Journal. 15:272-78. Aug. 1927. illus.

1561 House of William Penn's secretary. Touchstone. 5:64-69. Apr. 1919. illus.
Stenton, 1727.

1562 HUTCHINS, FRANK W. The Washington house in Philadelphia. D. A. R.
magazine. 61:34-40. Jan. 1927; 61:123-29. Feb. 1927; 61:198-203.
Mar. 1927.
House occupied by Washington as president.

1563 KIMBALL, SIDNEY FISKE. Belmont, Fairmount Park. Pennsylvania museum.
Bulletin. 22:333-45. Mar. 1927. illus.

1564 ——. Philadelphia's Colonial chain. Art and archaeology. 21:150-54.
Apr.-May 1926. illus.
Houses in Fairmount Park.

1565 KIMBALL, MARIE G. Revival of the Colonial; Philadelphia restores its old
houses on the Schuylkill. Architectural record. 62:1-17. July 1927. illus.

1566 ——. Roughing it in Philadelphia: Mount Pleasant. Virginia quarterly
review. 14:416-24. July 1938.

1567 LAW, MARGARET LATHROP. Philadelphia's Colonial chain. Architecture.
56:1-7, 85-92. July, Aug. 1927. illus.

1568 LIPPINCOTT, HORACE MATHER. Some old Quaker houses in the Philadelphia
neighborhood. Friends' historical association. Bulletin. 24:57-76. 1935.

1569 (Loxley house. Contemporary description.) Atkinson's casket. 9:409. Sept.
1830. illus.

1570 LUDLUM, MABEL STEWART. The story of Strawberry mansion. Pennsylvania
museum. Bulletin. 26:pt.2. 1931. 14p. illus.
1797. Benjamin Latrobe, architect. Probably the first Gothic Revival structure in
United States.

1571 Mount Pleasant, Fairmount Park, Philadelphia. Philadelphia, Pennsylvania
museum and school of industrial art, 1927. 31p. illus.

1572 The Papen-Johnson house in existence 1698-1883; the first specimen of
German architectural skill in stone in Germantown, Pennsylvania. Americana. 7:1123-26. Dec. 1912.

1573 PENNSYLVANIA MUSEUM OF ART. ASSOCIATE COMMITTEE OF WOMEN.
Chain of Colonial houses. Philadelphia, 1932. 25p. illus.
A guide book to the nine houses in Fairmount Park under the management of the
Pennsylvania Museum.

1574 PETERS, RICHARD, JR. Belmont mansion. Numismatic and antiquarian society of Philadelphia. Proceedings. v. 30. 1925.
1742 and later.

1575 Restoration of Kenwood, a Regency house; Leigh French, Jr., and Eberlein, Harold Donaldson, architects. Architectural forum. 51:519-28. Oct. 1929.
At Bethayres, near Philadelphia.

1576 (Robert Morris' house. Contemporary description.) Atkinson's casket. 2:73. Feb. 1832.

1577 TILLOTSON, HENRY S. Historic old Chew house. Mentor. 17:32-33. July 1929. illus.
(Begun 1761)

1578 WALLACE, PHILIP B. Colonial houses, Philadelphia, pre-revolutionary period. N. Y., Architectural Book Publishing Co., 1931. 248p. illus.
This is *Colonial Architecture in Old Philadelphia*, v.2.

Philadelphia—Public (*see also* 1462)

1579 (Academy of natural sciences. Contemporary description.) Atkinson's casket. 10:469. Oct. 1831.

1580 (Bank of the United States. Contemporary descriptions.) Atkinson's casket. 11:505. Nov. 1829; National register. 13:321. Nov. 20, 1819.
1818–24. Credited to William Strickland by Agnes Addison. *See* 2742.

1581 BIDDLE, EDWARD. Girard college. Numismatic and antiquarian society of Philadelphia. Proceedings. 28:199-215. 1919.

1582 BRABAZON, THOMAS. Our earliest civic center, the Independence hall group in Philadelphia. Architectural record. 34:1-19. July 1913. illus.

1583 CLARKE, J. SELLER. The old Independence hall group at Philadelphia. Western architect. 35:86-87. July 1926. illus.

1584 COHEN, CHARLES J. The origin of Carpenters' hall, Philadelphia, with incidents of the neighborhood. Numismatic and antiquarian society of Philadelphia. Proceedings. 28:123-66. 1919.
1770–92. Robert Smith, architect.

1585 Congress hall restored. Architectural record. 35:97-100. Jan. 1914. illus.

1586 (Dorsey's Gothic museum. Contemporary description.) Atkinson's casket. 10:457. Oct. 1830. illus.

1587 EBERLEIN, HAROLD DONALDSON. Fairmount waterworks, Philadelphia. Architectural record. 62:57-67. July 1927. illus.
(1815) Benjamin Latrobe, architect.

1588 EDMONDS, FRANKLIN DAVENPORT. Public school buildings of the city of Philadelphia from 1745 to 1845. Philadelphia, 1913. 18QD. illus.

1589 ETTING, FRANK. Historical account of the old Pennsylvania State house, now known as the Hall of Independence. Boston, J. R. Osgood and Co., 1876. 204p. illus.

1590, 1591 (Exchange building. Contemporary descriptions.) Atkinson's casket. 2:74. Feb. 1833; Knickerbocker. 3:396. May 1834.
(1832–34. William Strickland, architect.)

1592 FITZ-GIBBON, COSTEN. Latrobe and the Center square pump house. Architectural record. 62:18-22. July 1927. illus.
1801.

1593 (Girard college.) Franklin institute of Philadelphia. Journal. v. 25-32. 1838-41.

1594 HAVILAND, JOHN. Description of Haviland's design for the new penitentiary, now erecting near Philadelphia, accompanied by a bird's eye view. Philadelphia, Robert Desilver, 1824. 12p. illus.

1595 KIMBALL, SIDNEY FISKE. The Bank of Pennsylvania, 1799, an unknown masterpiece of American classicism. Architectural record. 44:132-39. Aug. 1918. illus.
Benjamin Latrobe, architect.

1596 ———. The Bank of the United States, 1818-24. Architectural record. 58:581-94. Dec. 1925. illus.

1597 (Literary and scientific institutions of Philadelphia. Contemporary discussion.) Hazard's register of Pennsylvania. 12:294-95. Nov. 9, 1833.

1598 (Merchant's hotel. Contemporary description.) Atkinson's casket. 6:280-81. 1937. illus.

1599 (Masonic hall. Contemporary description.) Atkinson's casket. 5:217-18. May 1829.

1600 Mr. Nicholas Biddle and the architecture of Girard college. Pennsylvania magazine of history and biography. v. 18. 1894.

1601 (Naval asylum. Contemporary description.) Atkinson's casket. 12:553-54. Dec. 1832. illus.

1602, 1603 (Pennsylvania hotel. Contemporary description.) Hazard's register of Pennsylvania. 16:287. Oct. 31, 1835; Weekly magazine. 1:328-30. Apr. 14, 1798.
William Strickland, architect.

1604 (Philadelphia arcade. Contemporary description.) Atkinson's casket. 12:560. Dec. 1832. illus.

1605 (Philadelphia museum. Contemporary description.) Niles' weekly register. 54:356-57. Aug. 4, 1838.

1605A Reminiscences of Carpenters' Hall, in the city of Philadelphia, and extracts from the ancient minutes of the proceedings of the Carpenters' company of the city and county of Philadelphia. Philadelphia, Crissey and Markley, printers, 1858. p. 1-41, 1-21, 1-57.

Pages 1-57 contain catalogue of books in the library of the Carpenters' company in 1857. Also included are lists of officers and members from 1763.

1606 SCATTERGOOD, DAVID. Handbook of Girard college. Philadelphia, D. Scattergood, 1888. 64p. illus.

1607 ———. Handbook of the Statehouse at Philadelphia. Philadelphia, D. Scattergood, 1890. 64p. illus.

1608, 1609 (State house. Contemporary descriptions.) Atkinson's casket. 4:169-70. Apr. 1829; 12:553. Dec. 1831: Philadelphia monthly magazine. June 1798. p.333-34.

1610 WALTER, THOMAS USTICK. Report of the architect of the Girard college for orphans to the Building committee. (Philadelphia, 1834-50.) 14 pamphlets.

Philadelphia—Religious

1611 BARRATT, NORRIS STANLEY. Outline of the history of old St. Paul's church, Philadelphia, with an appeal for its preservation, together with articles of agreement, abstract of title, list of rectors, vestrymen, and inscriptions of tombstones and vaults. Colonial society of Pennsylvania, 1917. 327p. illus.

1612 FARIS, JOHN T. Old churches and meeting houses in and around Philadelphia. Philadelphia, J. B. Lippincott Co., 1926. 261p. illus.

1613 St. James of Kingsess church. The Old Swede's church of St. James of Kingsess, 1762. Philadelphia, M. C. Callahan, 1911. 13p. illus.

Lutheran.

1614 WATSON, JOHN FANNING. The Swede's church and house of Sven Sener. Philadelphia, G. E. Callahan and D. S. Callahan, 1907. 13p. illus.

1677. Reprinted from *Annals of Philadelphia* by John F. Watson. First edition, 1830.

Pittsburgh

1615 DAVIS, MRS. ELVERT M. Fort Fayette. Western Pennsylvania historical magazine. 16:65-84. Apr. 1927.

Before 1812.

1616 FEDERAL WRITERS' PROJECT. Tales of pioneer Pittsburgh. Philadelphia, William Penn association, *ca.*1937. 28p. illus.

1617 MACPHERSON, L. C. Monongahela house. Western Pennsylvania historical magazine. 3:194-97. Oct. 1920.

1618 MILLER, ANNIE CLARK. Old houses and estates in Pittsburgh. Western
Pennsylvania historical magazine. 9:129-68. July 1926.

1619 (St. Paul's. Contemporary description.) Niles' weekly register. 36:333.
July 18, 1829.

Pottstown

1620 Unknown historic mansion of Pennsylvania; Bessybell, near Pottstown, Pa.
Country life in America. 33:50-51. Jan. 1918. illus. only.

Sunbury

1621 BECK, LOUISE B. The old Scott house. Northumberland county historical
society. Proceedings. 6:226-32. 1934.
1796.

1622 GEARHART, HEBER G. Maclay-Wolverton house. Northumberland county
historical society. Proceedings. 5:149-59. 1933.
1773.

Valley Forge

1623 Washington's headquarters at Valley Forge. Antiques. 38:10, 18-19. July
1940. illus.
1758.

Warwick (*see* 1457)

SOUTHERN STATES

(Alabama, Arkansas, District of Columbia, Florida, Georgia, Kentucky, Louisiana, Maryland, Mississippi, North Carolina, South Carolina, Tennessee, Virginia, West Virginia)

GENERAL REFERENCES

1624 ALTSCHULER, J. A. Colonial architecture of the Carolinas. Architecture. v.43-49. June 1921—July 1924. illus. only.

1625 BIBB, A. B. Old Colonial works of Virginia and Maryland—in 7 parts. American architecture and building news. Part 1, 25:279-81. June 1889; part 2, 25:303-305. June 1889; part 3, 26:71-73. Aug. 1889; part 4, 26:123-24. Sept. 1889; part 5, 26:161-63. Oct. 1889; part 6, 31:133-35. May 1891; part 7, 34:130-32. Nov. 1891. illus.

1626 BOYNTON, HENRY DELANO. Capitols of the South. Philadelphia, The Edgell Co., 1917. 31p. illus.

1627 BROWN, GLENN. Old Colonial works in Virginia and Maryland. American architect and building news. 22:198-99, 242-43, 254. Oct.-Nov. 1887. illus.

1628 COFFIN, LEWIS A., JR., AND HOLDEN, ARTHUR C. Brick architecture of the Colonial period in Maryland and Virginia. N. Y., Architectural Book Publishing Co., 1919. 147p. illus.

1629 CORNER, JAMES M., AND SODERHOLTZ, ERIC ELLIS. Examples of domestic Colonial architecture in Maryland and Virginia. Boston, Boston architectural club, 1892. 53p. illus.

1630 CRANE, EDWARD ANDREW, AND SODERHOLTZ, ERIC ELLIS. Examples of Colonial architecture in Charleston, South Carolina and Savannah, Georgia. Boston, Boston architectural club, 1895. 52 illus.

1631 DAVIS, BRINTON B. Architecture of the old South. Methodist quarterly review. 69:238-43. Apr. 1920.

1632 DENMARK, E. R. Architecture of the old South, 1640-1850. Atlanta, Ga., Southern architect and building news, 1926. 75p. illus.

1633 ELWELL, NEWTON D. Architecture, furniture and interiors of Maryland and Virginia during the 18th century. Boston, G. H. Polley and Co., 1897. 63p. illus.

1634 Deep south; pilgrimage through the plantation country. House and garden. 76:28-49. Nov. 1939. illus.
Mississippi and Louisiana.

1635 Frances Benjamin Johnston: her photographs of our old buildings. Magazine of art. 30:548-55. Sept. 1937. illus.

1636 Historic and scenic reaches of the nation's capital. National geographic magazine. July 1938.

A spot map locating most of the important architectural examples in Delaware, Maryland, and Virginia.

1637 HORTON, CORINNE. Georgian houses of the far South. House and garden. 6:260-67. Dec. 1904. illus.

1638 HORTON, MRS. THADDEUS. Amateur architects of the South. Architecture. 37:127-32. May 1918. illus.

1639 ———. Colonial houses of the South. Country life in America. 12:639-44. Oct. 1907. illus.

1640 ———. Classic houses of the South, old and new. House beautiful. 12:84-90. July 1902. illus.

Covers President Polk house, Dunleith, Fort Hill, Hermitage, Arlington.

1641 ———. Old South in American architecture. Uncle Remus' home magazine. v.26-27. Oct. 1909—Apr. 1910. illus.

1642 Houses of the old South. American architect. 147:57-64. Sept. 1935. illus.

1643 KEMPTON, CHRISTINE HUDSON. Old mansions in environs of Washington. House beautiful. 54:364-65. Oct. 1923. illus.

Poplar Hill, Mount Airy, Lothian.

1644 KENNEDY, J. ROBIE, JR. Examples of Georgian and Greek revival work in the far South. Architectural record. 21:215-21. Mar. 1907. illus.

1645 (Lighthouse designed by B. H. Latrobe.) American register. 1:28-29. 1806-1807.

Designed for the government for an island in the Mississippi.

1646 MAJOR, HOWARD. Southern plantation homes. House and garden. 50:112-13, 126, 130. Nov. 1926. illus.

Classic revival, Mississippi and Louisiana.

1647 MUMFORD, LEWIS. The South in architecture. N. Y., Harcourt, Brace and Co., 1941. 147p. illus.

An estimate of the South's contribution to architecture. The Dancy lectures, Alabama College.

1648 NEWCOMB, REXFORD. Spanish-Colonial architecture in the United States. N. Y., J. J. Augustin, 1937. 169p. illus.

Some material on the southern states.

1649 PETERSON, CHARLES E. Ante-bellum houses of the Mississippi Valley, a catalogue of an exhibition of new photographs and measured drawings. St. Louis, Mo., U. S. Department of the interior, National park service, Historic American buildings survey, Central unit, Oct. 1940. 16p.

Mimeographed. Includes Ohio Valley.

1650 SALE, MRS. EDITH DABNEY (TUNIS). Colonial interiors. N. Y., William Helburn, 1930. 95p. illus.

This is *Colonial Interiors,* second series. Covers Virginia, Maryland, and North Carolina. *See also* 236, 258.

1651 SCHUYLER, MONTGOMERY. Architecture of American colleges. Part 8. The southern colleges. Architectural record. 30:57-84. July 1911.

1652 SMITH, J. FRAZER. White pillars. N. Y., William Helburn, 1941. 252p. illus.

Early life and architecture of the lower Mississippi Valley.

1653 SPRUILL, JULIA CHERRY. Virginia and Carolina homes before the revolution. North Carolina historical review. 12:320-40. 1935.

1654 UNITED STATES. NATIONAL PARK SERVICE. Region one, Richmond, Va. Regional review. v. 1, no. 1, July 1938.

Some scattered material on early architecture.

1655 WATERMAN, THOMAS TILESTON. Notes on decorative cast iron. Magazine of art. 32:584-87, 601. Oct. 1939. illus.

Alabama, Louisiana, North Carolina, and South Carolina.

1656 WAYLAND, JOHN WALTER. Historic homes of northern Virginia and the eastern panhandle of West Virginia. Staunton, Va., McClure Co., 1937. 625p. illus.

1657 WHITEHEAD, RUSSELL F. Old and new South; a consideration of architecture in the southern states. Architectural record. 30:1-40. July 1911. illus.

1658 WORTHINGTON, ADDISON F. Old Maryland and Virginia farms. Architectural review. n.s.6:71-72. Apr. 1918. illus.

Colonial.

ALABAMA

GENERAL REFERENCES (*see also* 1655)

1659 (Alabama architecture.) A series of seventy-two articles in the magazine section of the Birmingham news, between May 1934 and July 1937, the first twelve by E. Walter Burkhardt, the following sixty by Marian Feare.

1660 Alabama number. Southern magazine. v. 1, no. 5. 1934. 60p. illus.

Description of historic homes.

1661 BRANNON, PETER A. Some early taverns in Alabama. Arrow points. 5:52-58. Sept. 1922.

1662 CURTIS, N. C. Ante-bellum houses of central Alabama. American institute of architects. Journal. 8:388-98. Nov. 1920. illus.

1663 FEDERAL WRITERS' PROJECT. Alabama: a guide to the deep South. N. Y., Richard R. Smith Co., 1941. 442p. illus.

1664 KENNEDY, J. ROBIE, JR. Examples of the Greek revival period in Alabama— in 2 parts. Brickbuilder. Part 1, 13:121-24, June 1904; part 2, 13:144-47. July 1904. illus.

Part 1, Tuscaloosa; part 2, the Black belt. *Ca.*1820—*ca.*1840.

1665 ———. Greek revival of the far South—Tuscaloosa, Alabama. Architectural record. 17:388-99. May 1905. illus.

1666 NATIONAL LEAGUE OF AMERICAN PEN WOMEN. BIRMINGHAM BRANCH. Historic homes of Alabama and their traditions. Birmingham, Ala., Birmingham Publishing Co., 1935. 314p. illus.

1667 Story of Gaineswood; details of the building of a famous plantation house. House and garden. 76:41-43. Nov. 1939. illus.

1849 at Demopolis.

1668 WARREN, WILLIAM T. Address before the American institute of architects. The Octagon. May 1931.

Principally on Alabama architecture.

ARKANSAS

GENERAL REFERENCES

1669 Arkansas number. Southern magazine. v. 2, no. 4. 1935. 48p. illus.

1670 BROUGH, CHARLES HILLMAN. Points and places of historical interest in Arkansas. Arkansas historical association. Publications. 1:286-301. 1906.

1671 FEDERAL WRITERS' PROJECT. Arkansas: a guide to the state. N. Y., Hastings house, 1941. 447p. illus.

1672 VAUGHAN, MYRA MCALMONT. A history of the Old State house. Arkansas historical association. Publications. 3:249-55. 1911.

DISTRICT OF COLUMBIA

LOCATIONS

Washington—City (including *Georgetown*) (*See also* 272, 714, 716, 2232)

1673 BAKER, GEOFFREY. The Smithsonian. Magazine of art. 34:128-33. Mar. 1941. illus.

1852. James Renwick, architect.

1674 BLAIR, GIST. Lafayette square. Columbia historical society. Records. 28:133-73. 1926.

1675 BROWN, B. T. One of the finest examples of the early Federal home: Dumbarton house in Georgetown. Arts and decoration. 45:28-31. Nov. 1936. illus.

(Between 1780 and 1795) *See also* 2249.

1676 BROWN, GLENN. Brief description and history of the Octagon house, Dr. William Thornton, architect. Washington, D. C., 1903. 4p. illus.

1677 ———. The making of a plan for Washington city. Columbia historical society. Records. 6:1-10. 1903.

L'Enfant's plan.

1678 ———. The Octagon, Dr. William Thornton, architect. Washington, D. C., American institute of architects, 1915. 25p. illus.

(1799-1800)

1679 ———. The plan of L'Enfant for the city of Washington and its effect upon the future development of the city. Columbia historical society. Records. 12:1-20. 1909.

1680 BRYAN, WILHELMUS BOGART. Dreamers as capital city builders. Columbia historical society. Records. 40-41:53-61. 1940.

Brief sketches of Law, Blodget, and Thornton.

1681 ———. Hotels of Washington prior to 1814. Columbia historical society. Records. 7:71-106. 1904. illus.

1682 ———. Something about L'Enfant and his personal affairs. Columbia historical society. Records. 2:111-17. 1899.

1683 CAEMMERER, HANS PAUL. Manual on the origin and development of Washington. Washington, D. C., Government printing office, 1939. 365p. illus.

Seventy-fifth Congress, third session, Senate document 178.

1684 ———. The Federal city. D. A. R. magazine. 67:477-81. 1933.

1685 ———. Washington, the national capital. Washington, D. C., Government printing office, 1932. 736p. illus.

Seventy-first Congress, third session, Senate document 332. Contains a list of books on Washington, p.721-22.

1686 (Capital. Contemporary description.) Cabinet of religion, New York. 2:383-86. Oct. 6, 1829.

1687 Capital's most-haunted house to become a public monument: Octagon house. Newsweek. 16:35. July 29, 1940.

1688 CLARK, ALLEN C. The Abraham Young mansion. Columbia historical society. Records. 12:53-70. 1909.

1689 ———. Old mills. Columbia historical society. Records. 31-32:81-115. 1930.

District of Columbia and vicinity.

1690 ———. Suter's tavern. Columbia historical society. Records. 26:189-93.
1924.
Georgetown, *ca.*1800.

1691 Cox, William V. Celebration of the one hundredth anniversary of the
establishment of the seat of government in the District of Columbia.
Washington, D. C., Government printing office, 1901. 343p. illus.
Fifty-sixth Congress, second session, House document 552.

1692 Cunningham, Harry Francis. The old City hall, Washington, D. C.
Architectural record. 37:268-73. Mar. 1915. illus.
(1820. George Hadfield, architect.)

1693 ———; Younger, Joseph A.; and Smith, J. Wilmer. Measured drawings of Georgian architecture in the District of Columbia, 1750-1820.
N. Y., the Architectural Book Publishing Co., 1914. 66 illus.

1694 (Department of state building. Contemporary description.) Atkinson's casket.
no. 1:25-26. Jan. 1832.

1695 Eichler, Alfred W., and Huot, L. L. Entrance detail and mantle (sic),
Hood residence, Washington, D. C. Architecture. v. 40, no. 4. Oct.
1919. illus. only.

1696 Erb, Albert P. Early architecture of the District of Columbia. Architecture. v. 46-47. Oct. 1922—July 1923. illus. only.

1697 Famous Octagon house in Washington. House beautiful. 44:244-45. Oct.
1918. illus.

1698 Federal Writers' Project. Our Washington: a comprehensive album of
the nation's capital in words and pictures. Chicago, A. C. McClurg and
Co., 1939. 178p. illus.

1699 ———. Washington, city and capital. Washington, D. C., Government
printing office, 1937. 1141p. illus.

1700 Forney, R. W. Historic Octagon house. National republic. 20:23. July
1932. illus.

1701 Frye, Virginia King. St. Patrick's—first Catholic church of the Federal
city. Columbia historical society. Records. 23:26-51. 1920.
(First building 1810)

1702 Gordon, William A. Old homes on Georgetown Heights. Columbia historical society. Records. 18:70-91. 1915.

1703 Grant, Ulysses S., 3rd. Development of the plan of Washington. Americana. 24:370-85. July 1930.

1704 ———. The L'Enfant plan and its evolution. Columbia historical society.
Records. 33-34:1-25. 1932.

1705 GREENOUGH, HORATIO. Aesthetics at Washington, no. 1. Washington, D. C., John T. Towers, 1851. 22p.

1706 HALE, WILLIAM HARLAN. The grandeur that is Washington. Harper's. 168:560-69. 1934.
Discussion starts with 1792.

1707 HARVEY, FREDERICK L. (comp.) History of the Washington national monument society. Washington, D. C., Government printing office, 1903. 362p.
Fifty-seventh Congress, second session, Senate document 224. Cornerstone 1848. Robert Mills, architect.

1708 HUOT, L. L. Entrance detail, house at Georgetown, D. C. Architecture. v. 40, no. 6. Dec. 1919. illus. only.

1709 ———. Mantle (sic) in house at Georgetown, D. C. Architecture. v. 40, no. 4. Oct. 1919. illus. only.

1710 HUTCHINS, FRANK, AND HUTCHINS, CORTELLE. Washington's Washington. Washington, D. C., Historical research service, 1925. 12p. illus.

1711 JACKSON, CORDELIA. People and places in old Georgetown. Columbia historical society. Records. 33-34:133-62. 1932.

1712 ———. Tudor place. Columbia historical society. Records. 25:68-86. 1923.
(Between 1794 and 1814. Dr. William Thornton, architect.)

1713 JELLIFEE, L. C. The Octagon, headquarters of the American institute of architects. Architects and builders magazine. 3:440-42. Sept. 1902. illus.

1714 JUSSERAND, J. J. With Americans of past and present days. N. Y., Charles Scribner's Sons, 1916. 350p. illus.
Pages 135–95 on "Major L'Enfant and the Federal city."

1715 KIMBALL, SIDNEY FISKE. Origin of the plan of Washington. Architectural review. 7:41-45. Sept. 1918. illus.

1716 ———, AND BENNETT, WELLS. Competition for the Federal buildings, 1792-93. American institute of architects. Journal. 7:8-12, 98-102, 202-211, 355-61, 521, 527. Jan., Mar., May, Aug., Dec. 1919; 8:117-24. Mar. 1920. illus.

1717 KOCHKA, J. L. Photographing historic Washington landmarks. Photo-era. 63:121-24. Sept. 1929. illus.

1718 LATROBE, JOHN H. B. Construction of the public buildings in Washington. Maryland historical magazine. 4:221-28. Sept. 1909.
Read before Maryland Historical Society in 1865.

1718A LOCKWOOD, MARY S. Historic homes in Washington. . . . N. Y., *ca.* 1889. 304p. illus.

1719 MacFarland, Henry B. F. George Washington's plan for the capital city. American architect. 93:112-13. Apr. 1908.

1720 Mills, Robert. Water-works for the metropolitan city of Washington. Washington, D. C., L. Towers, 1853. 36p.

1721 Moore, Charles. Personalities in Washington architecture. Columbia historical society. Records. 37:38:1-15. 1937.

1722 ———. Washington, past and present. N. Y., Century Co., 1929. 340p. illus.

1723 Morris, Maud Burr. An old Washington mansion (2017 I Street, northwest). Columbia historical society. Records. 21:114-28. 1918.

1724 Moses, Lionel. The Octagon, Washington, D. C. Art world. 2:293-96. June 1917.

1725 Newell, Frederick Haynes (ed.). Planning and building the city of Washington. Washington, D. C., Ransdell, 1932. 258p. illus.
Published by the Washington Society of Engineers. George Washington as a city planner.

1726 Newton, Roger Hale. Bulfinch's designs for the Library of Congress. Art bulletin. 23:221-22. Sept. 1941. illus.

1727 Noel, F. Regis, and Downing, Margaret Brent. The Court-house of the District of Columbia. Washington, D. C., Judd and Detweiler, 1919. 105p. illus.

1728 The Octagon, number 1741 New York avenue, Washington, D. C. Art and progress. 6:129-33. Feb. 1915.

1729 Owen, Robert Dale. Hints on public architecture, containing, among illustrations, views and plans of the Smithsonian institution: together with an appendix relative to building materials. N. Y., G. P. Putnam, 1849. 119p. illus.

1730 (Patent office. Contemporary description.) Robert Merry's museum. 1:89-90. Apr. 1841. illus.

1731 Paxton, Annabel Betts. Washington doorways. Richmond, Va., Dietz press, 1940. 144p. illus.

1732 Peets, Elbert. Genealogy of L'Enfant's Washington. American institute of architects. Journal. 15:115, 151, 187. 1927.

1733 ———. L'Enfant's Washington; notes on redrafting of the autograph plan. Architectural record. 72:158-60. 1932.
Examination of the central part of L'Enfant's plan, with notes.

1734 The planners of the city of Washington—L'Enfant, the French Catholic, and Dermott, the Irish Catholic—"The Tin Case map of the city 1797-1798" as drawn by Dermott, and from which the city has been built. American Catholic historical research. n.s. 2:64-78. Jan. 1906.

1735 (Post office. Contemporary description.) National era. 11:198. Dec. 10, 1857.

1736 (Public buildings.) Niles weekly register. 25:349-50. Jan. 31, 1824.
Reports of Charles Bulfinch and James Hoban on the progress of the Capitol and the White House.

1737 RAINEY, ADA. The charm of old Washington. Washington, D. C., F. E. Sheiry, 1932. 62p. illus.
Early Republican houses.

1738 RUSK, WILLIAM SENER. The story of Washington. Americana. 28:498-505. 1934.

1739 SMITH, DARRELL HEVENOR. The Office of the supervising architect of the Treasury; its history, activities and organization. Baltimore, Md., The Johns Hopkins press, 1923. 138p.
Institute for Government Research. Service monograph of the United States government, no. 23. Includes bibliography.

1740 SMITH, HAL H. Historic Washington homes. Columbia historical society. Records. 11:243-67. 1908.

1741 (Smithsonian institution. Contemporary description.) National era. 1:3. Apr. 1, 1847.

1742 (Stephen A. Douglas house. Announcement of contract for building.) National era. 11:75. May 7, 1857.

1743 THAYER, R. H. History, organization and functions of the office of supervising architect of the Treasury department. Washington, D. C., Government printing office, 1886. 55p.

1744 TINDALL, WILLIAM. District buildings. Columbia historical society. Records. 26:146-56. 1924.

1745 TOPHAM, WASHINGTON. The Benning-McGuire house, E street and neighborhood. Columbia historical society. Records. 33-34:87-131. 1932.
Covers other houses.

1746 TORBERT, MRS. ALICE COYLE. Doorways and dormers of old Georgetown. Washington, D. C., 1932. 31p. illus.
A guide. First edition 1930.

1747 WALTER, THOMAS USTICK. Report on the new Treasury buildings and Patent office at Washington. . . . Philadelphia, L. R. Bailey, 1838. 18p.

1748-1750 (Washington. Contemporary descriptions.) Gazette of the United States. 3:185. Oct. 8, 1791; New Yorker. 6:332. Feb. 9, 1839; Portfolio. 2:154. Sept. 13, 1806.

1751 Washington homes. House and garden. 78:sec.2, 1-46. July 1940. illus.

1752 (Washington monument. Contemporary description.) Literary world. 2:540. Jan. 1, 1848.

1753 Washington, the Federal city. House and garden. 78:sec.1, 1-62. July 1940. illus.

1754 WENTZELL, VOLKMAR. The nation's capital by night. National geographical magazine. 77:514-30. Apr. 1940. illus.

1755 WIGHT, P. B. Government architecture and government architects. American architect and building news. 1:75-77, 83-85, 91-93. Mar. 18, 1876.

1756 WILCOX, U. V. Octagon house. Mentor. 17:23-28. July 1929. illus.

1757 WILLIAMS, EDWIN MELVIN. Building the Federal city, the first decade (1791-1801) of Washington, D. C. Americana. 22:174-226. 1928.

1758 YOUNGER, JOSEPH. Brentwood, Benjamin Latrobe, architect, Washington, 1818. Architecture. 37:55-56. Mar. 1918. illus.

1759 ZEVELY, DOUGLAS. Old residences and family history in the City hall neighborhood. Columbia historical society. Records. 6:104-122. 1903.

Washington—Capitol. Charles Bulfinch, Benjamin Latrobe, T. U. Walter and others, architects.

1760 ANDERSON, MARY FRANCIS. The old brick Capitol, Washington, D. C. Americana. 23:162-68. Apr. 1929.
     1812.

1761 ASHTON, EUGENE. The Latrobe corn-stalk columns. Magazine of American history. 18:128-29. Aug. 1887. illus.

1762 BENNETT, WELLS. Stephen Hallet and his designs for the national Capitol, 1791-1794. American institute of architects. Journal. 4:290-95, 324-30, 376-83, 411-18. July-Oct. 1916. illus.

1763 (Bronze balustrade of the Capitol. Contemporary information.) Peterson's magazine. 35:87. Jan. 1859.

1764 BROWN, GLENN. History of the United States Capitol. Washington, D. C., Government printing office, 1899-1904. 2v. illus.
     Fifty-sixth Congress, first session, Senate document 60.

1765 ———. United States Capitol in 1800. Columbia historical society. Records. 4:128-34. 1901.

1766 BRYAN, WILHELMUS BOGART. History of the National capitol from its foundation through the period of the adoption of the organic act. N. Y., Macmillan Co., 1914-16. 2v. illus.

     (Capitol.) *See* United States Architect of the Capitol, annual report for various years. Washington, D. C., Government printing office.

1767-1776 (Capitol. Contemporary descriptions.) American register. 1809. p.372-73; Atkinson's casket. 1:25, 7:314-15. Jan., July 1832; Monthly repository and library of entertaining knowledge. 3:229-32. Dec. 1832; National era. 6:103. June 25, 1852, 11:127. Aug. 6, 1857, 13:88. June 2, 1859; National register. 8:130-31. Aug. 28, 1819; New mirror. 3:308-309. Aug. 17, 1844; Niles' weekly register. 10:382-83. Aug. 1816; Parley's magazine. 4:222-23. July 1836; Sartain's union magazine of literature and art. 10:193. Feb. 1852; Western miscellany. 1:98. Oct. 1848.

1777 Documentary history of the construction and development of the United States Capitol, building and grounds. Washington, D. C., Government printing office, 1904. 1312p. illus.

Fifty-eighth Congress, second session, House reports 646, v. 9.

1778 ERB, ALBERT P. Original posts and fence from the United States Capitol. Architecture. v. 52, no. 3. Sept. 1925. illus. only.

1779 FAIRMAN, CHARLES EDWIN. Art and artists of the Capitol of the United States of America. Washington, D. C., Government printing office, 1927. 526p. illus.

Sixty-ninth Congress, first session, Senate document 95.

1780 FRARY, IHNA THAYER. They built the Capitol. Richmond, Va., Garrett and Massie, 1940. 324p. illus.

1781 GROSVENOR, GILBERT. The Capitol, wonder building of the world. National geographic magazine. 43:603-616. June 1923. illus.

1782 HAMLIN, TALBOT FAULKNER. Birth of American architecture. Parnassus. 10:8-12. Nov. 1938. illus.

Concerning the architects.

1783 HAZELTON, GEORGE COCHRANE, JR. The national Capitol, its architecture, art and history. N. Y., J. F. Taylor and Co., 1897. 301p. illus.

1784 HOWARD, JAMES Q. The architects of the American Capitol. International review. 1:736-53. Nov. 1874.

1785 KIMBALL, SIDNEY FISKE, AND BENNETT, WELLS. William Thornton and his design for the national Capitol. Art studies. v. 1. 1923. illus.

Subsequently issued as an extra number of American Journal of Archaeology.

1786 LATROBE, BENJAMIN HENRY. A private letter to the individual members of Congress on the subject of the public buildings of the United States at Washington. Washington, D. C., S. H. Smith, 1806. 32p.

A report of work on the Capitol.

1787 LATROBE, JOHN HAZLEHURST BONNEVAL. The Capitol and Washington at the beginning of the present century. Baltimore, Md., W. K. Boyle, 1881. 30p. illus.

An address delivered before the American Institute of Architects, 1881.

1788 MILLS, ROBERT. Guide to the Capitol of the United States. Washington, D. C., J. C. Greer, printer, 1854. 82p. illus.
First edition, 1834. For varying titles and editions *see* 2773.

1789 PAGE, WILLIAM TYLER. The story of the nation's Capitol. Alexandria, Va., Washington-Mt. Vernon memorial book corporation, 1932. 184p. illus.
History and description.

1790 WALTER, THOMAS USTICK. Letter to the Committee of the United States Senate on public buildings, in reference to an enlargement of the Capitol. . . . Washington, Towers, printer, 1850. 7p.

1791 ———. Report of the architect of the United States Capitol extension and the new dome. . . . Washington, D. C., Government printing office, 1864. 10p.

1792 Who was the architect of the United States Capitol extension? Architecture. 36:138-39. July 1917.

Washington—White House. James Hoban and Benjamin Latrobe, architects.

1793 BAKER, ABBY GUNN. The erection of the White House. Columbia historical society. Records. 16:120-29. 1913.

1794 BIBB, A. BURNLEY. Restoration of the White house. House and garden. 3:127-39. Mar. 1903. illus.

1795 BRYAN, WILHELMUS BOGART. The name White house. Columbia historical society. Records. 1932. p.33-34, 306-307.

1796 CHITTENDEN, CECIL ROSS. The White house and its yesterdays; a narrative of an American home. Alexandria, Va., Washington-Mt. Vernon memorial book corporation, 1932. 155p. illus.

1797 GRIFFIN, M. I. J. Irish builders of the White house. American-Irish historical society. Journal. v.7. 1907.

1798 ———. James Hoban, the architect and builder of the White house. American Catholic historical researches. Jan. 1907.

1799 KIMBALL, SIDNEY FISKE. The genesis of the White house. Century. 95: 523-28. Feb. 1918.

1800 LEWIS, ETHEL. The White house, an informal history of its architecture, interiors and gardens. N. Y., Dodd, Mead and Co., 1937. 330p. illus.

1801 MEHAFFEY, JOSEPH C. Early history of the White house. Military engineer. 20:201-206. May-June 1928.

1802 MOORE, CHARLES. The restoration of the White house. Century. 65:807-831. Apr. 1903.

1803 ———. The restoration of the White house. D. A. R. magazine. 57:513-44. Sept. 1923.

1804 NEWLANDS, FRANCIS GRIFFITH. White house restoration. Washington, D. C., Government printing office, 1904. 31p.

1805 The restoration of the White house. American architect. 79:67-70. Feb. 28, 1903.

1806 The restoration of the White house. Message of the President of the United States, transmitting the report of the architects. Washington, D. C., Government printing office, 1903. 51p. illus.
Fifty-seventh Congress, second session, Senate document 197.

1807 SCHUYLER, MONTGOMERY. The new White house. Architectural record. 13:358-88. Apr. 1903. illus.

1808 SINGLETON, ESTHER. The story of the White house. N. Y., S. S. McClure Co., 1907. 2v. illus.

1809 SMALLEY, E. V. The White house. Century magazine. 27:805-815. Apr. 1884. illus.

1810 (White house. Contemporary descriptions.) American penny magazine. 2:333-34. June 27, 1846; Atkinson's casket. 9:409. Sept. 1831; Merry's museum. 9:183. June 1845; National register. 4:176. Sept. 13, 1817.

1811 (White house. 1823.) Niles' weekly register. 25:349-50. Jan. 31, 1824.
Copy of a letter from Charles Bulfinch to Joseph Elgar, Commissioner of Public Buildings, enclosing report on progress on the President's house.

FLORIDA

1812 CONNOR, JEANNETTE THURBER. Nine old wooden forts of St. Augustine. Florida historical society. Quarterly. 4:103-111. Jan. 1926; 4:171-80. Apr. 1926.

1813 FEDERAL WRITERS' PROJECT. Florida: a guide to the southernmost state. N. Y., Oxford university press, 1939. 600p. illus.

1814 ———. Seeing Saint Augustine. Saint Augustine, Fla., The Record Co., 1937. 73p. illus.

1815 Gregory house being restored in Torreya state park. Museum news. 18:1, 5. May 15, 1940.

1816 JONES, E. ALFRED. A drawing of the Governor's house at St. Augustine in east Florida in 1764. Art in America. 10:82-85. Feb. 1922. illus.

1817 MATSCHAT, CECILE HULSE. Suwannee River. N. Y., Farrar and Rinehart, 1938. 296p. illus.
Rivers of America series.

1818 PHINNEY, A. H. Florida's Spanish missions. Florida historical society. Quarterly. 4:15-21. July 1925.

1819 REYNOLDS, CHARLES B. The oldest house in the United States, St. Augustine, Fla. N. Y., The Foster and Reynolds Co., 1921. 31p.

> An examination of the St. Augustine Historical Society's claim that its house on St. Francis Street was built in the year 1565 by the Franciscan monks.

1820 THOMAS, DAVID Y. Report upon the historic buildings, monuments and local archives of St. Augustine, Florida. American historical association. Reports. 1:339-52. 1905.

1821 UNITED STATES. NATIONAL PARK SERVICE. Fort Marion and Fort Matanzas national monuments. Washington, D. C., Government printing office, 1940. 16p. illus.

> St. Augustine.

GEORGIA

(See also 1630)

1822 CORRY, JOHN P. Houses of Colonial Georgia. Georgia historical quarterly. 14:181-201. Sept. 1930.

> Savannah.

1823 FEDERAL WRITERS' PROJECT. Augusta. Augusta, Ga., Tidwell printing supply Co., 1938. 218 p. illus.

1824 ———. Georgia: a guide to its towns and countryside. Athens, Ga., University of Georgia press, 1940. 559p. illus.

1825 ———. Savannah. Savannah, Ga., Review printing Co., 1937. 208p. illus.

1826 HINES, NELLE WOMACK. Treasure album of Milledgeville and Baldwin county, Georgia. Milledgeville, Ga., J. W. Burke Co., 1936. 52p. illus.

1827 HOWARD, MRS. ANNIE HORNADY (ed.). Georgia homes and landmarks. Atlanta, Ga., Southern features syndicate, 1929. 186p. illus.

1828 LANNING, JOHN TATE. Spanish missions of Georgia. Chapel Hill, N. C., University of North Carolina press, 1935. 321p. illus.

> Bibliography of other states.

1829 Master detail series: historic American buildings; Westover, Milledgeville, Baldwin county; Davenport house, Savannah, Chatham county. Architectural forum. 64:499-508. June 1936. illus.

1830 New England in Georgia. House and garden. 42:50-51. July 1922. illus.

1831 ROSS, MARY. Restoration of the Spanish missions in Georgia—1598-1606. Georgia historical quarterly. 10:171-99.

1832 Southern romanticism. House and garden. 77:16-26. Mar. 1940. illus.

> Savannah.

KENTUCKY

GENERAL REFERENCES

1833 COLEMAN, J. WINSTON, JR. Stage coach inns in Kentucky. Kentucky progesss magazine. 7:144-48. 1936.

1834 (Doorways. Illustrations.) Kentucky progress magazine. 6:74-77. Winter 1934. illus. only.

1835 EMBRY, JACQUELINE. Romantic houses in the gallant bluegrass. Kentucky progress magazine. 6:22-24. Fall 1933. illus.
Review of 1850.

1836 FARRELL, JOSEPHINE. Some old Kentucky homes. Country life. 49:49-51. Apr. 1926. illus.

1837 FEDERAL WRITERS' PROJECT. Kentucky: a guide to the blue-grass state. N. Y., Harcourt, Brace and Co., 1939. 489p. illus.

1837A HAMLIN, TALBOT F. The A. I. A. meets in Kentucky. Pencil points. 21:279-93. May 1940. illus.

1838, 1839 HOWE, AMANDA. Some historic Kentucky inns. Kentucky progress magazine. 6:25-27, 45. Fall 1933. illus.
Reprinted from the *Automobile Bulletin*, November, 1932.

1840 LEWIS, GEORGE A. Old Innes fort on Elkhorn Creek. Kentucky state historical society. Register. 19:29-31. Jan. 1921.

1841 McDONALD, JOSEPHINE FARRELL. Some old Kentucky homes. Kentucky progress magazine. 6:15-18, 44. Fall 1933. illus.

1842 MORGAN, FREDERIC L. Public buildings of old Kentucky. Kentucky progress magazine. 6:18-22. Fall 1933. illus.
Classic revival.

1843 NEWCOMB, REXFORD. Architecture of old Kentucky. Kentucky state historical society. Register. 31:185-200. July 1933. illus.

1844 ———. Architecture in Kentucky. Kentucky progress magazine. 6:4-13, 42, 43. Fall 1933. illus.

1845 ———. Old Kentucky architecture. N. Y., William Helburn, 1940. 13p. of text. 223 illus.
Colonial, Early Republican, Greek revival, Gothic, and other styles, erected prior to the war between the states.

1846 ———. Small houses of old Kentucky. Kentucky progress magazine. 6:112-17. Spring 1934. illus.

1847 Old Kentucky homes. House and garden. 78:34-37. Sept. 1940. illus.

1848 PIRTLE, ALFRED. Some early engineers and architects in Kentucky. Kentucky historical society. Register. 12:37-53. Sept. 1914.

1849 Reid, Kenneth. Background in old Kentucky. Pencil points. 21:262-78. May 1940. illus.

1850 Simpson, Elizabeth. Bluegrass houses and their traditions. Lexington, Ky., Transylvania press, 1933. 408p. illus.

> History of the ownerships and descriptions of the physical characteristics of about 52 Kentucky houses and one college.

1851 Stratton, H. O. Kentucky doorways. House beautiful. 77:80-81. Mar. 1935. illus.

1852 Thomas, Mrs. Elizabeth Patterson. Old Kentucky homes and gardens. Louisville, Ky., Standard printing Co., 1939. 180p. illus.

Locations

Bardstown

1853 Jillson, Willard Rouse. House of J. Rowan where "My old Kentucky home" was written. Kentucky state historical society. Register. 19:1-8. May 1921.

> Reprinted in pamphlet form at Frankfort, Kentucky.

1854 Sherlock, Chelsa C. My old Kentucky home. Better homes and gardens. 2:14, 15, 40, 41. Mar. 1924. illus.

> Federal Hill, 1795 and later. (*Better Homes and Gardens* published under the name of *Fruit, Garden and Home* in March, 1924).

Covington

1855 Bullock, William T. Sketches of a journey. London, John Miller, 1827.

> Includes a plan by J. B. Papworth of a projected town to be named Hygeia. Reprinted in 2407.

Crab Orchard

1856 Burch, Esther Whitley. First brick house in Kentucky. D. A. R. magazine. 51:214-17. Oct. 1917. illus.

> Whitley house, 1783, near Crab Orchard.

1857 Herring, Eliza A. Whitley mansion. Kentucky historical society. Register. 15:25-26. 1917. illus.

> 1786–87, restored. (1783?)

Frankfort

1858 Georgian mansion built in 1796: designed by Thomas Jefferson. Pencil points. 16:109-110. Mar. 1935. illus. only.

> Liberty Hall.

1859 Liberty Hall. Kentucky state historical society. Register. 34:392-94. Oct. 1936. illus.

1860 Master detail series, historic American buildings: Liberty hall, Frankfort; Thomas Jefferson, architect. Architectural forum. 61:205-209. Sept. 1934. illus.

Harrodsburg

1861 Harrodsburg number. Kentucky progress magazine. Fall 1934. illus.

1862 Old mud meeting house. Harrodsburg herald, 1900. 40p.

1863 Replica of Fort Harrod, Harrodsburg, 1923-28. Historical quarterly. 3:19-22. Oct. 1928.

1864 STEPHENSON, W. W. Historic homes of Harrodsburg, Kentucky. Kentucky state historical society. Register. 10:9-14. Sept. 1912.

Jefferson County

1865 ELLWANGER, ELLA HUTCHISON. Oxmoor, its builder and its historian. Kentucky state historical society. Register. 17:8-21. Jan. 1919. illus.

Lexington

1866 CAPEN, OLIVER BRONSON. Country homes of famous Americans, part 7. Henry Clay. Country life in America. 6:158-62. June 1904. illus.
Contains illustration of Ashland as built by Henry Clay.

1867 FEDERAL WRITERS' PROJECT. Lexington and the Blue Grass country. Lexington, Ky., E. M. Glass. 149p. illus.

1868 GOODE, CLARA. Chaumiére des Prairies, Lexington, Kentucky. Journal of American history. 16:325-31. Oct.-Dec. 1922.
Little on the building.

1869 HARRISON, MRS. IDA WITHERS. Chaumiére du Prairie, home of David Meade. Journal of American history. 9:563-73. Oct.-Dec. 1915.
Little on the building.

1870 Master detail series: historic American buildings; Rose Hill, Mulberry Lane, Lexington, Kentucky. Architectural forum. 62:567-68. June 1935.
(1818)

1871 NEWCOMB, REXFORD. Transylvania college and her century-old Greek revival building, Gideon Shryock, architect. Art and archaeology. 29:250-55, 285. June 1930. illus.
(1833)

1872 SHERLOCK, CHELSA C. Ashland. Better homes and gardens. 2:13, 35-36. May 1924. illus.
Design credited to Latrobe, 1806. Reconstructed 1857.

Louisville

1873 ANDERSON, KITTY. Soldiers' Retreat, a historical house and its famous people. Kentucky historical society. Register. 17:67-77. Sept. 1919.
Near Louisville.

1874 FEDERAL WRITERS' PROJECT. Centennial history of the University of Louisville. Louisville, Ky., The University of Louisville, 1939. 301p. illus.

1875 HUTCHINGS, E. T. Louisville. Pencil points. 21:295-308. May 1940. illus.

1876 PIRTLE, ALFRED. Mulberry Hill; the first home of George Rogers Clark in
Kentucky. Kentucky historical society. Register. 15:49-54. Sept. 1917.
Destroyed, near Louisville.

Madison County

1877 Castlewood, Madison county, Kentucky, Gideon Shryock, architect. Archi-
tural forum. 61:210-16. Sept. 1934. illus.
(*Ca.*1820) at Richmond.

Mason County

1878 LEE, LUCY C. Historic homes in Mason county, Kentucky. Kentucky historical society. Register. 7:43-47. Sept. 1909.

Nelson County

1879 WICKLIFFE, JOHN D. Pioneer stations in Nelson county. Historical quarterly. 2:129-33. Apr. 1928.
Forts. *Historical Quarterly* published by Filson Club, Louisville, Kentucky.

New Haven

1880 Abbey of Our Lady of Gethsemani, Order of reformed Cistercians, commonly
called Trappists. 1924. 39p.
(1851-66)

Oldham County

1881 TRABUE, ALICE ELIZABETH. Spring Hill, Oldham county, Kentucky, home
of Major W. Berry Taylor. Kentucky state historical society. Register.
18:23-29. May 1920.
*Ca.*1800.

Pleasant Hill

1882 WOOD, HENRY CLEVELAND. Pleasant Hill and the Shaker folk. Kentucky
progress magazine. 6:234-37. Fall 1934. illus.

Shelbyville

1883 (C. B.) Historic home. Kentucky state historical society. Register. Jan.
1909. p.38.
Nineteenth century home of Mark Hardin.

Washington County

1884 RANDOLPH, COLEMAN. The old house on the hill; a brief historical sketch
issued as a souvenir. Morristown, N. J., 1921. 23p. illus.
Thomas Marshall house, after 1780.

LOUISIANA

GENERAL REFERENCES (*see also* 1634, 1646, 1655)

1885 FEDERAL WRITERS' PROJECT. Louisiana: a guide to the state. N. Y., Hastings house, 1941. 746p. illus.

1886 KNIFFEN, FRED B. Louisiana house types. American association of geographers. Annals. 26:179-93. Dec. 1936.

1887 KOCH, RICHARD. Ceramic materials of old Louisiana buildings. American ceramic society. Bulletin. 17:329-31. Aug. 1938.
Technical description from Historic American Buildings Survey.

1888 MURPHY, HELEN S. Souls of old houses. Louisiana historical quarterly. 13:59-63. Jan. 1930.
Five plantation houses.

1889 Old Louisiana buildings. Photographs by the Historic buildings survey in Louisiana. Richard Koch, photographer. Southwest review. 20:169-83. 1935. illus.

1890 Portfolio of old plantation houses reflecting the glory that was Louisiana's. Country life in America. 58:51-54. Oct. 1930. illus.

1891 REYNOLDS, JAMES. Plantations on the bayous. House beautiful. 82:34-35. July-Aug. 1940. illus.
Octave, Domingo, Praline, Rosewood. 1780–*ca.*1850.

1892 RIES, MAURICE. Mississippi Fort, called Fort-de-la Boulaye (1700-1715): first French settlement in present day Louisiana; a report by Gordon W. Callender, Prescott H. F. Follett, Albert Lieutaud and Maurice Ries. Reprinted from the Louisiana historical quarterly. 19:829-99. Oct. 1936. illus.

1893 SAXON, LYLE. Old Louisiana. N. Y., Century Co., 1929. 388p. illus.

1894 ———. Vanished paradise—The Shadows, 1830; Madewood, 1848; Belle Grove; Three Oaks; Uncle Sam plantation; Oak Lawn manor, 1827. Country life. 67:34-41. Nov. 1934. illus.

1895 SPRATLING, WILLIAM P. Old plantation architecture in Louisiana. Architectural forum. 44:217-24, 301-306. April-May 1926. illus.

1896 ———, AND SCOTT, NATALIE. Old plantation houses in Louisiana. N. Y., William Helburn, 1927. 162p. illus.

1897 TEBBS, ROBERT W. Louisiana plantations. Pencil points. 19:249-64. Apr. 1938. illus.

Locations

Baton Rouge

1898 Noll, Arthur Howard. Some southern capitols—part 2. Louisiana's Capitol. American architect and building news. 30:145-46. Dec. 6, 1890. illus.

  1847. Burned in 1862, rebuilt in 1882. Supposedly a reconstruction of the 1847
  building.

New Iberia

1899 Laist, Theodore F. The architecture of the Bayou Teche country. Western
architect. 37:51-56. Mar. 1928. illus.

  Covers Oaklawn, Franklin; Weeks house, New Iberia; Dabney plantation house, near
  New Iberia; and others.

New Orleans

1900 Arthur, Stanley Clisby. New Orleans: history of the Vieux Carré, its
ancient and historical buildings. New Orleans, H. Harmanson, 1936.
246p. illus.

1901 (Cathedrals, new and old. Contemporary descriptions.) Debow's review.
10:366-67. Mar. 1851.

1902 (Coleman, John P. Old New Orleans homes. Clippings in the New
Orleans state scrapbooks at Howard library, New Orleans.)

1903 Curtis, Nathaniel Cortlandt. Creole architecture of old New Orleans.
Architectural record. 43:435-46. May 1918. illus.

  Illustrations of wrought and cast iron from the collection of photographs at Newcomb
  College.

1904 ———. Dome of the old St. Louis hotel, New Orleans. Architectural
record. 39:355-58. Apr. 1916. illus.

  1840.

1905 ———. Early small dwellings and shops in the French quarter of New
Orleans. American institute of architects. Journal. 16:27-31. Jan. 1928.
illus.

1906 ———. New Orleans, its old houses, shops and public buildings. Philadelphia, J. B. Lippincott Co., 1933. 267p. illus.

1907 ———, and Spratling, W. P. Architectural tradition in New Orleans.
American institute of architects. Journal. 13:279-96. Aug. 1925. illus.

1908 Delcroix, Eugene A. Map of old New Orleans, showing locations of old
houses. Pencil points. 19:203-204. Apr. 1938. illus.

  With sixteen photographs, p.204–220.

1909 ———. Patios, stairways and iron-lace balconies of old New Orleans: a
series of photographs. New Orleans, H. Harmanson, 1938. 92p. illus.

1910 EMBURY, AYMAR II. Old New Orleans, the picturesque buildings of the French and Spanish regime. Architectural record. 30:85-98. July 1911. illus.

1911 (Exchange hotel. Contemporary description.) Niles' weekly register. 52: 224. June 3, 1837.

1912 FAVROT, CHARLES A. Historical sketch on the construction of the Custom house of the city of New Orleans. Louisiana historical quarterly. 3:467-74. Oct. 1920. illus.

1913 FEDERAL WRITERS' PROJECT. New Orleans city guide. Boston, Houghton Mifflin Co., 1938. 430p. illus.

1914 FEITEL, ARTHUR. New Orleans beckons you. Pencil points. 19:221-23. Apr. 1938. illus.

1915 GENTHE, ARNOLD. Impressions of old New Orleans—a book of pictures. N. Y., George H. Doran Co., 1926. 250p. illus.

1916 GOLDSTEIN, MOISE H. The architecture of old New Orleans. New Orleans, La., Tulane University press, 1902. 17p. illus.
Prize Senior Essay, Class of 1902, Tulane University.

1917 Historic New Orleans. American ceramic society. Bulletin. 16:306-309. July 1937. illus.
Brief discussion of the sights.

1918 IRELAND, IRMA THOMPSON. Arabesque: ornamental iron work of the French quarter in New Orleans. Design. 36:3-11. Feb. 1935. illus.

1919 JOOR, HARRIET. New Orleans, the city of iron lace. Craftsman. 11:172-80. Nov. 1906. illus.

1920 KENDALL, JOHN S. Old houses of New Orleans. Louisiana historical quarterly. 17:680-705. Oct. 1934. illus.

1921 ———. Old New Orleans houses and some of the people who lived in them. Louisiana historical quarterly. 20:794-820. July 1937.

1922 ———. The Pontalba buildings. Louisiana historical quarterly. 19:119-49. Jan. 1936.
1846.

1923 KING, GRACE. New Orleans, the place and the people. N. Y., The Macmillan Co., 1902. 404p. illus.
First edition 1895.

1924 KOCH, RICHARD. Architectural highlights of the Vieux Carré. Pencil points. 19:231-46. Apr. 1938. illus.

1925 Master detail series: historic American buildings: Beauregard house, 1113 Chartres street, New Orleans. Architectural forum. 63:495-506. Nov. 1935. illus.

1926 Old New Orleans. American architect. 146:49-56. June 1935. illus.

1927 OWEN, ALLISON. Architectural charm of old New Orleans. American institute of architects. Journal. 1:426-35. Oct. 1913. illus.

1928 RICCIUTI, ITALO WILLIAM. New Orleans and its environs, the domestic
architecture—1727-1870. N. Y., William Helburn, 1938. 160p. illus.

1929 SAUER, LILLIAN BREWSTER. Sidelights on the haunted house. New Orleans,
1930. 30p. illus.
Warrington house.

1930 SHUEY, MARY WILLIS. Ironwork of old New Orleans. Antiques. 18:224-27.
Sept. 1930. illus.
Ca.1795-1860.

1931 SPAULDING, SUMNER. New Orleans and the Vieux Carré. California arts
and architecture. 53:7-39. June 1938.

1932 SPRATLING, WILLIAM P. Picturesque New Orleans. New Orleans, Tulane
university press, 1923. 4p. illus.

1933 STEIN, JOSEPH A. New Orleans. Pencil points. 19:195-202. Apr. 1938.
illus.
The plan of the city.

1934 SUYDAM, EDWARD HOWARD. Portfolio of old plantation houses reflecting the
glory that was Louisiana's. Country life. 58:51-54. Oct. 1930. illus.
only.
Pencil sketches.

1935 TUNNELL, BARBARA MADISON. Aristocrat of the Vieux Carré: Grima house,
a beautiful example of Georgian architecture. House beautiful. 66:68-69.
July 1929. illus.
1823.

1936 WOOD, MINTER. Life in New Orleans in the Spanish period. Louisiana
historical society. Publications. 22:642-47. July 1939. illus.

Saint Francisville

1937 LEWIS, ADDIE L. Afton villa. St. Francisville, La., 1935. 13p.

1938 Rosedown, built in 1835 at Saint Francisville, La. Arts and decoration.
39:12-13. Oct. 1933. illus.

1939 YOUNG, STARK. Deep South notes—part 2. New Republic. 71:343-44.
Aug. 10, 1932.
Rosedown plantation, 1835. *See also* 113.

Saint James Parish

1940 YOUNG, STARK. Deep South notes—part 1. New Republic. 71:315-16.
Aug. 3, 1932.
Uncle Sam's plantation.

MARYLAND

GENERAL REFERENCES (*see also* 150, 153, 184A, 207, 228, 258, 1636, 1650, 1658)

1941 BERKLEY, HENRY J. Colonial ruins, Colonial architecture and brickwork of the Chesapeake Bay section. Maryland historical magazine. 19:1-10. Mar. 1924.

1942 (Colonial architecture of Maryland.) Architectural record. 3:337-46. 1894. illus. only.

1943 EARLE, SWEPSON, AND SKIRVEN, PERCY G. (eds.). Maryland's Colonial eastern shore. Baltimore, Md., Munder, Thomsen press, 1916. 203p. illus.

1944 ERB, ALBERT P. Early architecture of Maryland. Architecture. v.48-50. Sept. 1923—Sept. 1924. illus. only.

1945 FEDERAL WRITERS' PROJECT. Maryland: a guide to the old line state. N. Y., Oxford university press, 1940. 561p. illus.

1946 FORMAN, HENRY CHANDLEE. Early manor and plantation houses of Maryland—1634-1800. Easton, Md., The Author, 1934. 271p. illus.

1947 KEISTER, J. L.; MUNSON, O. J.; SALOMONSKY, EDGAR; AND SALOMONSKY, VERNA COOK. Early architecture of Maryland. Architecture. v.36-40. Nov. 1917—July 1919. illus. only.

1948 RUSK, WILLIAM SENER. Early Maryland architects. Americana. 35:265-75. Apr. 1941.
Extracts from architects' advertisements in Colonial newspapers.

1949 SCARBOROUGH, KATHERINE. Homes of the cavaliers. N. Y., The Macmillan Co., 1930. 392p. illus.
Covers 1740–90.

1950 SCARFF, JOHN H. Some houses of Colonial Maryland. Monograph series. 16:253-77. Aug. 1930. illus.

1951 SILL, HOWARD. Some old Maryland houses. American institute of architects. Journal. 13:5-7. Jan. 1925. illus. only.
Covers Baltimore, Ellicott City, and Prince Georges County.

1952 SMITH, DELOS HAMILTON. Old Maryland churches. D. A. R. magazine. 59:5-14. Jan. 1925.

1953 SWANN, DON. Colonial and historic homes of Maryland. Baltimore, Md., Etchcrafters art guild, 1939. 2v. illus.
One hundred original etchings.

1954 WILSTACH, PAUL. Tidewater Maryland. Indianapolis, Ind. Bobbs-Merrill Co., 1931. 383p. illus.

1955 WORTHINGTON, ADDISON F. Twelve old houses west of the Chesapeake Bay. Boston, Rogers and Manson Co., 1918. 51p. illus.

Some Virginia examples included.

1956 ZIEGLER, CHARLES A. An architectural ramble through Maryland. American architecture and architectural review. 125:237-44. Mar. 1, 1924. illus.

1957 ———. Colonial architecture of the eastern shore of Maryland. White pine series of architectural monographs. v. 2, no. 6. Dec. 1916. 15p. illus.

LOCATIONS

Annapolis

1958 CAVANAGH, CATHERINE FRANCES. Ancient abodes of Annapolis. Americana. 4:819-28. Nov. 1909.

1959 DESMOND, EFFINGHAM C. Pre-revolutionary Annapolis house, designed by Matthew Buckland for Matthias Hammond, esquire—in 2 parts. Monograph series. Part 1, v. 15, no. 4. 1929. 24p; part 2, v. 15, no. 5. 1929. 25p. illus.

Part 2 by R. T. H. Halsey.
Now credited to William, not Matthew, Buckland.

1960 EBERLEIN, HAROLD DONALDSON. The Harwood house, Annapolis. Architectural forum. 37:159-70. Oct. 1922. illus.

Commonly called the Hammond-Harwood house (1770-74).

1961 KEY, REBECCA. A notice of some of the first buildings. . . . Maryland historical magazine. 14:258-71. Sept. 1919.

1962 MAGRUDER, P. H. Colonial government house of Maryland. U. S. Naval institute. Proceedings. 61:1405-1411. 1935.

1963 MARSH, J. H. America's finest Georgian architecture; Hammond house, Annapolis. Arts and decoration. 30:84. Nov. 1928. illus.

1964 RAMSBURGH, EDITH ROBERTS. Annapolis and its early American homes. D. A. R. magazine. 61:652-59. Sept. 1927; 61:735-42. Oct. 1927.

1965 RANDALL, T. HENRY. Colonial Annapolis. Architectural record. 1:309-343. Jan. 1891. illus.

1966 SMITH, DELOS HAMILTON. Annapolis on the Severn. Monograph series. 15:141-68. 1929. illus.

1967 ———. Colonial houses at Annapolis. Architectural review. 10:69-72, 91, 96. Mar. 1920. illus.

1968 Society of Colonial Wars. Maryland State house, memorial to John Appleton Wilson. Baltimore, Md., Society of Colonial wars in the state of Maryland, 1931. 59p. illus.
History of Maryland's capitols.

1969 Stephens, M. Watts. The Colonial council house. Patriotic Marylander. 1:7-10. June 1915.

1970 Thom, DeCourcy W. The old Senate chamber. Maryland historical magazine. 25:365-84. Dec. 1930.

1971 ———. The restoration of the old Senate chamber in Annapolis. Maryland historical magazine. 2:326-35. Dec. 1907.

1972 Tilghman, J. Donnell. Bill for the construction of the Chase house. Maryland historical magazine. 33:23-26. 1938.
Detailed bill of costs.

1973 Tilghman, Oswald. Annapolis, history of ye ancient city and its public buildings. Annapolis, Md., Capital press, 1925. 47p. illus.
First edition 1914.

1974 Wilson, J. Appleton. Restoration of the Senate chamber. Maryland historical magazine. 22:54-62. Mar. 1927.

Anne Arundel County

1975 Holden, Arthur C. Domestic architecture of Anne Arundel county, Maryland. Monograph series. v. 17, no. 5. 1931. 26p. illus.

Baltimore and *Baltimore County* (*see also* 1951)

1976 (Battle monument. Contemporary description.) Atkinson's casket. 9:385. Sept. 1825.
1815. Maximilian Godefroy, architect. First Egyptian Revival attempt in United States.

1977 Buckler, Riggin. Colonial doorways of Baltimore, Maryland. Brickbuilder. 23:140-43. June 1914. illus.

1978 ———. Early American details. Architectural forum. 41:199-202. Oct. 1924. illus.
Mantels.

1979 ———. Mantel at Evergreen, Baltimore. Brickbuilder. 24:37-38. Feb. 1915. illus.

1980 ———. Spring house, Goodloe-Harper estate, Roland Park, Baltimore. Architectural forum. 45:61-62. July 1926. illus.

1981 Erb, Albert P. Mount Claire, home of Charles Carroll, Baltimore, Maryland. Architecture, v. 51, no. 2. Feb. 1925. illus. only.
See also 219.

1982 HALL, B. F. Adventure with an old house: Atamasco, Green Spring Valley. House beautiful. 77:91-92. May 1935. illus.
1750 and later, near Baltimore.

1983 HAMMOND, JOHN MARTIN. Homewood, Baltimore, Maryland—in 2 parts. Architectural record. 41:435-47, 525-35. May, June 1917. illus.
(Variously dated 1798–1809. William Edwards, builder.)

1984 HOWARD, MCHENRY. The Washington monument and squares. Maryland historical magazine. 13:179-82. June 1918.

1985 HOYT, WILLIAM D., JR. Bill for the carpenter work on Hampton. Maryland historical magazine. 33:352-71. 1938.
Itemized bill.

1986 KIMBALL, SIDNEY FISKE. Latrobe's designs for the Cathedral of Baltimore. Architectural record. 42:541-50; 43:37-45. Dec. 1917, Jan. 1918. illus.
(1806)

1987 LUCKETT, MRS. EDMOND B. The history of the Washington monument in Baltimore. Patriotic Marylander. 1:55-61. June 1915.
(1815–29. Robert Mills, architect.)

1988 Opening of the Homewood house. Johns Hopkins alumni magazine. 21:127-51. 1933.

1989 Robert Mills and the Washington monument in Baltimore. Maryland historical magazine. 34:144-60. June 1939; 35:178-89. June 1940.
Documents.

1990 RUSK, WILLIAM SENER. Some buildings of old Baltimore. Americana. 27:300-305. July 1933.

1991 (Shot tower. Contemporary description.) Ariel. 2:159. Jan. 24, 1829.

1992 SIOUSSAT, ANNIE LEAKIN. The old Carroll homestead, Mount Clare—Maryland Colonial dames headquarters. Antiquarian. 2:24-25. July 1924.
1754.

1993 STEFFENS, D. H. Colonial doorways and doorsteps in Baltimore. House beautiful. 46:72-73, 110-11. Aug. 1919. illus.

Bladensburg

1994 ERB, ALBERT P. House in Bladensburg, Md., built by Christopher Lownes in 1746. Architecture. v. 51, no. 4. Apr. 1925. illus. only.

1995 ———. House in Bladensburg, Md., on the Annapolis road, built *ca.*1750. Architecture. v. 52, no. 1. July 1925. illus. only.

1996 KEMPTON, CHRISTINE. Colonial homes of old Bladensburg, Md. House beautiful. 48:105-107. Aug. 1920. illus.

Calvert County

1997 FOOTNER, HULBERT. Charles' gift. Saturday evening post. 212:23, 80-83. July 1, 1939. illus.
1650.

Chestertown

1998 SKIRVEN, PERCY G. Old court house, Chestertown, built before 1698. Patriotic Marylander. 3:51-54. Sept. 1916.

Dorchester

1999 DOWNING, MARGARET B. First church in Maryland. Commonweal. 5:402-404. Feb. 16, 1927.
St. Mary's church, known as Queen's chapel, 1769.

Easton

2000 Oldest frame building in America. Current opinion. 71:381-82. Sept. 1921.
Meeting house, 1683. (Is it?)

Frederick

2001 DELAPLAINE, E. S. Historic shrine in Maryland: Taney home at Frederick. National republic. 22:12-13. Oct. 1934. illus.
(1815)

2002 ———. Visiting the Taney home. National republic. 18:20-21. Sept. 1930. illus.
1799.

Prince Georges County (see also 1951)

2003 BROWN, WARD. Montpelier, the Snowden-Long house, Prince Georges county, Maryland. Monograph series. 16:169-96. 1930. illus.
Before 1751, near Laurel.

2004 CRENSHAW, MARY MAYO. Dower house, Calvert family mansion, Maryland. St. Nicholas. 52:496-99. Mar. 1925.
Near Rosaryville. Once known as Mt. Airy.

2005 ERB, ALBERT P. Mantels in Tavern, the Marlboro house, in Upper Marlboro, Prince Georges county, Maryland, built *ca.*1712. Architecture. v. 52, no. 5. Nov. 1925. illus. only.

2006 FERGUSON, ALICE L. Susquehannock fort on Piscataway Creek. Maryland historical magazine. 36:1-9. Mar. 1941. illus.

2007 Mount Airy, the provincial home of the Calverts of Maryland. D. A. R. magazine. 56:715-22. Dec. 1922.
1660 and later.

2008 THURMAN, FRANCIS LEE. Little known and unfrequented haunts of Washington. Virginia magazine of history. 43:139-43. 1935.
Material on Thornton and Montpelier.

Saint Mary's County

2009 NAIRN, FRASER. Mr. Satterlee of Sotterley in St. Mary's county, Maryland. Country life in America. 65:56-58. Mar. 1934. illus.

1730.

2010 SMITH, DELOS HAMILTON. Old landmarks in Maryland's oldest county, Saint Mary's county. Art and archaeology. 33:243-51, 265. Sept. 1932. illus.

Talbot

2011 CHISLING, ELLIOTT L. Wye house, home of the Lloyd's, Talbot county, Maryland. Monograph series. v. 16, no. 5. 1930. 23p. illus.

Ca.1782.

2012 HOWARD, MCHENRY. Wye house. Talbot county, Maryland. Maryland historical magazine. 18:293-99. Dec. 1923.

MISSISSIPPI

GENERAL REFERENCES (*see also* 1634, 1646)

2013 DEUPREE, MRS. N. D. Some historic homes in Mississippi. Mississippi historical society. Publications. 6:245-64. 1902; 7:325-47. 1903. illus.
Brief sketches of 21 houses.

2014 FEDERAL WRITERS' PROJECT. Mississippi: a guide to the magnolia state. N. Y., Viking press, 1938. 545p. illus.

2015 SUTTON, CANTEY VENABLE (ed.). History of art in Mississippi. Gulfport, Miss., Dixie press, 1929. 177p. illus.

LOCATIONS

Biloxi

2016 SMITH, KATHERINE LOUISE. Home of Jefferson Davis. House beautiful. 15:272-74. Apr. 1904. illus.
Beauvoir (1852–54).

Jackson

2017 NOLL, ARTHUR HOWARD. Some southern Capitols—part 1, Mississippi's capitol. American architect and building news. 29:84-86. Aug. 9, 1890. illus.
(1836–39. William Nichols, architect.)

2018 TAYLOR, J. R. Capitol buildings of Mississippi. Mississippi Department of archives and history. Register. 1904:577-67.

Natchez

2019 CUTTS, ANSON BAILEY. America preserved. Architectural review (London).
83:183-86. Apr. 1938. illus.
Colonial and Classic revival, in and near Natchez.

2020 DUPEE, FREDERICK. Colonnades in the deep South: Natchez, the Versailles
of a vanished empire of cotton. Travel. 66:13-14, 51. Feb. 1936. illus.
Monteigne, Longwood, Magnolia Hall, Revena, Greenleaves.

2021 FAUST, M. E. Some historic houses of Natchez. House beautiful. 67:310-12.
Mar. 1930. illus.

2022 HERING, OSWALD. Plantation homes of the Mississippi: princely mansions
of Natchez—what they stand for in American tradition—the origin
of their architecture. Arts and decoration. 43:10-13. Oct. 1935. illus.
Classic revival.

2023 Melrose—symbolic of the South—built in 1845. Country life. 66:58-63.
Oct. 1934.
(1840's)

2024 Natchez. House beautiful. 81:62-63. Mar. 1939. illus.
Ca. 1780—*ca.*1850.

2025 Natchez pilgrimage. Antiques. 37:140-41. Mar. 1940. illus.

2026 NEWELL, MRS. GEORGIA (WILLSON), AND COMPTON, CHARLES CROMARTIE.
Natchez and the pilgrimage. Kingsport, Tenn., Southern publishers,
1935. 39p. illus.

2027 OLIVER, NOLA NANCE. Natchez—symbol of the old South. N. Y., Hastings
house, 1940. 101p. illus.

2028 RONIM, E. E. Quaint houses of the South—Colonial homes of Natchez.
House and garden. 11:59-64. Feb. 1907. illus.

2029 WILLINK, CECILE. Historic houses of old Natchez. Country life in America.
47:51-54. Dec. 1924. illus.

NORTH CAROLINA

GENERAL REFERENCES (*see also* 1624, 1650, 1653, 1655)

2030 FEDERAL WRITERS' PROJECT. North Carolina: a guide to the old north
state. Chapel Hill, N. C., University of North Carolina press, 1939.
600p. illus.

2031 HENDERSON, ARCHIBALD, AND WOOTTEN, BAYARD. Old homes and gardens
of North Carolina. Chapel Hill, N. C., University of North Carolina
press, 1939. 250p. illus.

2032 Historic homes in North Carolina. North Carolina booklet. v. 2, Jan. 1903.
25p.
Covers The Groves, Wakefield, houses in the Cape Fear country.

2033 Historic homes in North Carolina. North Carolina booklet. v. 3. Oct. 1903.
37p.
Covers Fort Defiance, Panther Creek, Clay Hill.

2034 JOHNSTON, FRANCES BENJAMIN, AND WATERMAN, THOMAS TILESTON. The
early architecture of North Carolina. Chapel Hill, University of North
Carolina press, 1941. 300p. illus.

2035 North Carolina number. Southern magazine. v. 2, no. 5. 1935.
Material on the restoration of Fort Raleigh.

LOCATIONS

Bath

2036 RODMAN, LIDA TUNSTALL. Historic homes and people of old Bath town.
North Carolina booklet. 2:3-13. 1902.

Brunswick County

2037 CURTIS, N. C. Saint Philip's church, Brunswick county, North Carolina.
Architectural record. 47:181-82. Feb. 1920. illus.
Colonial.

Durham

2038 Open to visitors: Johnston house, Durham, North Carolina. Christian science
monitor. Jan. 18, 1939. p. 13.

Edenton

2039 CHAPPELL, MACK. The Cupola house and its associations. North Carolina
booklet. 15:203-217. Apr. 1916.
1758.

Lincolnton

2040 HINTON, MARY HILLIARD. Ingleside, home of Colonel John Ingles. North
Carolina booklet. 15:158-65. Jan. 1916.

New Bern

2041 CLARK, KENNETH. Eastern North Carolina town house, the Smallwood-
Jones residence. White pine series of architectural monographs. v. 13,
no. 3. 1927. 19p. illus.

2042 HANNIGAN, CHARLES FRANCIS. New Bern, the Athens of North Carolina—
in 2 parts. White pine series of architectural monographs. Part 1, v. 13,
no. 1. 1927. 19p; part 2, v. 13, no. 2. 1927. illus.
Colonial.

2043 KIMBALL, SIDNEY FISKE, AND CARRAWAY, GERTRUDE S. Tryon's palace. N. Y. historical society. Quarterly bulletin. 24:13-22. Jan. 1940. illus. 1767. John Hawks, architect.

Raleigh

2044 (Capitol. Contemporary description.) Niles' weekly register. 44:114. Apr. 20, 1833. 1833–40. Ithiel Town and David Patton, architects.

2045 DEVEREUX, ANNIE LANE. Historic homes. Part 5—Welcome. North Carolina booklet. 11:115-16. Oct. 1911.

2046 Home of a president: cottage in which Andrew Johnson was born, in Raleigh, North Carolina. Christian science monitor. Jan. 12, 1938. p. 15.

2047 PAULSON, J. D. Jewel of the Greek revival style. Art and archaeology. 35:69-75. Mar.-Apr. 1934. illus. Capitol.

Statesville

2048 CLARK, ROSAMOND. A sketch of Fort Dobbs. North Carolina booklet. 19:133-38. Apr. 1920. 1755. Destroyed.

2049 HARRILL, FANNIE GERTRUDE. Old Fort Dobbs. D. A. R. magazine. 45: 299-303. Dec. 1914.

Wilmington

2050 HUNT, H. L., JR. Orton plantation. Country life. 71:31-33. Jan. 1937. illus. 1725.

Winston-Salem

2051 CREWS, HALL. Old Salem, now a part of Winston-Salem, North Carolina. Monograph series. v. 15, no. 2. 1929. 21p. illus.

SOUTH CAROLINA

GENERAL REFERENCES (*see also* 184A, 1624, 1655)

2052 BAUM, DWIGHT JAMES, AND SALOMONSKY, VERNA COOK. Early architecture of South Carolina. Architecture. v. 43-44. Feb.-Sept. 1921. illus. only.

2053 FEDERAL WRITERS' PROJECT. South Carolina: a guide to the Palmetto state. N. Y., Oxford university press, 1941. 514p. illus.

2054 HARRIS, ESTELLE. First homes in Carolina. D. A. R. magazine. 62:613-24. 1929.

2055 LEIDING, HARRIETTE KERSHAW. Historic houses of South Carolina. Phila-
      delphia, J. B. Lippincott Co., 1921. 318p. illus.

2056 RUTLEDGE, ARCHIBALD. Home by the river, the story of Hampton planta-
      tion. N. Y., Bobbs-Merrill Co., 1941. 167p. illus.

2057 SALLEY, ALEXANDER S., JR. The state houses of South Carolina, 1751-1936.
      Columbia, Cary Printing Co., 1936. 39 p. illus.

2058 South Carolina number. Southern magazine. v. 1, no. 1. 1934. 60p. illus.
      Some material on Colonial churches in Charleston.

2059 STONEY, SAMUEL GAILLARD. Plantations of the Carolina low country.
      Charleston, S. C., Carolina art association, 1938. 243p. illus.
      Second edition, 1939.

2060 TODD, JOHN R., AND HUTSON, FRANCIS M. Prince William's parish and
      plantations. Richmond, Va., Garrett and Massie, 1935. 266p. illus.
      More material on the lands than the buildings.

2061 WILLIS, BESSIE H. Colonial and Revolutionary homes in South Carolina.
      D. A. R. magazine. 43:377-79. July 1913.

LOCATIONS

      Beaufort

2062 FEDERAL WRITERS' PROJECT. Beaufort and the sea islands. Savannah, Ga.,
      Review Printing Co., 1938. 47p. illus.

2063 HARRILL, SOPHIE C. Beaufort, South Carolina; the second oldest town in
      the United States. House beautiful. 49:299-300. Apr. 1921. illus.
      Colonial houses.

2064 SALOMONSKY, VERNA COOK. Two Colonial interiors from Beaufort, South
      Carolina. Architectural record. 49:267-71. Mar. 1921. illus.

      Charleston (*see also* 196, 1630)

2065 CASEY, WILLIAM. Charleston doorways, entrance motives from a South Caro-
      lina city. White pine series of architectural monographs. 14:241-64.
      1928. illus.
      Covers 1706–1772.

2066 CHANDLER, JOSEPH EVERETT. Some Charleston mansions. White pine series
      of architectural monographs. v. 14, no. 4. 1928. 19p. illus.
      Covers 1757–1811.

2067 Charleston houses. House and garden. 49:198-200. May 1926. illus.

2068 Charleston opens historic playhouse with historic play. Architectural record.
      83:20-25. Jan. 1938. illus.
      In Planters' Hotel, 1806.

2069 Charm of old Charleston, new world city of old world memories. White pine series of architectural monographs. v. 14, no. 2. 1928. 19p. illus.

2070 CURTIS, MRS. ELIZABETH (GIBBON). Gateways and doorways of Charleston, South Carolina, in the eighteenth and nineteenth centuries. N. Y., Architectural Book Publishing Co., 1926. 68p. illus.

2071 DAWSON, C. STUART. Gateways of old Charleston. Country life in America. 39:48-49. Jan. 1921. illus.

2072 FRASER, CHARLES. A Charleston sketchbook, 1796-1806. Charleston, S. C., Carolina art association, ca. 1940. 40p. illus.

2073 FURMAN, SARA. Harrietta, an old plantation house on the Santee River. House beautiful. 70:475-80. Dec. 1931. illus.
Eighteenth century. Forty miles from Charleston.

2074 HEYWARD, D. Dock street theatre, Charleston, an artistic and intellectual center. Magazine of art. 31:10-15. Jan. 1938. illus. (1735–36)

2075 HORTON, CORINNE. Old Charleston gateways. House and garden. 8:245-50. Dec. 1905. illus.

2076 JOHNSON, GEORGE, AND MELCHERS, SAINT JOHN. Glimpses of old residences in Charleston. House beautiful. 46:96-97. Aug. 1919. illus.
Covers 1767–1830.

2077 KENNEDY, J. ROBIE, JR. Examples of Georgian work in Charleston, South Carolina. Architectural record. 19:283-94. Apr. 1906. illus.

2078 LAPHAM, SAMUEL, JR. Architectural significance of the rice mills of Charleston, S. C. Architectural record. 56:178-84. Aug. 1924. illus.
Ante-bellum.

2079 ———, AND SIMONS, ALBERT. Development of Charleston architecture—in 3 parts. Architectural forum. Part 2, 39:299-306. Dec. 1923; part 3, 40:33-40. Jan. 1924. illus.
For part 1, see 2093.

2080 LEIDING, HARRIETTE KERSHAW. Charleston, historic and romantic. Philadelphia, J. B. Lippincott Co., 1931. 293p. illus.

2081 MacELWEE, R. S. Preservation and restoration of Charleston's fine old architecture. American city. 42:134-35. Feb. 19, 1930.

2082 MARVIN, ROY. Town house of Charleston, South Carolina, William Gibbes residence. White pine series of architectural monographs. v. 14, no. 3. 1928. 20p. illus.
Before 1776.

2083 McCORMACK, HELEN G. An architectural inventory for Charleston. American society of architectural historians. Journal. v. 1, no. 3-4. p. 21-23. July-Oct. 1941.

2084 Mechlin, Leila. Glimpse of old Charleston and the nearby rice plantations. American magazine of art. 14:475-85. Sept. 1923. illus.

2085 Murphy, Christopher, Jr. Memories of the old South: plantation homes. Country life. 57:60-61. Jan. 1930. illus.
Harrietta. Forty miles from Charleston.

2086 Old slave quarters. Charleston. House and garden. 75:70. Mar. 1939. illus.

2087 Oldest theatre: opening of the restored Dock street theatre. Time. 30:41-42. Dec. 6, 1937.

2088 Old town houses and famous landmarks. House and garden. 75:40-44, 48-49. Mar. 1939. illus.
1750–1850.

2089 Plantation houses; saga of Charleston's glory told in these great river estates. House and garden. 75:28-33. Mar. 1939. illus.

2090 Ravenel, Harriott H. (Mrs. St. Julien). Charleston, the place and the people. N. Y., The Macmillan Co., 1931. 528p. illus.

2091 Roberts, D. M. Dock street theatre rebuilt; Federal project restores first real theatre in our country. Scholastic. 31:10-11. Jan. 15, 1938. illus.

2092 Robie, Virginia. Bull-Pringle house (Miles Brewton), Charleston, South Carolina. Antiques. 5:168-71. Apr. 1924. illus.
(Ca.1765)

2093 Simons, Albert. Development of Charleston architecture—part I. Architectural forum. 39:153-60. Oct. 1923. illus.
For parts 2 and 3, see 2079.

2094 ———. Edwards-Smyth house, Charleston, South Carolina. White pine series of architectural monographs. 14:265-87. 1928. illus.

2095 ———. Some minor Charleston houses. Architectural forum. 42:81-88. Feb. 1925. illus.

2096 ———, and Lapham, Samuel. Charleston, South Carolina. N. Y., American institute of architects, 1927. 200p. illus.
Octagon library of early American architecture.

2097 Smith, Alice Ravenel Huger. Twenty drawings of the Pringle house on King street, Charleston, South Carolina. Charleston, S. C., Lanneau's art store, 1914. 24p. illus.
(Ca. 1765). Includes article: Colonial House of Miles Brewton with Some Account of Their Owners, by Daniel Elliott Huger Smith.

2098 ———, and Smith, Daniel Elliott Huger. Dwelling houses of Charleston, South Carolina. Philadelphia, J. B. Lippincott Co., 1917. 386p. illus.

2099 Vanderhorst Row, Charleston, South Carolina; a prototype of the modern apartment house. Architectural forum. 39:59-61. Aug. 1923. illus. (1800)

2100 WILLIS, E. Two historic restorations enshrining the beauty of Charleston. Country life in America. 55:41-42. Apr. 1929. illus.

2101 WOOTTEN, MRS. BAYARD (MORGAN), AND STONEY, SAMUEL GAILLARD. Charleston, azaleas and old bricks. Boston, Houghton Mifflin Co., 1937. 24p. illus.

2102 WRIGHT, RICHARDSON. Charles-town (sic) houses. House and garden. 75: 27-44. Mar. 1939. illus.

Columbia

2103 GREEN, EDWIN LUTHER. History of the buildings of the University of South Carolina. Columbia, S. C., R. L. Bryon, 1909.

John's Island

2104 LAPHAM, SAMUEL, JR. Architectural specifications of a century ago, being a copy, with commentary, of documents and drawings for a church on John's Island, South Carolina, by Robert Mills, architect (1781-1855). Architectural record. 53:239-44. Mar. 1923. illus.

Sumter County

2105 SAUNDERS, ANN CATHERINE ANDERSON. Hill Crest, the old Anderson homestead in Sumter county, South Carolina. D. A. R. magazine. 45:3-6. July 1914.

TENNESSEE

GENERAL REFERENCES

2106 BRANDAU, ROBERTA SEAWELL (ed.). History of homes and gardens of Tennessee. Nashville, Tenn., Garden study club of Tennessee, 1935. 503p. illus.

2107 FEDERAL WRITERS' PROJECT. Tennessee: a guide to the state. N. Y., Viking press, 1939. 558p. illus.

2108 MATHEWS, MAXINE. Old inns of east Tennessee. East Tennessee historical society. Publications. 2:22-33. 1930.

2109 SCOFIELD, EDNA. Evolution and development of Tennessee houses. Tennessee academy of science. Journal. 11:229-39. 1936.
Starts with one-room log houses.

Locations

Chattanooga

2110 ALLEN, PENELOPE JOHNSON (comp.). Guide book of Chattanooga and vicinity. Chattanooga, Tenn., 1935. 27p.

Published under the auspices of Volunteer chapter United States Daughters of 1812.

Franklin

2111 McGANN, WILL SPENCER. Old Carter house at Franklin, Tennessee. Tennessee historical magazine. Ser. 2. 3:40-44. Oct. 1932. illus.

Hartsville

2112 YOUNG, S. M. Old rock house. Tennessee historical magazine. Ser. 2. 3:59-64. Oct. 1932. illus.

Late eighteenth century, between Hartsville and Dixon Springs.

Knoxville

2113 CATES, ALICE SMITH. Blount mansion—the cradle of Tennessee. D. A. R. magazine. 69:344-49. 1935.

1792.

2114 PORTER, MATILDE A. Swan Pond, the Ramsey home. Tennessee historical magazine. Ser. 2. 3:283-86. 1932. illus.

1797.

Maury County

2115 POLK, GEORGE W. St. John's church. Tennessee historical magazine. 7:147-53. Oct. 1921. illus.

Near Columbia. Gothic, 1839–41.

Nashville

2116 ANDERSON, MARY F. Jackson's Hermitage—an intimate record of its builder. Americana. 26:502-515. 1932. illus.

(Begun 1819)

2117 The architecture of Nashville. American institute of architects. Journal. 7:159-70, 251-58. June 1919. illus.

2118 BEARD, MRS. WILLIAM EWING. The Capitol, Nashville, Tennessee. Nashville, Tenn., Davie Printing Co., 1912.

(Finished 1855. William Strickland, architect.)

2119 BEARD, WILLIAM EWING. Nashville, the home of history makers. Nashville, Civitan club, 1929. 93p.

2120 CALDWELL, MRS. JAMES E. (comp.). Historic and beautiful homes near Nashville. Nashville, Tenn., 1911.

2121 CALDWELL, MRS. MARY FRENCH. Andrew Jackson's Hermitage. Nashville, Tenn., Ladies' hermitage association, 1933. 106p. illus.

2122 DAVENPORT, F. G. Cultural life in Nashville, 1825-1860. Chapel Hill, University of North Carolina press, 1941. 246p. illus.
Some material on architects.

2123 Hermitage. Antiques. 22:96-97. 1932. illus.

2124 HORN, STANLEY F. The Hermitage, home of Old Hickory. Richmond, Va., Garrett and Massie, 1938. 225p. illus.

VIRGINIA

GENERAL REFERENCES (*see also* 150, 153, 228, 1625, 1627-29, 1633, 1636, 1650, 1653, 1656, 1658, 1955)

2125 ALLEN, EDWARD B. Chimneys of Colonial days. International studio. 77: 156-59. May 1923. illus.

2126 ANDREWS, MARIETTA MINNIGERODE. George Washington's country. N. Y., E. P. Dutton Co., 1930. 318p. illus.

2127 Architecture in Virginia. Virginia historical register. 6:37-42 (no. 1). Jan. 1853.
The progress of architecture in Virginia.

2128 (Architecture in Virginia from preservation standpoint.) *See* Association for preservation of Virginia antiquities. Yearbook, 1896——.

2129 ARTHUR, ROBERT. Tidewater forts of Colonial Virginia. Coast artillery journal. 57:3-20. July 1922.

2130 CARSON, WILLIAM E. Historic shrines of Virginia. Richmond, Va., State commission on conservation and development, 1933. 76p. illus.

2131 CHANDLER, J. A. C., AND THAMES, T. B. Colonial Virginia. Richmond, Va., Times-Dispatch Co., 1907. 388p. illus.

2132 CLARK, KENNETH. Architectural inspiration from northern Virginia. Monograph series. v. 17, no. 3. 1931. 26p. illus.
Covers 1757–1805 in Fairfax and Stafford counties.

2133 FEDERAL WRITERS' PROJECT. Virginia: a guide to the Old Dominion. N. Y., Oxford university press, 1940. 699p. illus.

2134 GOODWIN, RUTHERFOORD. Brief history of and guide book to Jamestown, Williamsburg and Yorktown. Richmond, Va., Cottrell Cooke, 1930. 63p. illus.

2135 Houses of the old South. American architect. 147:57-64. Sept. 1935. illus.

2136 HUMPHREY, HENRY B., JR. Homes of our presidents. Country life in America. 49:53-55, 60-62. Mar.-Apr. 1926; 50:37-39, 65-66, 70-76. May-Aug. 1926. illus.
Mount Vernon and Monticello.

2137 JAMES RIVER GARDEN CLUB, RICHMOND. Historic gardens of Virginia. Richmond, Va., William Byrd press, 1923. 355p. illus.
E. T. Sale (ed.).

2138 KEISTER, J. L.; MUNSON, O. J.; AND WEBER, J. A. Early architecture of Virginia. Architecture. 34:262-64, 266. Dec. 1916; 35:34, 35, 88, 89. Mar. 1917; 36:90, 91, 161, 179. July-Oct. 1917. illus. only.

2139 KIBLER, JAMES LUTHER. Colonial Virginia shrines. Richmond, Va., Garrett and Massie, 1936. 98p. illus.
Guidebook to Jamestown, Williamsburg, and Yorktown.

2140 ———. Historic Virginia landmarks from Cape Henry to Richmond. Richmond, Va., Garrett and Massie, 1929. 141p. illus.

2141 LANCASTER, ROBERT A., JR. Historic Virginia homes and churches. Philadelphia, J. B. Lippincott Co., 1915. 527p. illus.

2142 NASH, MRS. SUSAN HIGGINSON. Paints, furniture and furnishings. Architectural record. 78:447-58. Dec. 1935. illus.
Concerning Colonial use of color in Virginia.

2143 (Negro cabin. Contemporary description.) Dollar magazine. 1:129-31. May 1841.

2144 NILES, BLAIR. The James. N. Y., Farrar and Rinehart, 1939. 359p. illus.
Rivers of America series.

2145 PATTERSON, BRUCE V. Guide book of the Virginia Peninsula. Newport News, Va., Franklin Printing Co., 1935. 94p. illus.

2146 ROTHERY, AGNES. New roads in old Virginia. N. Y., Houghton Mifflin Co., 1929. 223p. illus.

2147 SALE, EDITH TUNIS. Manors of Virginia in Colonial times. Philadelphia, J. B. Lippincott Co., 1909. 310p. illus.

2148 SQUIRES, W. H. T. Days of yesteryear in colony and commonwealth. Portsmouth, Va., Printcraft press, 1928. 301p. illus.

2148A SWEM, E. G. Virginia historical index. Roanoke, Va., Stone Printing Co., 1934-36. 2v.

2149 TYLER, LYON G. Colonial brick buildings. Tyler's quarterly historical and genealogical magazine. 17:69-70. 1935.

2150 Virginia number. Southern magazine. v. 2, no. 3. 1935.
Material on the capitols and Stratford.

2151 Wales, Dinwiddie county, Virginia and Dr. Hugh Mercer's apothecary shop, Fredericksburg, Va. American architect. 143:69-72. May 1933. illus.

2152 WATERMAN, THOMAS TILESTON. The bay system in Colonial Virginia building. William and Mary quarterly. 2d ser. 15:117-22. 1935.

2153, 2154 WILSTACH, PAUL. Potomac landings. N. Y., Tudor Publishing Co., 1937. 378p. illus.
Appeared serially in *Country Life in America.* v. 39, 1920-21.

2155 ———. Tidewater, Virginia. Indianapolis, Ind., Bobbs-Merrill Co., 1929. 326p. illus.

2156 ZIEGLER, CARL A. An architectural ramble through Virginia—in two parts. American architecture and architectural review. Part 1, 123:531-34. June 1923; part 2, 124:141-51. Aug. 1923. illus.

DOMESTIC

2157 BALDWIN, FRANK CONGER. Early architecture of the Rappahannock Valley. American institute of architects. Journal. 3:113-18, 234-40, 329-36. Mar., June, Aug. 1915.
Covers Kenmore (begun 1752), Fredericksburg; Cleve manor (*ca.*1754); Gaymont (1725), Caroline County; and Belle Grove (1830), Frederick County.

2158 LANCASTER, R. A., JR. Historic houses and homes of Virginia. Richmond, Va., Bell Book and Stationery Co., 1912. 450p. illus.

2159 LYNE, CASSIE MONCURE. Lee homes in Virginia. Confederate veteran. 36:288-89. Aug. 1928.
Covers Stratford, Ditchley, and Arlington.

2160 MASSIE, SUZANNA W., AND CHRISTIAN, FRANCES A. (eds.). Homes and gardens in old Virginia. Richmond, Va., Garrett and Massie, 1931. 355p. illus.
Earlier edition, Richmond, J. W. Ferguson Co., 1930. 211p. illus.

2161 Master detail series: historic American buildings. Architectural forum. 66: 53-60. Jan. 1937. illus.
Covers Mary Washington house, Fredericksburg; Folly Farms, Folly Mills; Greenway, Charles City County.

2162 Measured drawings of early American architecture. Architectural record. 67:587-90. June 1930. illus.
Covers Martha Washington's kitchen and Galt house.

2163 Old Virginia houses. American architect. 148:51-58. May 1936. illus.

2164 SALE, EDITH TUNIS. Interiors of Virginia houses of Colonial times, from the beginnings of Virginia to the revolution. Richmond, Va., William Byrd press, 1927. 503p. illus.

2165 ———. Manors of Virginia in Colonial times. Philadelphia, J. B. Lippincott Co., 1909. 309p. illus.

2166 WATERMAN, THOMAS TILESTON, AND BARROWS, JOHN A. Domestic Colonial architecture of tidewater Virginia. N. Y., Charles Scribner's Sons, 1932. 191p. illus.

2167 WATERMAN, THOMAS TILESTON. English antecedents of Virginia architecture. American philosophical society. Proceedings. 80:57-63. 1939. illus.

2168 WHITE, GODDARD M. Details of early southern architecture; two famous mansions of Virginia. Architectural forum. 34:139-42. 35:67-70. Apr., Aug. 1921. illus.

Covers Sabine Hall, Westover, and Shirley.

RELIGIOUS

2169 ANDERSON, MARY F. Old parish churches in Virginia. Americana. 24:151-58. Apr. 1930.

2170 BROCK, HENRY IRVING. Colonial churches in Virginia. Richmond, Va., Dale press, 1930. 94p. illus.

2171 Colonial churches in Virginia; a series of sketches. Richmond, Va., Southern Churchman Co., 1907. 319p. illus.

2172 DAVIS, MARGARET. Tidewater churches. South Atlantic quarterly. 35:86-97. 1936.

2173 JOHNSTON, MRS. S. LACEY. Historic churches of Virginia. American monthly magazine. 39:49-54. Aug. 1911.

2174 MEADE, WILLIAM. Old churches, ministers and families of Virginia. Philadelphia, J. B. Lippincott Co., 1857. 2v. illus.

Other editions to 1897.

2175 WIGMORE, FRANCIS MARION. Old parish churches of Virginia. Washington, D. C., Government printing office, 1929. 46p. illus.

A pictorial historic exhibition of photographs in color, lent to the Library of Congress by Francis M. Wigmore.

LOCATIONS

Albemarle County (*see also* 2136, 2370)

2176 ADAMS, HERBERT BAXTER. Thomas Jefferson and the University of Virginia . . . Washington, D. C., Government printing office, 1888. 308p. illus.

2177 ALBEMARLE CLUB OF COLONIAL DAMES. Historical guide to Albemarle county. Charlottesville, Va., Albemarle club of Colonial dames, 1924. 64p. illus.

2178 BROWN, GLENN. Letters from Thomas Jefferson and William Thornton, architect, relating to the University of Virginia. American institute of architects. Journal. 1:21-27. Jan. 1913. illus.

2179 (CARLTON, MABEL MASON). Thomas Jefferson; an outline of his life and service with the story of Monticello, the home he reared and loved. The

Monticello papers, no. 1. N. Y., The Thomas Jefferson Memorial foundation, 1924. 21p. illus.

2180 FRARY, IHNA THAYER. Salvation of a Virginia mansion: Glen Echo, near Charlottesville. Arts and decoration. 53:29-31, 44. Feb. 1941. illus.

2181 GLENN, GARRARD. University of Virginia. Geographical magazine. 3:58-72. 1936.
Influence of Jefferson.

2182 GREENLEAF, MARGARET. Castle Hill, Virginia. Country life in America. 26:41-43. Oct. 1914. illus.
Colonial.

2183 HARNIT, FANNY. Monticello. D. A. R. magazine. 50:158-62. Feb. 1917.

2184 KIMBALL, MARIE G. Jefferson's furniture comes home to Monticello. House beautiful. 66:164, 165, 186, 188, 190. Aug. 1929. illus.

2185 KIMBALL, SIDNEY FISKE. Church designed by Jefferson. Architectural record. 53:184-86. Feb. 1923. illus.
Episcopal Church, Charlottesville, 1824.

2186 ———. Genesis of Jefferson's plan for the University of Virginia. Architecture. 48:397-99. Dec. 1923. illus.

2187 ———. Monticello, the home of Jefferson. American institute of architects. Journal. 12:174-81. Apr. 1, 1924. illus.

2188 ———. Thomas Jefferson as architect of Monticello and Shadwell. Harvard architectural quarterly. 2:89-137. June 1914. illus.

2189 MUIRHEAD, JAMES F. Jefferson's Virginian home. Landmark. 4:103-107. Feb. 1922.

2190 PATTON, JOHN SHELTON. Jefferson, Cabell and the University of Virginia. N. Y., and Washington, D. C., Neale Publishing Co., 1906. 380p. illus.

2191 ———. Monticello. University of Virginia alumni bulletin. Third series. 7:633-46. Oct. 1914.

2192 ———, AND DOSWELL, SALLIE J. Monticello and its master. Charlottesville, Va., Michie Co., 1925. 78p. illus.

2193 ———. University of Virginia: glimpses of its past and present. Lynchburg, Va., J. P. Bell and Co., printers, 1900. 96p. illus.

2194 ———, AND CRENSHAW, LEWIS D. (eds.). Glimpses of the past and present of the University of Virginia. Charlottesville, Va., Michie Co., printers, 1915. 97p. illus.

2195 RHODES, THOMAS L. Story of Monticello. Washington, D. C., American Publishing Co., 1928. 94p. illus.

2196 SADLER, MRS. ELIZABETH HATCHER. Bloom of Monticello. Richmond, Va., Whittet and Shepperson, 1925. 20p. illus.

2197 ST. CLAIRE, EMILY ENTWISLE. Beautiful and historic Albemarle. Richmond, Va., Appeals press, 1932. 110p. illus.

2198 WILSTACH, PAUL. Jefferson and Monticello. Garden City, N. Y., Doubleday, Page and Co., 1925. 258p. illus.
Limited edition same as first edition. Second revised edition, Doubleday, Doran and Co., 1931. 262p. illus.

2199 ———. Jefferson's little mountain. National geographic magazine. 55:481-503. Apr. 1929. illus.

Alexandria (see *Fairfax County*)

Arlington (see *Fairfax County*)

Augusta County
2200 VAN DEVANTER, JAMES NICHOLS. History of the Augusta church, from 1737 to 1900. Staunton, Va., Rose Printing Co., 1900. 71p. illus.

Bedford County
2201 WILSTACH, PAUL. Thomas Jefferson's secret home; Poplar Forest, Bedford county, Virginia. Country life in America. 53:41-43. Apr. 1928. illus. Also: St. Nicholas. 55:699-700. July 1928.
Near Lynchburg (1806).

Campbell County
2202 CHRISTIAN, WILLIAM ASBURY. Lynchburg and its people. Lynchburg, Va., J. P. Bell Co., 1900. 463p. illus.

Charles City County (*see also* 2161, 2168)
2203 BROWN, B. T. Shirley on the royal James. Arts and decoration. 38:36-37. Feb. 1933. illus.
(Between 1720 and 1740.)

2204 Details of early southern architecture. Architectural forum. 35:67-70. Aug. 1921. illus.
Shirley.

2205 TYLER, LYON GARDINER. Weyanoke, the oldest church plate and the first wind mill. Tyler's quarterly historical and genealogical magazine. 16:85-88. 1934.
Description of an early windmill.

2206 Westover restored. Country life in America. 30:25-27. Aug. 1916. illus.

2207 WILLEY, DAY ALLEN. Westover. House and garden. 11:231-35. June 1907. illus.
(*Ca.*1730 and later.)

Charlotte County

2208 Government to purchase Patrick Henry's estate. Museum news. 17:1. Feb. 15, 1940.
Red Hill.

Charlottesville (see *Albemarle County*)

Clarke County

2209 HUGHES, CHARLES RANDOLPH. Old chapel, Clarke county, Virginia. Berryville, Va., Blue Ridge press, 1906. 74p. illus.

Culpeper County

2210 HANES, BLANCHE FITZHUGH. Salubria, the Colonial home of Mrs. Thompson (Lady Spottswood), and the stopping place of Thomas Jefferson and other notables. Journal of American history. 11:252-56. Apr. 1917.
1739.

Dinwiddie County (*see also* 2151)

2211 DAVIS, MARGARET. Doorways to yesterday. Catholic world. 142:74-79. 1935.
Seventeenth and eighteenth century houses.

2212 LANCASTER, ROBERT A., JR. Wales, Dinwiddie county, Virginia. Virginia magazine of history. 44:232-37. 1936.
Late eighteenth century.

2213 Story of old Petersburg and southside Virginia. Petersburg, Va., J. T. Morriss and Sons, *ca.* 1940. 34p. illus.

Essex County

2214 Bathurst, home of the Jones family of Virginia and Kentucky. Kentucky historical society. Register. 14:53-55. Sept. 1916. illus.
Near Tappahannock. Colonial.

Fairfax County (*see also* 1640, 2132, 2136, 2159)

2215 ANDERSON, MARY F. Restoration of Arlington mansion. Americana. 28:449-77. 1934.
(Remodeled 1820 by George Hadfield.)

2216 BALL, EMMA R. (MRS. C. B. BALL). Washington's home and the story of the Mount Vernon ladies' association of the Union. Richmond, Va., Whittet and Shepperson, printers, 1912. 18p. illus.

2217 Bill for acquisition by Federal government of Mount Vernon. National republic. 18:11. May 1930.

2218 BROWN, B. T. Restoration in Alexandria, Virginia; C. B. Moore home. House beautiful. 71:205-208. Mar. 1932. illus.

2219 BRUSH, WARREN D. The building of Mount Vernon mansion. House beautiful. 51:130-31, 162-64. Feb. 1922. illus.

2220 CAPEN, OLIVER BRONSON. Country homes of famous Americans. Part 5. George Washington. Country life in America. 5:499-504. Apr. 1904. illus.

2221 CHASE, ENOCH AQUILA. History of Arlington. Washington, D. C., National Art Service Co., 1929. 22p. illus.

2222 ———. Restoration of Arlington house. Columbia historical society. Records. 33-34:239-65. 1932.

2223 CONNOR, HARRY R. Gunston hall, Fairfax county. Monograph series. v. 16, no. 3. 1930. 27p. illus.
    Ca.1758.

2224 CRAWFORD, M. D. C. Alexandria: an old Virginia classic. Arts and decoration. 15:108-109. June 1921. illus.

2225 CRENSHAW, MARY MAYO. Gunston hall. St. Nicholas. 52:938-42. July 1925. illus.

2226 ———. Stately Woodlawn mansion. Antiquarian. 7:41-44. Sept. 1926.
    Built by Lawrence Lewis (1805). Dr. William Thornton, architect.

2227 DODGE, HARRISON HOWELL. Mount Vernon, its owner and its story. Philadelphia, J. B. Lippincott Co., 1932. 232p. illus.

2228 DUHAMEL, JAMES F. Belvoir. Columbia historical society. Records. 35-36: 146-53. 1935.

2229 DUKE, JANE TAYLOR. Gunston hall. House beautiful. 83:50-52, 127-31. May 1941. illus.

2230 FLOURNOY, MRS. WILLIAM CABELL. Arlington. Confederate veteran. 31: 134-36. Apr. 1923.

2231 Gadsby's tavern. D. A. R. magazine. 67:71-74. 1933.
    Alexandria (1752).

2232 GAHN, BESSIE WILMARTH. Mystery house in Alexandria. D. A. R. magazine. 66:412-14. 1932.
    Describes a sketch similar to Washington headquarters house in Georgetown.

2233 George Washington, country gentleman; an account of a visit to Mount Vernon from the diary of Benjamin Latrobe. Country life in America. 41:34-41. Dec. 1921. illus.
    Sketches by Latrobe.

2234 GORDON, JOHN B. Alexandria's old meeting house. D. A. R. magazine. 63:538-41. Sept. 1929.
    Presbyterian meeting house, 1774.

2235 Gunston hall. Life. v. 11, no. 24. Dec. 15, 1941. p. 118-21. illus.

2236 HAMILTON, J. G. DEROULHAC. Arlington; a national memorial. Current history. 24:720-23. Aug. 1926.

2237 HARCOURT, HELEN. Mount Vernon, the American mecca. New Age. 6:319-24. Apr. 1907.

2238 KOPP, C. B. Salona, historic refuge of Dolly Madison. National republic. 20:6-7. July 1932. illus.
1801, near McLean.

2239 LEE, CUSTIS. Arlington house and its associations. Washington, D. C., United States quartermaster corps, 1932. 45p. illus.

2240 LINDSEY, MARY. Historic homes and landmarks of Alexandria, Virginia. Alexandria, Va., Newell-Cole Co., 1931. 52p. illus.

2241 LOSSING, BENSON. Home of Washington; or, Mount Vernon and its associations. . . . N. Y., Virtue and Yorston, 1871. 446p. illus.
First edition, 1870; also published Hartford, Conn., G. W. Rogers, 1870. A revision of his *Home of Washington and Its Associations*. . . . N. Y., W. A. Townsend, 1865 and 1866.

2242 LOWTHER, MINNIE KENDALL. Mount Vernon, Arlington and Woodlawn; history of these national shrines from the earliest titles of ownership to the present, with biographical sketches, portraits, and interesting reminiscences of the families who founded them. Washington, D. C., C. H. Potter and Co., 1922. 83p. illus.

2243 ———. Mount Vernon; its children, its romances, its allied families and mansions. Philadelphia, John C. Winston Co., 1930. 282p. illus.
Second edition 1932. 302p. illus.

2244 LYNE, MRS. WILLIAM H. Gunston hall—famous estate of George Mason. Confederate veteran. 36:210-12. June 1928.

2245 MCGROARTY, WILLIAM BUCKNER. Old Presbyterian meeting-house at Alexandria, Virginia, 1774-1874. Richmond, Va., William Byrd press, 1940. 81p. illus.

2246 MATHEWS, JAMES T., JR. Romance of old Christ church, Alexandria, Virginia. Washington, D. C., Park press, 1926. 31p. illus.

2247 MILLER, WILHELM. Mount Vernon as Washington would have had it. Country life in America. 26:no. 2, p. 49-52; no. 3, p. 48-49, 80, 82; no. 4, p. 43-45, 82, 84; no. 6, p. 58-59. June-Oct. 1914. illus.

2248 MOORE, CHARLES. Gunston hall. D. A. R. magazine. 61:678-80. Sept. 1927.

2249 Mount Vernon, Arlington house, Dumbarton house. House and garden. 78:sup. 20-26. July 1940. illus.

2250 Mount Vernon: the garden, the home, the builders. Garden and home builder. 45:456-80. July 1927. illus.

2251-2257 (Mount Vernon. Contemporary descriptions.) Atkinson's casket. 11: 505. Nov. 1829; Dollar magazine. 1:147-48. May 1841; Ladies' companion. 12:101. Jan. 1840; New World. 3:322. Nov. 20, 1841; Southern literary messenger. 18:53-57. Jan. 1852; Western miscellany. 1:74-76. Sept. 1848; Yale literary magazine. 23:354-57, 24:19-20. Aug., Oct. 1858.

2258 PAGE, THOMAS NELSON. Mount Vernon and its preservation, 1858-1910; the acquisition, restoration and care of the home of Washington by the Mount Vernon ladies' association of the Union for over half a century. N. Y., Knickerbocker press, 1910. 84p. illus.

2259 Rededication exercises of restored Virginia landmark; old church built in 1774 abounds in associations with George Washington and his contemporaries. Minute man. 23:114-18. June 1928.
Presbyterian meeting house, Alexandria.

2260 Robert E. Lee's home at Arlington. Antiques. 27:26-27. Jan. 1935. illus.
1803, portico 1826.

2261 ROBERTSON, THOMAS B. Ruins of old church at old Arlington gate. William and Mary quarterly. 21:67-70. July 1912.

2262 ROBINSON, BERTHA LOUISE. Old Southern mansion of Gunston hall. Journal of American history. 4:94-100. 1910.

2263 ROGERS, ALLA HARMAN. History of Mount Vernon, America's patriotic shrine. Washington, D. C., National Art Service Co., 1932. 27p. illus.

2264 SAYLOR, HENRY H. Alexandria, Virginia. White pine series of architectural monographs. v. 12, no. 4. 1926. 19p. illus.

2265 SHOULTS, W. E. Home of the first farmer of America. National geographic magazine. 53:602-628. May 1928. illus.
Mount Vernon.

2266 SCHULZ, EDWARD HUGH. Belvoir on the Potomac. . . . Fort Humphreys, Virginia, 1933. 14p. illus.

2267 SHERMAN, CAROLINE BALDWIN. Old Virginia landmark. William and Mary quarterly. 2nd ser. 7:87-91. Apr. 1927.
Ash Grove (1790 and later).

2268 SMITH, DELOS. Abington of Fairfax county. D. A. R. magazine. 63:325-30. June 1929.

2269 SMOOT, MRS. BETTY CARTER. Days in an old town. Alexandria, Va., 1934. 189p. illus.
Notes on Alexandria houses.

2270 SPENCER, RICHARD HENRY. The Carlyle house and its associations—Braddock's headquarters—here the Colonial governors met in council, April, 1755. William and Mary quarterly. 18:1-17. July 1909.
Alexandria (1752).

2271 STAPLEY, MILDRED. The house of George Washington. Country life in America. 26:39-44. May 1914. illus.

2272 STEPHENSON, JEAN. Mount Vernon: a monument to American idealism. D. A. R. magazine. 62:85-92. Feb. 1928.

2273 STRICKLAND, WILLIAM. The tomb of Washington at Mt. Vernon. Philadelphia, Carey and Hart, 1940. 76p. illus.

2274 STUNTZ, S. C. The Carlyle house, Alexandria, Virginia. D. A. R. magazine. 50:4-9. Jan. 1917.

2275 Through Virginia to Mount Vernon; extracts from the Journal of Benjamin Henry Latrobe, friend of Washington and architect of the Capitol. Appleton's book-lovers' magazine. 6:3-17. July 1905.

2276, 2277 (Tomb of Washington. Contemporary descriptions.) Cabinet of religion, New York. 2:479-80. Oct. 24, 1829; Rural repository. 25:137-38. May 1849.

2278 WILSTACH, PAUL. Country home of George Washington. Country life in America. 29:23-26. Apr. 1916. illus.

2279 ———. Mount Vernon, Washington's home and the nation's shrine. N. Y., Doubleday, Page and Co., 1916. 301p. illus.

Fauquier County
2280 PEAK, MAYME OBER. Oak Hill, the Fauquier home of chief justice Marshall. House beautiful. 49:288-89, 330. Apr. 1921. illus.
(1818)

Fluvanna County
2281 Bremo, designed and built by Thomas Jefferson in 1815. Arts and decoration. 39:10-11. Oct. 1933. illus.
See also 113.

Fredericksburg (see *Spotsylvania County*)

Gloucester County
2282 CATES, ALICE SMITH. Rosewell, the ancestral home of the Pages of Virginia. D. A. R. magazine. 57:451-59. Aug. 1923.
(Begun 1725, destroyed 1916.)

2283 CROWDER, R. T. First manor-houses in America and estates of the first Americans; a journey to the historic mansions along the York river in Gloucester county, Virginia. Journal of American history. 3:283-95. 1909.

2284 (Rosewell. Contemporary description.) Southern literary messenger. 10: 41-42. Jan. 1844.

2285 WATERMAN, THOMAS TILESTON. Rosewell, Gloucester county. Architectural forum. 52:17-20. Jan. 1930. illus.

Henrico County (*see also* 213, 2150)

2286 ALBRIGHT, C. LEONARD. Historic Mason's hall at Richmond, Virginia. Grand lodge bulletin. 31:404-405. Jan. 1930.
Called oldest Masonic hall in the United States.

2287 BRAGG, L. M. Virginia house in the Regency style, Wickham-Valentine house in Richmond. International studio. 97:21-24. Sept. 1930. illus.
(1812, Robert Mills, architect.)

2288 BUCHANAN, JAMES, AND HAY, WILLIAM. Copy of letter to Thomas Jefferson relocating Virginia capitol buildings. Virginia magazine of history. 41: 158-59. 1933.

2289 CHRISTIAN, WILLIAM ASBURY. Richmond, her past and present. Richmond, Va., L. H. Jenkins, 1912. 618p. illus.

2290 KIMBALL, SIDNEY FISKE. Thomas Jefferson and the first monument of the classic revival in America—in 3 parts. American institute of architects. Journal. Part 1, 3:371-81. Sept. 1915; part 2, 3:421-33. Oct. 1915; part 3, 3:473-91. Nov. 1915.
The Capitol, begun 1785.

2291 LANCASTER, ROBERT A., JR. Wilton. Virginia magazine of history. 41:310-17. 1933.
1747-53.

2292 Letters to Jefferson relative to the Virginia Capitol. William and Mary quarterly. 2nd ser. 5:95-98. Apr. 1925.
1785.

2293 (Monumental church. Contemporary discussion and illustration.) American pioneer. 1:371. Nov. 1842. illus.
Richmond, 1813-14. Robert Mills, architect.

2294 ROBINS, SALLY NELSON. Oldest house in Richmond, Virginia, now called the Edgar Allen Poe shrine. House beautiful. 54:488, 544. Nov. 1923. illus.
(*Ca.*1686)

2295 RYAN, EDWARD L. Singleton house. Virginia magazine of history. 41:102-108. 1933.
Late eighteenth century.

2296 ———. State Court house. Virginia magazine of history. 41:280-88. 1933.

2297 ————. Warsaw. Virginia magazine of history. 40:347-54. 1932.
Richmond, John Harmer Gilmer house. Nineteenth century.

2298 SCOTT, MARY WINGFIELD. Houses of old Richmond. Richmond, Va., Valentine museum, 1941. 332p. illus.

2299 Scraps from a note book—the Capitol, Virginia. Historical register. 1:169. Oct. 1848.
A letter from Jefferson to Madison to 1788 from Paris, describing the model for the Capitol.

2300 WEDDELL, ALEXANDER WILBOURNE. Richmond, Virginia in old prints, 1737-1887. Richmond, Va., Johnson Publishing Co., 1932. 254p. illus.

James City County (*see also* 2134, 2139, 2150, 2395)

2301 BROWN, BARBARA TRIGG. A small house restored in old Williamsburg. Good housekeeping. 99:78. Dec. 1934. illus.
73 Francis Street.

2302 ————. Restoration of Colonial Williamsburg. Good housekeeping. 99: 70-71, 125. Nov. 1934. illus.
Carter-Saunders house, before 1761.

2303 ————. Restoring historic Williamsburg. Good housekeeping. 99:74-75, 152. July 1934. illus.
St. George Tucker house, 1790 and earlier.

2304 ————. Williamsburg, a shrine for American patriots. American home. 12:349-51. Nov. 1934. illus.

2305 BROWN, GLENN. Jamestown. Architectural record. 63:78-79. Jan. 1928. illus.
Church, *ca.*1637.

2306 CHORLEY, KENNETH. Progress in the restoration of Colonial Williamsburg. Architectural record. v. 80. Nov. 1936. illus.
Photographs of details.

2307 COLEMAN, CHARLES WASHINGTON. The Wythe house, Williamsburg, Virginia. Magazine of American history. 7:270-75. Oct. 1881. illus.

2308 Colonial capitol of Virginia. American architect and building news. 16:198-99. Oct. 25, 1884. illus.

2309 COLONIAL WILLIAMSBURG, INC. A brief and true report for the traveller concerning Williamsburg in Virginia. . . . Richmond, Va., Dietz press, 1935. 192p. illus.

2310 ————. An album of Williamsburg restoration photographs. Williamsburg, Colonial Williamsburg, inc., 1933. illus.
Mounted photographs showing stages of restoration.

2311 ———. The Capitol. . . . Williamsburg, Colonial Williamsburg, inc., 1934. 43p. illus.
(1751. Destroyed 1832.)

2312 ———. The Governor's palace. Williamsburg, Colonial Williamsburg, inc., 1934. 14p. illus.
(Destroyed 1781.)

2313 ———. Guide book for Williamsburg, Virginia. Colonial Williamsburg, inc., 1935. 47p. illus.

2314 ———. The Raleigh tavern. Williamsburg, Colonial Williamsburg, inc., 1934. 30p. illus.
(Before 1742.)

2315 ———. Travis house. Williamsburg, Colonial Williamsburg, inc., 1933. 15p. illus.

2316 ———. Williamsburg restoration; a brief review of the plan, purpose, and policy of the Williamsburg restoration. Williamsburg, Colonial Williamsburg, inc., 1933. 24p. illus.

2317 DUELL, PRENTICE. Excavations at Williamsburg. Architectural record. 69: 16-17. Jan. 1931. illus.

2318 GOODWIN, WILLIAM ARCHER RUTHERFOORD. Bruton Parish Church restored, and its historic environment. Petersburg, Va., Franklin press, 1907. 205p. illus.

2319 Governor's palace, Colonial Williamsburg; measured drawings and views— in 4 parts. Architectural record. Part 1, 78:378-81; part 2, 78:395-409; part 3, 80:354-63, 368; part 4, 80:370-71. Dec. 1935—Nov. 1936. illus.

2320 GRAF, DON. Origin of present-day architecture; characteristics of the Colonial style. American home. 11:338-39. May 1934. illus.

2321 GREGORY, GEORGE C. Jamestown first brick State house. Virginia magazine of history. 43:193-99. 1935.
1631–96.

2322 ———. Log houses at Jamestown, 1607. Virginia magazine of history. 44:287-95. 1936.

2323 HEATWOLE, C. J. Historic Williamsburg to be the national museum of '76. Virginia journal of education. 21:439-43. June 1928.

2324 Historic residences in Williamsburg. Tyler's quarterly historical and genea-logical magazine. 11:73-84. Oct. 1929.
Tucker house, Blair house, and Peyton Randolph house.

2325 LEE, W. D. Renascence of Carter's Grove on the James River, now the home of A. M. McCrea. Architecture. 67:185-94. Apr. 1933. illus.
(1751.)

2326 Measured drawings of early American architecture: Galt house, Williamsburg. Architectural record. 67:587-90. June 1930. illus.

2327 OLDS, NATHANIEL S. Williamsburg and its restoration. Philadelphia, Privately printed, 1929. 11p. illus.

2328 OSBORNE, JOSEPH ALEXANDER. Williamsburg in Colonial times. Richmond, Va., Dietz press, 1935. 166p. illus.

2329 PARK, EMILY HARDEE. Old Williamsburg. American monthly magazine. 31:527-32. Sept. 1907.

2330 PERRY, W. G. Notes on the architecture of Colonial Williamsburg. Architectural record. 78:363-77. Dec. 1935. illus.

2331 POWER, ETHEL B. Colonial stage reset for action. House beautiful. 76:54-57. July 1934. illus.

2332 REEVE, E. A. Inside a Virginia Colonial house in Williamsburg. House and garden. 64:28-29. Nov. 1933. illus.

2333 Restoration at Williamsburg; Perry, Shaw and Hepburn, architects. Pencil points. 17:224-46. May 1936. illus.
Measured drawings and photographs.

2334 Restoration of Colonial Williamsburg in Virginia; Perry, Shaw and Hepburn, architects, with portfolio of buildings, maps and plans, measured drawings and working details—in 2 parts. Architectural record. Part 1, 78:359-458. Dec. 1935; part 2, 80:337-84. Nov. 1936. illus.

2335 Restoration of Williamsburg, Virginia; Perry, Shaw and Hepburn, architects. American architect. 147:10, 36-52. Dec. 1935. illus.

2336 ROSÉ, GRACE N., AND ROSÉ, J. M. Williamsburg today and yesterday. N. Y., G. P. Putnam's Sons, 1940. 77p. illus.

2337 Some notes on Green Spring. Virginia magazine of history. 37:289-300. Oct. 1929.
Home of Sir William Berkeley, the Ludwells, and the Lees. Destroyed.

2338 STANSBURY, CHARLES FREDERICK. The Jamestown tower. Eclectic magazine. 146:470-75. June 1906.

2339 TYLER, LYON GARDINER. Williamsburg, the old Colonial capital. William and Mary quarterly. 16:1-65. July 1907.

2340 ———. Williamsburg, the old Colonial capital. Richmond, Va., Whittet and Shepperson, 1907. 285p. illus.

2341 WALL, ALEXANDER J. Restoration of Williamsburg, Va. N. Y. historical society. Bulletin. 16:3-9. 1932.

2342 (William and Mary College. Contemporary description.) Southern literary messenger. 30:382-83. May 1860.

2343 WILLIAMSBURG GARDEN CLUB. Williamsburg scrap book. Richmond, Va.,
Dietz press, 1932. 97p. illus.

2344 WILLIAMSBURG HOLDING CORPORATION. Williamsburg restoration; a brief
review of the plan, purpose and policy of the Williamsburg restoration;
an authoritative statement issued by those in charge of the undertaking.
Williamsburg, Va., Williamsburg holding corp., 1931. 31p. illus.

2345 Williamsburg—what it means to architecture, to gardening, to decoration.
House and garden. 72:37-67. Nov. 1937. illus.

King George County

2346 BALDWIN, FRANK CONGER. Early architecture of the Rappahannock Valley,
Marmion, 1750. American institute of architects. Journal. 4:87-95.
Mar. 1916. illus.

King William County

2347 (Augustine Moor house. Contemporary description.) American penny magazine. 1:772. Jan. 10, 1846.

2348 CLARKE, PEYTON NEALE. Old King William homes and families. Louisville,
Ky., J. P. Morton Co., 1897. 211p. illus.

2349 LANCASTER, ROBERT A., JR. Pampatike and Winton. Virginia magazine of
history. 41:223-30. 1933.

Loudoun County

2350 LAMB, MRS. MARTHA J. Oak Hill, the house of President Monroe. Magazine of American history. 21:381-85. May 1889. illus.
(1820–23. James Hoban.)

Nansemond County

2351 MASON, GEORGE C. Colonial churches of Nansemond county. William and
Mary quarterly. 21:37-54. Jan. 1941.

Norfolk (see *Norfolk County*)

Norfolk County

2352 House of F. K. Barbour built about 1750, moved thirty miles, re-erected in
1935; R. M. Carrere, architect. American architect and architecture.
148:71-74. Jan. 1936. illus.

Northampton County

2353 ROBERTSON, T. B. Court houses of Northampton county. William and Mary
quarterly. 23:51-58. July 1914.

Petersburg (see *Dinwiddie County*)

Prince George County

2354 LUTZ, EARLE. Appomattox manor. Mentor. 17:34-35. July 1929. illus.
1651, near Hopewell.

2355 ROBERTS, MARY FANTON. Brandon, with its memories of perukes and farth-
ingales. Arts and decoration. 43:6-9, 43. Jan. 1936. illus.
(First half eighteenth century, with additions.)

Prince William County

2356 HARRISON, FAIRFAX. Landmarks of old Prince William; a study of origins in
northern Virginia. Richmond, Va., Privately printed, Old Dominion
press, 1924. 2v. illus.

2357 SALE, MRS. EDITH DABNEY (TUNIS). Upper Brandon; James River home
of F. O. Byrd. House beautiful. 68:50-52. July 1930. illus.
(Early nineteenth century.)

Princess Ann County

2358 KELLAM, SADIE SCOTT, AND KELLAM, V. HOPE. Old houses in Princess Ann.
Portsmouth, Va., Printcraft press, 1931. 235p. illus.

Richmond (see *Henrico County*)

Richmond County

2359 BALDWIN, F. C. Early architecture of the Rappahannock Valley; Mount Airy.
American institute of architects. Journal. 4:448-54. Nov. 1916. illus.
(1758.)

2360 BROOKE, ARTHUR. Colonial mansion of Virginia. Architectural record. 1:
91-95. Aug. 1899.
Mount Airy.

2361 DABNEY, EDITH. Historic mansions of the Rappahannock—Sabine Hall.
American homes and gardens. 6:197-200. May 1909. illus.
1730. *See also* 2168.

2362 GHEQUIERE, T. BUCKLER. Richmond county Court house, Virginia. American architect and building news. 2:199. June 28, 1877. illus.
1748 at Warsaw.

Smithfield (see *Surry County*)

Spotsylvania County (*see also* 2151, 2157, 2161)

2363 AVIS, A. The saving of Kenmore. Woman citizen. n. s. 9:12. Jan. 24, 1925.
illus.

2364 BALDWIN, FRANK CONGER. Early architecture of the Rappahannock Valley—
Kenmore (1753-1777). American institute of architects. Journal. 3:
113-18. Mar. 1915. illus.

2365 BERRYMAN, FLORENCE SEVILLE. Kenmore, Fredericksburg, Va., an example
of early American art. American magazine of art. 16:301-306. June
1925. illus.

2366 CRENSHAW, MARY MAYO. Saving the Fielding Lewis home. Antiquarian.
9:56-59. Sept. 1927.
Kenmore, Fredericksburg.

2367 DUKE, JANE TAYLOR. Kenmore, the home of George Washington's sister and her husband, Fielding Lewis, patriot. House beautiful. 81:24-27, 81-82. Feb. 1939. illus.

2368 FLEMING, MRS. VIVIAN MINOR. Kenmore mansion, built 1752, home of Colonel Fielding Lewis and his wife, Betty Washington. Fredericksburg, Va., Kenmore association, 1924. 23p. illus.

2369 GOOLRICK, JOHN T. Old homes and history around Fredericksburg. . . . Richmond, Va., Garrett and Massie, 1929. 105p. illus.

2370 MILLEN, ROGER. Six old Virginia houses. American institute of architects. Journal. 13:61-66. Feb. 1925. illus. only.
Braxton house, Rising Sun tavern, bank building, Mary Washington house, and the sentry box in Fredericksburg, and Weaver Tree in Albemarle County.

2371 PIPER, ADALINE D. Charm of Chatham, an historic mansion of the South, recently restored. House beautiful. 59:437-41. Apr. 1926. illus.
1721.

2372 ———. A famous Virginia house opens its doors. Arts and decoration. 52:10-12, 44. Aug. 1940. illus.
Doggett house, 1780.

2373 POWELL, D. V. M. Colonial churches in Spotsylvania county. William and Mary quarterly, 2nd ser, 11:3-6. 1931.

2374 STERN, PHILIP N. Ornamental stuccowork at Kenmore. Antiques. 27:16-18. Jan. 1935. illus.
Stuccowork, 1775.

Stafford County (*see also* 2132)

2375 WATERMAN, THOMAS TILESTON. Old court house buildings, Stafford Court house, Virginia. William and Mary quarterly. 2nd ser. 16:247, 587-88. 1936.

Staunton (see *Augusta County*)

Surry County

2376 BOHANNON, A. W. Old Surry: thumb-nail sketches of places of historic interest in Surry county, Virginia. Petersburg, Va., Plummer Printing Co., 1927. 74p. illus.

2377 HAMMOND, JOHN MARTIN. Claremont manor on the James: an historic brick house of Queen Anne type. House beautiful. 51:564-65. June 1922.
(Seventeenth century and later.)

2378 MILLAR, DONALD. Jacobean house in Virginia. . . . Architectural record. 57:220, 285-88. Mar. 1925. illlus.
Bacon's castle, Smithfield (*ca.*1655). *See also* 196.

2379 MOOREHEAD, SINGLETON P., AND KENDREW, A. EDWIN. Restoration work at the Warren house. Virginia magazine of history. 43:204-208. 1935.

Westmoreland County (*see also* 2150, 2159)

2380 ALEXANDER, FREDERICK WARREN. Stratford hall and the Lees connected with its history. Oak Grove, Va., The Author, 1912. 332p. illus. (*Ca.*1729.)

2381 ARMES, ETHEL. Stratford on the Potomac. Greenwich, Conn., United daughters of the Confederacy, 1928. 40p. illus.

2382 ———. Stratford on the Potomac. Antiques. 23:175-77. 1933.

2383 CAPEN, OLIVER BRONSON. Country homes of famous Americans. Part 10. Robert E. Lee. Country life in America. 6:432-34. Sept. 1904. illus.

2384 CUMMIN, HAZEL E. Home of the Westmoreland Lees. Stratford hall, Va. Country life in America. 77:28-31. Apr. 1940. illus.

2385 ———. Stratford hall, seat of the Westmoreland Lees, restored. American home. 22:15-17. Sept. 1939. illus.

2386 HOPPIN, CHARLES ARTHUR. Origin of Wakefield, Washington's birthplace. Tyler's quarterly historical and genealogical magazine. 8:217-41. Apr. 1927.

2387 ———. Seven old houses on the Wakefield estate. Tyler's quarterly historical and genealogical magazine. 11:85-93. Oct. 1929.

2388 ———. The simple glory that was Wakefield to be restored. Tyler's quarterly historical and genealogical magazine. 9:219-24. Apr. 1928.

2389 KENNEDY, MRS. S. D. Stratford, Westmoreland county, Virginia. Journal of American history. 17:333-36. 1923.

2390 PERRY, ARMSTRONG. Stratford, Va., birthplace of the Lees. D. A. R. magazine. 59:27-30, 64-69. Jan. 1925.

2391 (Stratford hall. Contemporary description.) Southern literary messenger. 6:800-803. Dec. 1840.

Williamsburg (see *James City County*)

York County (*see also* 2134, 2139)

2392 KENNEDY, WILL P. Restoring Yorktown shrines. D.A.R. magazine. 61: 799-809. Nov. 1927; 61:887-95. Dec. 1927.

2393 Restoration of a southern Colonial estate, York hall, the residence of Captain George P. Blow, Yorktown, Va. Architectural forum. 35:211-20. Dec. 1921. (1740–41.)

2394 TRUDELL, CLYDE F. Colonial Yorktown. Richmond, Va., Dietz press, 1938. 206p. illus.
"Being a brief historie of the place; together with something of its houses and publick buildings. With manie illustrations in pen and ink by ye author."

2395 UNITED STATES. NATIONAL PARK SERVICE. Colonial national historical park. Washington, D. C., United States Government printing office, 1940. 16p. illus.

Jamestown excavations and Yorktown houses.

2396 York hall restored. Country life in America. 40:52-55. Oct. 1921. illus.

Also known as the Nelson house.

Yorktown (see *York County*)

WEST VIRGINIA

2397 CARPENTER, CHARLES. Story of historic Harewood. National republic. 21:15-16. Aug. 1933. illus.

Near Charles Town, *ca*.1770.

2398 FEDERAL WRITERS' PROJECT. Historic Romney, 1762-1937. Romney, W. Va., 1937. 67p. illus.

2399 ———. West Virginia: a guide to the mountain state. N. Y., Oxford university press, 1941. 559. illus.

2400 HUNTER, KATHERINE M., AND HUNTER, BERNARD C. Some notes on Berkeley Springs, West Virginia. William and Mary historical quarterly. ser. 2, 16:347-51. July 1936. illus.

Ca.1780 and classic revival.

2401 THURSTON, MYNNR. The Washingtons and their Colonial homes in West Virginia. Charles Town, W. Va., 1936. 29p. illus.

2402 (West Virginia.) Some West Virginia material included in Virginia entries, e.g., 1656.

2403 West Virginia number. Southern magazine. v. 2, no. 9. 1936. 48p.

NORTH CENTRAL STATES

(Illinois, Indiana, Iowa, Kansas, Michigan, Minnesota, Missouri, Nebraska, Ohio, Wisconsin)

GENERAL REFERENCES *(see also* 1649)

2404 BUSHNELL, DAVID I. Villages of the Algonquian, Siouan, and Caddoan tribes west of the Mississippi. Washington, D. C., Government printing office, 1922. 211p. illus.
United States. Bureau of American Ethnology, Bulletin 77.

2405 COLE, HARRY ELLSWORTH. Stage coach and tavern tales of the Old Northwest. Cleveland, Ohio, Arthur H. Clark Co., 1930. 376p. illus.

2406 HAVINGHURST, WALTER. Upper Mississippi. N. Y., Farrar and Rinehart, 1937. 258p. illus.
Rivers of America series.

2407 THWAITES, REUBEN GOLD. Early western travels, 1748-1846. Cleveland, Ohio, Arthur H. Clark Co. 32v. 1904-1907.
Reprints from early travel books, indexed. Many houses mentioned.

ILLINOIS
GENERAL REFERENCES

2408 COLBY, LYDIA. An elastic sod house. Illinois state historical society. Journal. 18:1035-38. Jan. 1926.
1855.

2409 CUSTER, MILO (ed.). Some pioneer buildings of central Illinois. Bloomington, Ill., Central Illinois historical society. Publication no. 2. 1924. 21 illus.

2410 ELDER, PAUL WILSON. Early taverns and inns in Illinois. Illinois state historical society. Journal. 20:578-83. Jan. 1928.

2411 FEDERAL WRITERS' PROJECT. Illinois: descriptive and historical guide. Chicago, A. C. McClurg and Co., 1939. 687p. illus.

2412 HURIE, ANNA KATHRYN. Early mills in Illinois. Illinois state historical society. Journal. 22:593-600. Jan. 1930. illus.

2413 O'DONNELL, THOMAS EDWARD. Outline of the history of architecture in Illinois. Illinois state historical society. Transactions. 32nd. meeting. p. 124-43. 1931.

2414 ——. A proposed survey of the architectural development in Illinois. Illinois state historical society. Transactions. 38:75-79. 1926.

2415 ——. Recording the early architecture of Illinois in the historic American buildings survey. Illinois state historical society. Transactions. p.185-213. 1934.

2416 REED, EARL H. Historic American buildings survey; northern Illinois, 1716-1867. Chicago, 1934. 50 illus.
Another set of plates issued 1937.

2417 SCHNAPP, MARGARET KATHERINE. Historic churches in Illinois. Illinois state historical society. Journal. 21:525-33. Jan. 1929.

LOCATIONS

Albion

2418 O'DONNELL, THOMAS EDWARD. Albion, an early English settlement in southern Illinois. Western architect. 35:123-26. Oct. 1926. illus.
Ca.1820—ca.1860.

Cahokia

2419 BABB, MARGARET E. Mansion house of Cahokia and its builder—Nicholas Jarrot. Illinois historical society. Transactions, for the year 1924:78-93.

Cairo

2420 FEDERAL WRITERS' PROJECT. Cairo guide. Nappanee, Ind., E. V. publishing house, 1938. 62p. illus.

Chicago

2421 ANDREAS, ALFRED THEODORE. History of Chicago. Chicago, Ill., A. T. Andreas Co., 1884-86. 3v. illus.
See especially 1:504–506; 2:562–67; 3:62–74.

2422 CURREY, JOSIAH SEYMOUR. Story of old Fort Dearborn. Chicago, McClurg, 1912. 173p. illus.

2423 DRURY, JOHN. Old Chicago houses. Chicago, University of Chicago press, 1941. 518p. illus.

2424 FEDERAL WRITERS' PROJECT. Selected bibliography; Illinois, Chicago and its environs. Chicago, 1937. 58p.

2425 SPARKS, EDWIN E. The beginnings of Chicago. American architect. 81:101-104. Sept. 26, 1903.

2426 ——. The beginnings of Chicago. Western society of engineers. Journal. 1903. p. 357-72. illus.

2427 TALLMADGE, THOMAS EDDY. Architecture in old Chicago. Chicago, University of Chicago press, 1941. 218p. illus.

Coles County

2428 BALCH, ALFRED B. Pioneer log church, Coles county, Illinois. Illinois historical society. Journal. 13:85-86. Apr. 1921.

Evanston

2429 TALLMADGE, THOMAS E. Architectural history of a western town. American architect. 115:443-51. Mar. 26, 1919. illus.
Covers *ca.*1840–1919.

Galena

2430 BALE, FLORENCE GRATIOT. The Branton tavern. Illinois state historical society. Journal. 29:151-60. 1936.
Mid-nineteenth century, near Galena.

2431 FEDERAL WRITERS' PROJECT. Galena guide. Chicago (?), 1937. 79p. illus.

Galesburg

2432 Log city days. Galesburg, Ill., Knox college centenary publications, 1937. 79p. illus.

Metamora

2433 IRVING, J. C., AND OTHERS. Old court house at Metamora presented to the state of Illinois. Illinois historical society. Journal. 14:365-81. Oct. 1921, Jan. 1922.

Nauvoo

2434 FEDERAL WRITERS' PROJECT. Nauvoo guide. Chicago, A. C. McClurg and Co., 1939. 49p. illus.

New Salem

2435 BOOTON, JOSEPH F. Record of the restoration of New Salem: New Salem state park near Petersburg, Illinois, 1932-1933. State of Illinois, Department of public works and buildings. 88p. illus.

2436 POND, FERN NANCE. New Salem memorial. D. A. R. magazine. 69:101-102. 1935.

Princeton

2437 FEDERAL WRITERS' PROJECT. Princeton guide. Princeton, Ill., Republican printing Co., 1939. 48p. illus.

Sangamon County

2438 SALE, MRS. ANTHONY W. Old Mills of Sangamon county. Illinois state historical society. Journal. 18:1056-58. Jan. 1926.

Springfield

2439 ILLINOIS. GENERAL ASSEMBLY. Information on Illinois State house. In five parts. 1:347-75. 1869; 1:731-66. 1871; 1:407-427. 1873; 1:479-500. 1875: 2:Doc.F, 1879.

2440 ILLINOIS. SECRETARY OF STATE. Guide to Illinois Capitol and other buildings at Springfield. Springfield, Ill., 1938. illus.

Virginia

2441 MARTIN, LORENE. Allendale, an old adobe house. Illinois historical society. Journal. 28:110-14. July 1935.
1852, near Virginia.

INDIANA

GENERAL REFERENCES

2442 BURNS, LEE. Early architects and builders of Indiana. Indiana historical society. Publications. 11:179-215. 1935. illus.
Contains a number of biographies and documentary information.

2443 COTTMAN, GEORGE STREIBY. Centennial history and handbook of Indiana. Indianapolis, Max R. Hyman, 1915. 464p. illus.
Illustrations of many public buildings, p.203–464.

2444 DUNN, JACOB PIATT. Indiana and Indianans, a history of aboriginal and territorial Indiana and the century of statehood. Chicago and N. Y., American historical society, 1919. 5v. illus.
Illustrates early statehouses. Old Capitol, 1832-36, Ithiel Town, architect.

2445 FEDERAL WRITERS' PROJECT. Indiana: a guide to the Hoosier state. N. Y., Oxford university press, 1941. 548p. illus.

2446 FRITSCH, WILLIAM AUGUST. German settlers and German settlements in Indiana. Evansville, Ind., 1915. 61p. illus.

2447 Homes along the Ohio. House and garden. 78:55. Sept. 1940. illus.
Lanier house, 1844, and Shrewsbury house, Madison; Starks house, Aurora.

2448 INDIANA FEDERATION OF ART CLUBS. Art guide to Indiana. Extension division, Indiana university. Bulletin. v. 16, no. 8. Bloomington, Ind. Apr. 1931. 184p. illus.

2449 Indiana gazetteer, or topographical dictionary of the state of Indiana. Indianapolis, E. Chamberlain, 1849. 440p. illus.
Contemporary illustrations of buildings.

2450 KNOX, JULIA LECLERC. Pioneer homesteads. Indiana magazine of history. 18:371-80. Dec. 1922.

2451 LOUCKS, KENNETH. John Elder: pioneer builder. Indiana magazine of history. 26:25-33. Mar. 1930.

2452 RIFNER, BEN. Early architecture of Indiana. 1942. Master's thesis, the Ohio State University.

2453 SIMPICH, FREDERICK. Indiana journey. National geographic magazine. 70:267-320. Sept. 1936. illus.

LOCATIONS

Corydon

2454 CLELAND, ETHEL. New facts about the Corydon State house. Indiana magazine of history. 9:14-19. Mar. 1913.
(1811–12.)

2455 COLEMAN, CHRISTOPHER B. Restoration of the Capitol at Corydon. Indiana magazine of history. 30:255-58. Sept. 1934.

2456 COTTMAN, GEORGE STREIBY. Corydon State house: Hoosier shrine. . . . Department of conservation, State of Indiana, Division of lands and waters. Publication no. 94. 1930. 53p. illus.

2457 Indiana's first State Capitol at Corydon. Indiana historical bulletin. 7:6-7. Oct. 1929.
Account of the restoration of the Capitol. 1825.

2458. MOORES, CHARLES. Old Corydon. Indiana magazine of history. 13:20-41. Mar. 1917.

Crawfordsville

2459 KNOX, JULIA LeCLERC. Some interesting Crawfordsville people and their homes. Indiana magazine of history. 22:285-96. Sept. 1926.

Franklin County

2460 BOSSERT, MICHAEL. Early schools of Franklin county. Indiana magazine of history. 26:218-36. Sept. 1930.

Goshen

2461 BARTHOLOMEW, H. S. K. Old landmarks of Goshen. Indiana magazine of history. 29:198-202. Sept. 1933.

Indianapolis

2462 BURNS, LEE. Indianapolis: the old town and the new, Indianapolis, Ind., Cornelius Printing Co., 1923. 44p. illus.

2463 LOUCKS, KENNETH. Hoosier hostelry a hundred years ago. Indiana historical bulletin. 8:313-15. 1931.
Union inn, 1824–36.

Jackson County

2464 BURGE, WARREN. An historic cabin. Knightstown, Ind., The Thornwood printery, 1914. 31p. illus.
1807. Claimed to be oldest log cabin in Indiana.

Madison (see also 2447)

2465 COTTMAN, GEORGE STREIBY. James F. D. Lanier home. Department of conservation, State of Indiana, Division of Lands and waters. Publication no. 64, 1927. 43p. illus.
1843. Francis Costigan, architect.

2466 ———. James F. D. Lanier house, an Indiana memorial, Madison, Indiana. Department of conservation. Publication no. 59, 1927. 11p.

2467 GARBER, BLANCHE GOODE. Lanier family and Lanier home. Indiana magazine of history. 22:277-84. Sept. 1926.

2468 KNOX, JULIA LeCLERC. Old Sullivan home, Madison, Indiana. Indiana magazine of history. 31:109-111. June 1935.
1816.

2469 ———. Quaint little old Indiana city. Indiana magazine of history. 28: 88-95. June 1932.

Michigan Hill (near *Madison*)

2470 KNOX, JULIA LeCLERC. Cravenhurst. Indiana magazine of history. 29:339-42. Dec. 1933.

New Albany

2471 KNOX, JULIA LeCLERC. Old Phineas Kent mansion of New Albany. Indiana historical bulletin. 9:405-407. Apr. 1932.
*Ca.*1852.

New Harmony

2472 FREYTAGOET, NORA C. Historic New Harmony: a guide. Mount Vernon, Ind., The Western star, 1923. 66p. illus.
First edition, 1914.

2473 KNOX, JULIA LeCLERC. Unique little town of New Harmony. Indiana magazine of history. 32:52-58. Mar. 1935.

2474 LOCKRIDGE, ROSS F. Old Fauntleroy home. New Harmony, New Harmony memorial commission, 1939. 219p. illus.
(1815.)

Paoli

2475 NEWCOMB, REXFORD. Greek revival courthouse in southern Indiana. Architectural forum. 48:177-80. Feb. 1928. illus.
(1850.)

Rush County

2476 DOGGETT, DENZIL. Water-powered mills of Flat Rock River. Indiana magazine of history. 32:319-59. 1936.
*Ca.*1820.

Salem

2477 HOBBS, MARTHA SAYLES. Historic homes of Salem, Indiana and vicinity. Indiana magazine of history. 21:33-59. Mar. 1925.
1814-60.

Switzerland County

2478 DUFOUR, PERRET. Swiss settlement of Switzerland county, Indiana. Indianapolis, Indiana historical society, 1925. 446p.

2479 Knox, Julia LeClerc. Two pioneer homesteads of Switzerland county. Indiana magazine of history. 28:247-50. Dec. 1932.
John David Dufour house and David Blunk house.

Vevay

2480 Knox, Julia LeClerc. Century old Wright home. Indiana magazine of history. 32:380-83. 1936.

2481 ———. Old Jean Daniel Morerod home, Vevay, Ind. Indiana magazine of history. 27:125-28. June 1931.

2482 ———. Some interesting pioneer homesteads in and around Vevay. Vevay, Ind., n.d. 22p. illus.

Vincennes

2483 Burns, Lee. Life in old Vincennes. Indiana historical society. Publications. 8:437-60.
Description and history.

2484 Gavisk, Francis H. Old Vincennes cathedral. Vincennes, Indiana. 7p. 1934.
George Rogers Clark national memorial leaflets, no. 3. (1825)

2485 O'Donnell, Thomas Edward. Historic cathedral and library, Vincennes, Ind. Architectural forum. 45:81-84. Aug. 1926. illus.

2486 Van Natter, Francis Marion. Cathedral of old Vincennes. National republic. 20:6-7. Apr. 1933.

2487 Vincennes Fortnightly Club. Historic Vincennes: tourists' guide. 7th ed. Vincennes, Ind., 1939. 40p. illus.

IOWA

General References

2488 Dubell, Susan I. Pioneer home. Palimpsest. 12:445-54. Dec. 1931.
General discusion of pioneer log construction.

2489 Duffield, George C. An Iowa settler's homestead. Annals of Iowa. ser. 3. 6:206-215. Oct. 1903.

2490 Federal Writers' Project. Iowa: guide to the Hawkeye state. N. Y., Viking press, 1938. 583p. illus.

2491 Hoffman, M. M. John Francis Rague (1799-1877) pioneer architect of Iowa. Annals of Iowa. 3rd ser. 19:444-48. 1934.

2492 Sharp, Mildred J. Early cabins in Iowa. Palimpsest. 2:16-29. Jan. 1921.
Discussion of pioneer log structures.

Locations

Bloomington

2493 MAHAN, BRUCE E. Three early taverns. Palimpsest. 3:250-60. Aug. 1922.

Burlington

2494 FEDERAL WRITERS' PROJECT. Guide to Burlington, Iowa. Burlington, Ia., Acres-Blackmar Co., 1938. 72p. illus.

Cedar Rapids

2495 FEDERAL WRITERS' PROJECT. Guide to Cedar Rapids and northeast Iowa. Cedar Rapids, Ia., Laurance press, 1937. 79p. illus.

Des Moines

2496 SWISHER, JACOB A. Capitols at Des Moines. Iowa journal of history and politics. 39:52-87. Jan. 1941. illus.
Covers 1857 building and present building, 1888.

Dubuque

2497 FEDERAL WRITERS' PROJECT. Guide to Dubuque. Dubuque, Ia., Hoermann press, 1937. 32p. illus.

2498 GALLAHER, RUTH A. First church in Iowa. Palimpsest. 7:1-10. Jan. 1926. illus.
Log church, 1834.

Estherville

2499 FEDERAL WRITERS' PROJECT. Guide to Estherville, Iowa, Emmet county and Iowa great lakes region. Estherville, Iowa, Estherville enterprise print, 1939. 36p. illus.

Iowa City

2500 Old Capitol. Iowa city, Ia., State university of Iowa, 1928. 16p.

2501 SHAMBAUGH, BENJAMIN FRANKLIN. Founding of Iowa City. Palimpsest. 20:137-76. May 1939. illus.
Contains an account of the building of the Iowa state capitol (cornerstone, 1840) and its architect, John Francis Rague.

2502 ———. The old stone Capitol remembers. Iowa city. State historical society of Iowa, 1939. 435p.
Material on Father Mazzuchelli, John Francis Rague, and the Capitol.

McGregor

2503 FEDERAL WRITERS' PROJECT. Guide to McGregor. McGregor, Ia., J. F. Widman and Sons Co., 1938. 24p. illus.

KANSAS

2504 CALDWELL, MARTHA B. Annals of Shawnee Methodist mission and Indian manual labor school. Topeka, Kansas, Kansas state historical society, 1939. 120p. illus.

2505 DICK, EVERETT NEWTON. Sod-house frontier, 1854-1890; a social history of the northern plains from the creation of Kansas and Nebraska to the admission of the Dakotas. N. Y., D. Appleton-Century Co., 1937. 550p. illus.

2506 DOYLE, W. E. Indian forts and dwellings. Annual report of the board of regents of the Smithsonian Institution for the year 1876. p. 460-65. Wichita.

2507 FEDERAL WRITERS' PROJECT. Kansas: guide to the Sunflower state. N. Y., Viking press, 1939. 538p. illus.

2508 ISELY, BLISS. Grass wigwam at Wichita. Kansas historical quarterly. 2:66-71. 1933.

2509 KANSAS STATE HISTORICAL SOCIETY. Old Pawnee Capitol, an account of the first Capitol building of Kansas, the town of Pawnee, initial sessions of the first territorial legislature, destruction of the town of Pawnee, ruins of the Capitol building. Topeka, Kan., Kansas state printing plant, 1928. 38p. illus.

2510 ROSS, MRS. EDITH CONNELLEY. Old Shawnee mission. Topeka, Kan., Kansas state printing plant, 1928. 28p. illus.

2511 SHERLOCK, CHELSA CLELLA. Old John Brown's cabin, Osawatomee, Kansas. Better homes and gardens. Dec. 1926. illus.

2512 TAFT, ROBERT. Photographic history of early Kansas. Kansas historical quarterly. 3:3-14. Feb. 1934.
Photographs by Alexander Gardener of buildings standing in Kansas in 1868.

2513 WHITTEMORE, MARGARET. Sketchbook of Kansas landmarks. Topeka, Kan., College press, 1936. 125p. illus.
Second edition 1937.

MICHIGAN

2514 American home pilgrimages—part 5—Michigan. American home. 20:29-30, 101-103. Oct. 1938. illus.

2515 BURTON, CLARENCE MONROE. Detroit in earlier days; a few notes on some of the old buildings in the city. Detroit, Mich., Burton abstract and title Co. 36p. illus.

2516 CLARK, E. M. Restoration of old Fort Holmes on Mackinac Island. Michigan historical magazine. 20:295-300. 1936.

2517 FEDERAL WRITERS' PROJECT. Michigan: a guide to the Wolverine state. N. Y., Oxford university press, 1941. 682p. illus.

2518 HAIGH, HENRY A. Henry Ford's typical American village at Dearborn. Michigan historical magazine. 13:506-543. 1929.

2519 ———. Old Ten Eyck tavern. Michigan historical magazine. 15:441-45. 1931.
Detroit.

2520 KIMBALL, SIDNEY FISKE. Old houses of Michigan. Architectural record. 52:227-40. Sept. 1922. illus.

2521 (LORCH, EMIL.) Report of the committee on Michigan architecture of the Michigan society of architects. American society of architectural historians. Journal. 2:34-35. Apr. 1942.

2522 MITCHELL, EDWIN VALENTINE. American village. N. Y., Stackpole Sons, 1938. 261p. illus.
Henry Ford's Greenfield Village at Dearborn.

2523 Old Fort Michilimackinac. Ann Arbor, Mich., University of Michigan press, 1938. 12p. illus.

2524 POOLE, S. ALICIA. Historic community house. Michigan historical magazine. 15:438-40. 1931.
John Jacob Astor house, Mackinac Island.

2525 QUAIFE, M. M. Mansion of St. Martin. Burton historical collections. 3:33-48. Jan. 1925.
Detroit, late eighteenth century.

2526 STRATTON, WILLIAM B. The growth of Detroit. Western architect. 24:126-28. Oct. 1916. illus.
Nineteenth century.

2527 VAN FLEET, JAMES ALVIN. Old and New Mackinac. Ann Arbor, Mich., Courier steam printing-house, 1870. 176p. illus.

MINNESOTA

2528 BURRIS, EVADENE A. Building the frontier home. Minnesota history. 15:43-55. Mar. 1924. illus.

2529 Chippewa mission. St. Paul, Minn., Minnesota historical records survey project, 1941. 42p. illus.
Near Watson. Report of the Chippewa mission archaeological investigation. Mimeographed.

2530 DEAN, WILLIAM BLAKE. History of the Capitol buildings of Minnesota. Minnesota historical society. Collections. 12:1-42. Dec. 1908. illus.
(First Capitol 1853.)

2531 Early historic structures: Faribault house; Afton octagonal house. Northwest architect. 4:4-5. Jan.-Feb. 1940.
(Faribault house, 1837, St. Paul. Afton octagonal house, 1860's.)

2532 FEDERAL WRITER'S PROJECT. Minnesota: a state guide. N. Y., Viking press, 1938. 523p. illus.

2533 LEACH, MRS. PAUL J. Haunted windmill. Minnesota history. 12:65-67. 1931.
Faribault county.

2534 MARIN, WILLIAM A. Sod houses and prairie schooners. Minnesota history. 12:135-56. June 1931.
Describes the typical sod house.

MISSOURI

GENERAL REFERENCES

2535, 2536 ANKENEY, J. S. Century of Missouri art. Columbia, Mo., 1922. 20p. illus.
Reprinted from the *Missouri Historical Review.* 16:481–501. July 1922. illus.

2537 BRYAN, JOHN ALBURY (ed.). Missouri's contribution to American architecture. St. Louis, Mo., St. Louis architectural club, 1928. 286p. illus.

2538 FEDERAL WRITERS' PROJECT. Missouri: a guide to the "Show me" state. N. Y., Duell, Sloan and Pearce, 1941. 611p. illus.

2539 ———. The Oregon trail; the Missouri River to the Pacific Ocean. N. Y., Hastings house, ca.1939. 244p. illus.

2540 PETERSON, CHARLES E. French houses of the Illinois country. Missouriana. 10:4-7. Aug.-Sept. 1938. illus.

2541 ROACH, CORNELIUS. Missouri's eleven state Capitols. Missouri historical review. 7:224-31. July 1913.
1820–1912.

2542 STEVENS, WALTER B. The Missouri tavern. Missouri historical review. 15:241-76. Jan. 1921. illus.
The tavern as an institution. *Ca.*1820—*ca.*1860.

2543 VAN RAVENSWAAY, CHARLES. Boon's Lick country. 1940. 21p. illus.
Historical and architectural guide for Cooper, Howard, and Saline counties. Mimeographed.

2544 VILES, JONAS. The capitals and Capitols of Missouri. Missouri historical review. 13:135-56, 232-50. Jan.-Apr. 1919.

2545 WILLIAMS, WALTER. The tavern on the Boon's Lick road. Overland. 2nd ser. 58:417-20. Nov. 1911.

LOCATIONS

Arrow Rock (Saline County)

2546 GRAVES, MRS. W. W. Old tavern at Arrow Rock. Missouri historical review. 19:256-61. Jan. 1925.

2547 GUITAR, SARAH. Arrow Rock tavern. Missouri historical review. 20:499-503. July 1926.
1830.

2548 TODHUNTER, MRS. RYLAND. Historic Arrow Rock tavern. D. A. R. magazine. 59:477-82. Aug. 1925.

Booneville

2549 Brief history of the Thespian hall, Booneville, Missouri. Thespian hall preservation committee, 1937. 16p. illus.
(1855-57.)

Fulton

2550 PAYNE, DAVID. Missouri family album; story of the James Robnett house near Fulton. House and garden. 79:48-49. Apr. 1941.
1858.

Herculaneum

2551 SHOEMAKER, FLOYD C. Herculaneum shot tower. Missouri historical review. 20:214-16. Jan. 1926.
1809.

Kansas City

2552 The United States Trading house or factory at Fort Osage, 1808-1827, a documentary history. Commission for the restoration of Ft. Osage, 1941. 16p. illus.
Mimeographed.

Ste. Genevieve

2553 CHILDS, M. W. Two centuries look down upon this home; Valle house, Ste. Genevieve, Missouri. Better homes and gardens. 12:34-35. Mar. 1934. illus.

2554 PETERSON, CHARLES E. Early Ste. Genevieve, Missouri and its architecture. Missouri historical review. 35:207-232. Jan. 1941. illus.

2555 ———. Guide to Ste. Genevieve with notes on its architecture. St. Louis, 1940. 21p. illus.

St. Louis

2556 The Berthold mansion. Missouri historical society. Collections. 4:290-94. 1914. illus.

2557 BRYAN, JOHN ALBURY. Outstanding architects in St. Louis between 1804 and 1904. Missouri historical review. 28:83-90. Jan. 1934.
Biographical sketches of nineteen architects with partial list of their works.

2558 DRUMM, STELLA M., AND VAN RAVENSWAAY, CHARLES. The old Court house. Missouri historical society. Glimpses of the past. v. 7, nos. 1-6. Jan.-June 1940.
(1839–62.)

2559 LEBAUME, LOUIS. Early architecture of St. Louis, 1764-1900. American architect. 133:713-18. June 5, 1928. illus.

2560 PETERSON, CHARLES E. The museum of American architecture: a progress report. American society of architectural historians. Journal. v. 1, no. 3-4. p. 24-26. July-Oct. 1941.
The Jefferson national expansion memorial on the St. Louis riverfront. *See* 59.

2561 ———. Old St. Louis riverfront. St. Louis public library. Bulletin. Apr. 11-30, 1938. 19p. illus.
Contains a short bibliography.

2562 POWELL, MARY. Public art: sculpture, mural decorations, stained glass and noteworthy buildings in St. Louis. St. Louis public library. Bulletin. Jan. 1921. 32p.

2563 St. Louis—new and old. Western architect. 23:49-50. June 1916. illus.

Washington

2564 McCLURE, MRS. ELEANOR B. Early history of Washington, Missouri. Washington, Mo., Washington Missourian, 1939. 48p. illus.

NEBRASKA

2565 BARNES, CASE G. Sod house (1862-97). Lincoln, Nebraska, 1930. 287p. illus.

2566 DORSEY, JAMES O. Omaha dwellings, furniture and implements. U. S. Bureau of American ethnology. 13th annual report, 1891-92. Washington, 1896. P.263-88. illus.
Aboriginal.

2567 FEDERAL WRITERS' PROJECT. Nebraska, a guide to the Cornhusker state. N. Y., Viking press, 1939. 424p. illus.

Ohio

GENERAL REFERENCES

2568 American home pilgrimages—Ohio. American home. Part 1, the Lakeshore. 19:25-36. Jan. 1938; part 2, Marietta, Zanesville, Columbus. 19:41-44. Feb. 1938; part 3, Scioto Valley and Cincinnati. 19:43-45. Mar. 1938. illus.

2569 BAREIS, GEORGE F. Pioneer cabin in the history of Madison township. Ohio state archaeological and historical society. Quarterly. 11:259-61.

2570 CLARK, EDNA MARIA. Ohio art and artists. Richmond, Va., Garrett and Massie, 1932. illus.
Chapters 3 and 14 briefly cover Ohio architecture.

2571 Famous houses of Ohio. D. A. R. magazine. 70:1113-15. 1936.

2572 FEDERAL WRITERS' PROJECT. The Ohio guide. N. Y., Oxford university press, 1940. 634p. illus.

2573 ——. Ohio's capitals. Columbus, O., Secretary of state, 1937. 12p. illus.

2574 FRARY, IHNA THAYER. Early domestic architecture in Ohio. American architect. 123:307-312. Apr. 11, 1923. illus.

2575 ——. Early homes of Ohio. Richmond, Va., Garrett and Massie, 1936. 336p. illus.

2576 ——. Old wall stencils of Ohio. Antiques. 38:169. 1940. illus.

2577 HATCHER, HARLAN HENTHORNE. The Buckeye country; a pageant of Ohio. N. Y., H. C. Kinsey and Co., 1940. 325p. illus.
Chapters on Ohio architecture.

2578 KING, I. F. Typical log cabin. Ohio state archaeological and historical society. Quarterly. 10:175-77.

2579 KNITTLE, RHEA MANSFIELD. Early Ohio taverns: tavern-sign, barge, banner, chair and settee painters. Ashland, O., Privately printed, 1937. 39p.

2580 O'DONNELL, THOMAS EDWARD. Influence of the carpenters' handbooks in the early architecture of Ohio. Architecture. 55:169-71. Mar. 1927. illus.

2581 ——. Mantel designs in the early architecture of Ohio. Architecture. 56:11-14. July 1927. illus.

2582 ——. Ornamental ironwork; early American examples in Ohio show New England influence. House beautiful. 64:694-95, 730. Dec. 1928. illus.

2583 ——. Ornamental ironwork in early Ohio architecture. Architecture. 54:299-302. Oct. 1926. illus.

2584 ———. Some Greek revival doorways in Ohio. Architectural forum. 49: 649-52. Nov. 1928. illus.

2585 OVERMAN, WILLIAM D. Index to materials for the study of Ohio history. Columbus, O., Ohio state archaeological and historical society. Quarterly. 44:138-55. 1935.

2586 ———. Select list of materials on Ohio history in serial publications. Ohio state archaeological and historical society. Quarterly. 50:137-70. 1941.

2587 ROBBINS, CARLE. Concerning the improver and front porch builder. Cleveland, O., The Bystander. Dec. 8, 1928. p.8-11. illus.
Early Ohio houses, with and without porches.

2588 ———. On a neglected heritage. Cleveland, O., The Bystander. Nov. 24, 1928. p.21-23. illus.
Early doorways.

2589 ROOS, FRANK JOHN, JR. An investigation of the sources of early architectural design in Ohio. 1938. illus.
Condensed in *Abstracts of Doctoral Dissertations*, no. 26. Columbus, Ohio, The Ohio State University Press, 1938.

2590 ———. Reflections of New England's architecture in Ohio. Old time New England. 28:40-48. Oct. 1937. illus.

2591 WEINY, DANIEL W. Early Colonial architecture of the Ohio Valley. Architecture. 41:pl.53. May 1920; 43:pl.65. May 1921; 45:pl.94. June 1922; 47:pl.95. June 1923; 51:pl.39, 40. Mar. 1925. illus. only.

LOCATIONS

Brecksville
2592 Master detail series: historic American buildings survey: the Congregational church, Brecksville, Cuyahoga county, Ohio. Architectural forum. 64: 187-88. Mar. 1936. illus.
(1844.)

Chillicothe
2593 FEDERAL WRITERS' PROJECT. Chillicothe, Ohio's first Capital. Chillicothe, Ohio, Chillicothe civic association, 1941. 32p. illus.

2594 ———. Chillicothe and Ross county. Columbus, O., F. J. Heer Printing Co., *ca.*1938. 91p. illus.

2595 O'DONNELL, THOMAS EDWARD. The Greek revival in Chillicothe—Ohio's old Capital city. Architecture. 52:355-60. Oct. 1925. illus.

Cincinnati
2596 FEDERAL WRITERS' PROJECT. They built a city; 150 years of industrial Cincinnati. Cincinnati, O., Cincinnati Post, 1938. 402p. illus.

2597 KIMBALL, SIDNEY FISKE. Masterpieces of early American art—part 1—a notable old house in Cincinnati. Art and archaeology. 8:297. Sept.-Oct. 1919. illus.
   The Taft house, ca.1820.

2598 ROOS, FRANK JOHN, JR. Cincinnati's Taft house. American magazine of art. 29:440-45. July 1936. illus.

2599 SCHUYLER, MONTGOMERY. The building of Cincinnati. Architectural record. 23:337-66. May 1908. illus.

2600 SIPLE, WALTER H. Taft museum. Cincinnati art museum. Bulletin. 14: 1-21. Jan. 1933. illus.

Columbus

2601 Capitol, Columbus, Ohio. American architect. 46:26-27. Oct. 1894. illus.

2602 O'DONNELL, THOMAS EDWARD. Greek revival Capitol at Columbus, Ohio. Architectural forum. 42:5-8. Jan. 1925.
   (1839–61. Henry Walter and others, architects.)

Findlay

2603 FEDERAL WRITERS' PROJECT. Findlay and Hancock county Centennial, 1937. Findlay, O., 1937. 52p. illus.

Fremont

2604 O'DONNELL, THOMAS EDWARD. Old Greek revival courthouse, Fremont, Ohio. Architectural forum. 45:221-24. Oct. 1926. illus.
   Ca.1840.

Granville

2605 SPENCER, EMA. New England town in Ohio. Ohio magazine. 1:215-24. Sept. 1906.
   Classic revival.

Hudson

2606 FRARY, IHNA THAYER. Ohio town of New England traditions. The home of the "Yale of the West." House beautiful. 52:36-37, 75-77. July 1922. illus.
   Classic revival.

2607 ———. Old Western Reserve college. Architectural record. 44:575-76. Dec. 1918. illus.

2608 O'DONNELL, THOMAS EDWARD. Early architecture in the state of Ohio: Hudson, a town of New England traditions. Western architect. 38: 138-40. Aug. 1929. illus.

Kirtland

2609 Master detail series: historic American buildings: Kirtland temple. Architectural forum. 64:177-83. Mar. 1936. illus.
   1833–36.

Lima

2610 FEDERAL WRITERS' PROJECT. Guide to Lima and Allen county. Lima, O., 1938. 64p. illus.

Manchester

2611 CARLISLE, MORTEN. Buckeye station, built by Nathaniel Massie in 1797. Ohio archaeological and historical society. Quarterly. 40:1-22. 1931.

Marietta

2612 BUELL, ROWENA. House of seven porches, Allen-Buell house, Marietta. Your garden and home. Jan. 1933. p.16.
1836.

2613 First Congregational church of Marietta, Ohio. Architectural record. 20: 116-20. Aug. 1906. illus.
1807.

2614 HAWES, E. M. Ohio's Campus Martius. Art and archaeology. 33:309-315. Nov. 1932. illus.
1788.

2615 HILDRETH, SAMUEL P. The old Court house and jail of Washington county, Ohio. American pioneer. 1:163-64. May 1842. illus.
1798. Griffin Green, architect.

2616 NYE, MINNA TUPPER. Campus Martius, Marietta, Ohio. American monthly magazine. 39:5-7. July 1911.

2617 O'DONNELL, THOMAS EDWARD. Early architecture of Marietta, the oldest city in Ohio. Architecture. 51:1-4. Jan. 1925. illus.

2618 SCHNEIDER, NORRIS FRANZ. Campus Martius state memorial museum. Marietta, Ohio, MacDonald printing Co., 1932.
Covers 1787–95.

2619 (WATERS, HARRIET). Old Marietta. Privately printed, 1934.
Photographs from an album owned by Miss Harriet Waters, taken between 1870 and 1890.

Milan

2620 O'DONNELL, THOMAS EDWARD. Early architecture of the state of Ohio: early houses in Milan. Western architect. 36:159-63. Oct. 1927. illus.
Ca.1830–1840.

Mount Vernon

2621 IZANT, GRACE GOULDER. Mount Vernon, Ohio—a study in architecture. Your garden and home. p.14, 22, 28. Apr. 1934. illus.

Newark

2622 WEINY, DANIEL W. Colonial architecture of Ohio: the Buckingham residence, Newark, Ohio. Architecture. v. 51, pl.39, 40. Mar. 1925. illus.
1842–43.

Schoenbrunn (near *New Philadelphia*)

2623 Ohio's first free schoolhouse to be restored. School life. 11:143. Apr. 1926.
1772.

2624 WEINLAND, JOSEPH E. Romantic story of Schoenbrunn, the first town in Ohio, a brief account of the town, its destruction and finding of the lost town after 146 years. Dover, O., Seibert Printing Co., 1928. 36p. illus.

Springfield

2625 Old tavern to be preserved: Pennsylvania house, Springfield, Ohio. Hobbies. 45:43. Sept. 1940.

Tallmadge (near *Akron*)

2626 Master detail series: historic American buildings survey: church of the Congregational society, Tallmadge, Summit county, Ohio. Architectural forum. 64:184-86. Mar. 1936. illus.
1822.

Tuscarawas County

2627 FEDERAL WRITERS' PROJECT. Guide to Tuscarawas county. New Philadelphia, O., Tucker Printing Co., 1939. 119p. illus.

Unionville

2628 CANTERBURY, BEULAH. Tavern by the side of the road. American cookery. 38:267-73. 1933.
1810.

Vermilion

2629 O'DONNELL, THOMAS EDWARD. Early architecture of the state of Ohio, part 4. Joseph Swift house, an example of Greek revival architecture. Western architect. 33:109-113. Oct. 1924. illus.
1840.

2630 ———. Early architecture of the state of Ohio. The Joseph Swift house, near Vermilion, Ohio. Western architect. 38:40-44. Mar. 1929. illus.

Warren

2631 FEDERAL WRITERS' PROJECT. Warren and Trumbull county. Warren(?), Ohio, 1938. 60p. illus.

Western Reserve (*see also* towns)

2632 CHERRY, MARJORIE LOOMIS. Blockhouses and military posts of the Firelands. Shippensburg, Pa. 94p. 1934.

2633 FRARY, IHNA THAYER. Group of early northern Ohio churches. American architect and the architectural review. 126:49-50. July 16, 1924. illus.

2634 ———. Two early Ohio churches. Architectural record. 56:286-88. Sept. 1924. illus.
Brief account of the Tallmadge Congregational church and the Claridon church.

2635 O'DONNELL, THOMAS EDWARD. Early architecture in the state of Ohio. Part I, the Western Reserve. Western architect. 31:112-15. Oct. 1922. illus.

Covers Carpenter house, near North Olmstead, and describes organization of Western Reserve.

2636 ———. Early architecture of the state of Ohio. Part 2, some old farmhouses of the Western Reserve. Western architect. 31:127-29. Nov. 1922. illus.

Covers Coe house, near North Olmstead, and Goodrich tavern, near Vermilion.

2637 ———. The early architecture in the state of Ohio. Part 3. Post-Colonial houses of the Western Reserve. Western architect. 32:103-105. Sept. 1923. illus.

Zanesville

2638 FEDERAL WRITERS' PROJECT. Zanesville and Muskingum county. Zanesville, O., 1937. 38p. illus.

WISCONSIN

2639 BARTON, A. O. Wisconsin's oldest courthouse. Wisconsin magazine of history. 2:332-34. Mar. 1919.

1859, Iowa County.

2640 BAUCHLE, MAY L. Wisconsin's rival houses. Wisconsin magazine. 2:14, 32 Nov. 1924.

Brisbois house, Prairie du Chien, oldest stone house (1815); Porlier house, Green Bay, oldest frame house (1780 and later).

2641, 2642 COLE, HARRY ELLSWORTH. Stage coach and tavern days in the Baraboo region. Baraboo, Wis., Baraboo news publishing Co., 1923. 72p. illus.

Also in: Wisconsin Academy of Sciences, Arts and Letters. *Transactions.* 22:1–8. 1926.

2643 FEDERAL WRITERS' PROJECT. Wisconsin: a guide to the Badger State. N. Y., Duell, Sloan and Pearce, 1941. 651p. illus.

2644 GUTH, ALEXANDER CARL. Early day architects in Milwaukee. Wisconsin magazine of history. 10:17-28. Sept. 1926.

Ca. 1848—*ca.* 1900.

2645 ———. Early day architects in Wisconsin. Wisconsin magazine of history. 18:141-45. Dec. 1934.

1830's–1850's. Greek revival.

2646 HARRIS, W. J. Greek revival in Wisconsin; Benjamin Church built Milwaukee's oldest house. House and garden. 78:59. Sept. 1940. illus.

2647 IVEY, ZIDA C. The famous octagon house at Watertown. Wisconsin magazine of history. 24:167-73. Dec. 1940. illus.

1853–56.

2648 JENKINS, PAUL B. A stove-wood house. Wisconsin magazine of history. 7:189-93. Dec. 1923. illus.
1848–49, near Williams Bay.

2649 KINGSLEY, I. T. Villa Louis, now known as Dousman municipal park, Prairie du Chien, Wisconsin. Country life in America. 72:35-37. Oct. 1937. illus.

2650 LARCHER, J. H. A. The taverns and stages of early Wisconsin. Wisconsin historical society. Proceedings. 62:117-67. 1915.

2651 Preservation of the old Indian agency house as an historical monument. Wisconsin archaeologist. n.s.10:77-79. Jan. 1931.
Portage (1832).

2652 TITUS, W. A. First concrete building in the United States, architect, Joseph Goodrich. Wisconsin magazine of history. 24:183-88. Dec. 1940. illus.
1844, Milton.

2653, 2654 ———. Helena shot tower. Wisconsin magazine of history. 11: 320-27. Apr. 1928.
(1831) Illustrated, *Wisconsin Magazine of History*. 8:68. Sept. 1924.

2655 ———. Three pioneer taverns. Wisconsin magazine of history. 17:179-86. 1933.
On the Sheboygan-Fond du Lac trail. Wade Tavern, Greenbush, 1850.

2656 TYLER, K. Captain John Winslow Cotton house, Green Bay, Wis. Hobbies. 45:44-45. July 1940.

ARCHITECTS

GENERAL REFERENCES

All titles including architects' names and locations are listed under locations. Cross references to these are always given here when the architects' names occur in the title. This list of architects obviously makes no pretension to completeness.

(Biographical sketches of American architects.) See standard biographical dictionaries: e.g., *Appleton's Cyclopaedia of American Biography; Dictionary of American Biography; National Cyclopaedia of American Biography*, indexed in *White's Conspectus of American Biography;* Thieme-Becker, *Allgemeines kunsterlexicon;* also such sources as *Proceedings of the American Institute of Architects* and 6. The *Dictionary of American Biography*, with articles by Talbot F. Hamlin, Fiske Kimball, and others, mentions the locations of numerous manuscript collections concerning the architects.

2657 EBERLEIN. HAROLD DONALDSON. Early American architects. Country life in America. 48:70-72. Oct. 1925. illus.
Brief survey, mentioning many men.

2658 HADDON, RAWSON W. First architectural society in America. Architectural record. 38:287-88. Aug. 1915.

2659 ROOS, FRANK J., JR. Concerning several American architectural leaders. Design. 37:3-5, 40. Dec. 1935. illus.

2660 RUSK, WILLIAM SENER. William Thornton, Benjamin H. Latrobe, Thomas U. Walter and the classical influence in their works. Baltimore, 1939. 77p. illus.
Doctoral dissertation at The Johns Hopkins University, 1933. Bibliography, including references to newspaper items and manuscript collections. Includes reprints of 2721, 2753, 2762.

2661 UPJOHN, H. Architect and client a century ago. Architectural record. 74: 377-82. Nov. 1933.

(Writings by American architects.) *See* 2773.

(*See also* 46, 255, 422, 942, 1523, 1524, 1541, 1721, 1755, 1760-92, 1848, 1948, 2442, 2451, 2557, 2644, 2709.)

ARCHITECTS

ALLIS, JOHN (b. 1642). Active Massachusetts. *See* 128, 159.

AUSTIN, HENRY (1804-1891). Active New Haven, Connecticut. *See* 2756 and *White's Conspectus of American Biography*.

BANNER, PETER (fl. 1794-1828). *See* 609, 655.

BARNETT, GEORGE I. (b. 1815). *See also* St. Louis, Missouri.

2662 BARNETT, TOM P. George I. Barnett, pioneer architect of the West. Western architect. 18:13-14, 23-24. Feb. 1912. illus.

BELCHER, SAMUEL (1779-1849). Active Connecticut. *See* 2756.

BENJAMIN, ASHER (1773-1845). *See also* 275, 584, 649, 894, 895, 1065, 2773.

2663 BACH, RICHARD FRANZ. Asher Benjamin revived. American architect. 112: 449-50. Dec. 19, 1917.

2664 Bible of classicism, the influence on today's decoration, of Asher Benjamin's *Builders' companion*. House and garden. 77:46-49. June 1940. illus.
Builders' Companion, 1827.

2665 EMBURY, AYMAR II. Asher Benjamin. N. Y., Architectural Book Publishing Co., 1917. 169p. illus.
Selected plates from five of the Benjamin handbooks.

2666 HADDON, RAWSON W. Mr. Embury's *Asher Benjamin*. Architectural record. 42:181-84. Aug. 1917.

2667 O'DONNELL, THOMAS EDWARD. Asher Benjamin. Architecture. 54:375-78. Dec. 1926. illus.

BLODGET, SAMUEL (1759-1814). *See* 1680 and Philadelphia, Pennsylvania.

BOGARDUS, JAMES (1800-1874). *See* 262, 280, 2773.

BRADY, JOSIAH (*ca.* 1760—*ca.* 1832). Active New York City. *See* 2756.

BROWN, JOSEPH (1733-1783). *See* 1041, 1045.

BRUNEL, SIR MARC ISAMBARD (1769-1849). Active New York City, *ca.* 1798. *See* 14, 267.

BUCKLAND, WILLIAM (1734-1774). *See* 90, 1959-67.

BULFINCH, CHARLES (1763-1844). *See also* 351, 447-51, 503, 578, 594, 599, 600, 604, 605, 608, 613, 621, 623, 628, 637, 759-61, 914, 1726, 1736, 1760-92, 1811.

2668 BULFINCH, ELLEN SUSAN. Life and letters of Charles Bulfinch. Boston, Houghton Mifflin Co., 1896. 323p. illus.

2669 Charles Bulfinch, architect. Brochure series of architectural illustration. 9:123-33. July 1903. illus.

2670 HOWELLS, JOHN MEAD. Charles Bulfinch, architect. American architect. 93:195-200. June 1908. illus.

2671 NEWCOMB, REXFORD. Charles Bulfinch, first American-born architect of distinction. Architect. 9:289-93. Dec. 1927. illus.

2672 PLACE, CHARLES A. Charles Bulfinch, architect and citizen. Boston, Houghton Mifflin Co., 1925. 294p. illus.

2673 ROTHSCHILD, LINCOLN. A triumphal arch by Charles Bulfinch. Old time New England. 29:161-62. Apr. 1939.

2674 SHANNON, MARTHA A. S. Architecture of Charles Bulfinch. American magazine of art. 16:431-37. Aug. 1925. illus.

2675 ———. Charles Bulfinch, the first American architect. Architecture. 52:431-36. Dec. 1925. illus.

2676 WILLARD, ASHTON R. Charles Bulfinch, the architect. New England magazine. 3:273-99. Nov. 1890. illus.

CANER, HENRY (1680-1731). *See 463.*

CARTER, ELIAS (1781-1864). *See 931.*

CHISLETT, JOHN (1800-1869). Active Pittsburgh, Pennsylvania. *See 1465.*

CLARK, EDWARD (b. 1824). Active Washington, D. C. See *White's Conspectus of American Biography.*

COSTIGAN, FRANCIS (1810-1865). *See 2465* and Louisville, Kentucky.

DAKIN, JAMES HARRISON. Active Louisiana, early nineteenth century. *See 1275, 1885.*

DAMON, ISAAC. Active Massachusetts, early nineteenth century. *See 128, 311.*

DAVIS, ALEXANDER JACKSON (1803-1892). *See also 1337-40, 1361, 2756.*

2677 DONNELL, EDNA. A. J. Davis and the Gothic revival. Metropolitan museum. Studies. 5:183-233. Sept. 1936. illus.

Includes a list of source books of Gothic revival ornament.

2678 PRATT, RICHARD H. Architect of the romantic era. House and garden. 52:122-23, 154-56. Oct. 1927. illus.

DE POUILLY, JACQUES N. B. Active New Orleans, early nineteenth century. *See 1885, 1913.*

DE POUILLY, JOSEPH ISADORE. Active New Orleans, early nineteenth century. *See 1885.*

DOWNING, ANDREW JACKSON (1815-1852). *See also* 1229, 2773, and Hudson Valley, N. Y.

2679 (Obituary.) Monell, Mrs. Knickerbocker magazine. Oct. 1852.

2680 PRATT, RICHARD H. In the days of Downing. House and garden. 52:102-103, 134, 136. Dec. 1927. illus.

ELDERKIN, JOHN. Active Connecticut, seventeenth century. *See* 128, 159, 402.

EMERY, MATTHEW G. (b. 1818). Active Washington, D. C. See *White's Conspectus of American Biography*.

FOWLER, ORSON SQUIRE (1809-1887). *See* 261, 2773.

2681 (O. S. Fowler.) The Harbinger. 8:14. Nov. 11, 1848.

GALLIER, JAMES, JR. (1827-1868). Active New Orleans, Louisiana. *See* 1885, 1913.

GALLIER, JAMES, SR. (1798-1868). Active New Orleans, Louisiana.

2682 GALLIER, JAMES, SR. Autobiography of James Gallier, architect. Paris, E. Brière, 1864. 150p. illus.

GILMAN, ARTHUR D. (1821-1882). Active Boston and New York. See *White's Conspectus of American Biography*.

GODEFROY, MAXIMILIAN (1781-1855). *See also* 1976. Active Baltimore, Maryland.

2683 DAVISON, CAROLINE V. (ed.). Maximilian Godefroy. . . . Maryland historical magazine. 29:1-20, 175-212. Sept. 1934.

GREENE, JOHN HOLDEN (1777-1850). Active Rhode Island and Georgia. *See* 128, 990, 993.

GREENOUGH, HENRY (1807-1883). See *White's Conspectus of American Biography*.

HADFIELD, GEORGE (*ca.* 1764–1826). *See also* 1692, 2215, 2221, 2222, 2236, 2239, 2242, 2249, 2260.

2684 (Obituary.) National journal. Washington, D. C., Feb. 6, 1826.

HALLET, STEPHEN (HALLET, ETIENNE SULPICE fl. 1789-1796). *See* 1762.

HAMILTON, ANDREW (d. 1741). *See also* 1524, 1582, 1583, 1585, 1589, 1607-1609.

2685 NEWCOMB, REXFORD. Architect of Independence hall. Western architect. 35:82-85. July 1926. illus.

2686 ———. Honorable Andrew Hamilton, barrister-gentleman-architect. Architect. 10:45-50. Apr. 1928. illus.

HARRISON, PETER (1716-1775). *See also* 1024, 1026, 1028.

2687 BACH, RICHARD FRANZ. Peter Harrison: pioneer American architect. Architectural record. 43:580-81. June 1918. illus.

2688 BATCHELDER, SAMUEL FRANCIS. Peter Harrison. Old time New England. 6:12-19. Jan. 1916. illus.

2689 HART, CHARLES HENRY. Peter Harrison, 1716-1775, first professional architect in America. Massachusetts historical society. Proceedings. Mar. 1916. p. 261-68.
Also issued as a reprint.

2690 KIMBALL, SIDNEY FISKE. Colonial amateurs and their models: Peter Harrison—in 2 parts. Architecture. Part 1, 53:155-60. June 1926; part 2, 54:185-90. July 1926. illus.

2691 NEWCOMB, REXFORD. Peter Harrison, early American classicist. Architect. 10:315-18. June 1928. illus.

HAVILAND, JOHN (1792-1852). *See also* 1594.

2692 NEWCOMB, REXFORD. John Haviland, early American architectural specialist. Architect. 11:285-88. Dec. 1928. illus.

2693, 2694 Obituary notice of John Haviland. Philadelphia, Isaac Ashmead, 1852. 14p. illus.
From the *Journal of Prison Discipline*, v. 7, July, 1852.

2695 (Obituary.) Daily national intelligencer, Washington, D. C., Apr. 16, 1852.

HAWKS, JOHN (1731-1790). Active North Carolina. *See* 2030, 2043, and *Dictionary of American Biography*.

HOADLEY, DAVID (1774-1839). *See also* 460.

2696 David Hoadley, architect. Art and progress. 3:545-46. Apr. 1912. illus.

HOBAN, JAMES (*ca.* 1762–1831). *See also* 1736, 1793-1811.

2697 OWEN, FREDERICK D. First government architect, James Hoban of Charleston, S. C. Architectural record. 11:581-89. Oct. 1901. illus.

HOOKER, PHILIP (1766-1836). *See also* 1187, 1189.

2698 ROOT, EDWARD WALES. Philip Hooker. N. Y., Charles Scribner's Sons, 1929. 242p. illus.

JAY, WILLIAM (b. 1796). Active Savannah, Georgia. *See* 1824.

JEFFERSON, THOMAS (1743-1826). *See also* 1858-60, 2176-99, 2281, 2288, 2290, 2292, 2299.

2699 FRARY, IHNA THAYER. Thomas Jefferson, architect and builder. Richmond, Va., Garrett and Massie, 1931. 139p. illus.

2700 HEATWOLE, C. J. Thomas Jefferson as an architect. Virginia journal of education. 19:361-63. May 1926.

2701 ISHAM, NORMAN MORRISON. Jefferson's place in our architectural history. American institute of architects. Journal. 2:230-35. May 1941.

2702 KIMBALL, SIDNEY FISKE. Jefferson the architect. Forum. 75:926-31. June 1926.

2703 ———. Jefferson's place in our architectural history. American institute of architects. Journal. 2:329-30. July 1914.

2704 ———. Thomas Jefferson and the origins of the classic revival in America. Art and archaeology. 1:219-27. May 1915. illus.

2705 ———. Thomas Jefferson, architect: original designs in the possession of Thomas Jefferson Coolidge, Jr. Cambridge, Mass., Riverside press, 1916. 205p. illus.

2706 LAMBETH, WILLIAM ALEXANDER. Thomas Jefferson and the arts. American institute of architects. Journal. 12:454-55. Oct. 1924. illus.
A letter concerning the hiring of two Italian sculptors.

2707 ———, AND MANNING, WARREN H. Thomas Jefferson as an architect and a designer of landscapes. Boston, Houghton Mifflin Co., 1913. 121p. illus.

2708 NEWCOMB, REXFORD. Thomas Jefferson, the architect. Architect. 9:429-32. Jan. 1928. illus.

2709 PRATT, RICHARD H. Jefferson and his fellow architects. House and garden. 51:74-75, 126, 148. July 1927. illus.

2710 RODMAN, W. S. Lighting schemes of Thomas Jefferson. Illuminating engineering society. Transactions. 12:105-121. 1917.

2711 SCHOULER, JAMES. Thomas Jefferson. N. Y., Dodd, Mead and Co., 1919. 252p. illus.

2712 STAPLEY, MILDRED. Thomas Jefferson, the architect, a tribute. Architectural record. 29:178-85. Jan. 1911.

JOY, THOMAS (1610-1678). See *White's Conspectus of American Biography.*

KEARSLEY, DR. JOHN (1684-1772). *See also* 1524.

2713 NEWCOMB, REXFORD. Dr. John Kearsley, physician-architect of Philadelphia. Architect. 10:177-81. May 1928. illus.

KNEASS, SAMUEL H. (1806-1858). Active Philadelphia. See *Dictionary of American Biography.*

LAFEVER, MINARD (1797-1854). *See* 275, 2773.

LATROBE, BENJAMIN HENRY (1764-1820). *See also* 290, 1473, 1523, 1524, 1570, 1580, 1587, 1592, 1595, 1596, 1645, 1718, 1758, 1760-1811, 1866, 1872, 1986, 2233, 2275.

2714 KIMBALL, SIDNEY FISKE. Benjamin Henry Latrobe and the beginnings of architectural and engineering practice in America. Michigan technic. 30:218-23. 1917. illus.

2715 Benjamin H. Latrobe. American architect and building news. 1:36-37. Jan. 29, 1876.

2716 Memoir of Benjamin Henry LaTrobe. Ackermann's repository. Jan. 1821.

2717 Latrobe, Benjamin Henry. Journal of Latrobe. N. Y., D. Appleton and Co., 1905. 269p. illus.
   "Being the notes and sketches of an architect, naturalist and traveler in the United States from 1796 to 1820 . . . with an introduction by J. H. B. Latrobe."

2718 ———. Oration before the Society of Artists of the United States. Portfolio. v. 5. 1811.

2719 LATROBE, FERDINAND C., II. Benjamin Henry Latrobe: descent and works. Maryland historical magazine. 33:247-61. 1938.
   List of works, dated.

2720 NEWCOMB, REXFORD. Benjamin Henry Latrobe, early American architect. Architect. 9:173-77. Nov. 1927. illus.

2721 RUSK, WILLIAM SENER. Benjamin H. Latrobe and the classical influence in his work. Maryland historical magazine. 31:126-54. 1936.

2722 SEMMES, JOHN EDWARD. Latrobe and his times, 1803-1891. Baltimore, Md., Norman, Remington Co., 1917. 601p. illus.
   Refers to J. H. B. Latrobe, with some information on B. H. Latrobe.

L'ENFANT, PIERRE CHARLES (1754-1825). *See also* 1342, 1366, 1677, 1679, 1682, 1703, 1704, 1714, 1715, 1732-34.

2723 KITE, ELIZABETH S. L'Enfant and Washington, 1791-1792. Baltimore, Md., The Johns Hopkins university press, 1929. 182p. illus.

2724 The story of L'Enfant. Western architect. 14:14-16. Aug. 1909.

LONG, ROBERT CAREY (1772-1849). Active Baltimore. *See* 267, 1948.

MANGIN, JOSEPH FRANCOIS (fl. 1794-1818). *See* 1345, 1348, 1358, 1363, 1367.

MANIGAULT, GABRIEL (1758-1809). Active Charleston, South Carolina. *See* 75.

McARTHUR, JOHN, JR. (1823-1890). Active Philadelphia. See *Dictionary of American Biography*.

McBEAN, JAMES (ac.1765). *See* 1381.

McCOMB, JOHN, JR. (1763-1853). *See also* 1299, 1345, 1348, 1358, 1363, 1367, 1372.

2725 McComb, John, Jr. Diary of John McComb, Jr. American architect. 93:15. Jan. 11, 1908.

2726 Wilde, Edward S. John McComb, Jr., architect. American architect. 94:49-53, 57-63. Aug. 1908.

McINTIRE, SAMUEL (1757-1811). *See also* 844, 852, 857, 860, 861, 862, 863, 866, 870, 872, 873, 879, 883, 887.

2727 Dyer, Walter A. Samuel McIntire, master carpenter. House beautiful. 37:65-69. Feb. 1915. illus.

2728 Kimball, Sidney Fiske. Estimate of McIntire. Antiques. 21:23-25. 1932. illus.

2729 Newcomb, Rexford. Samuel McIntire, early American architect. Architect. 9:37-43. Oct. 1927. illus.

2730 Pratt, Richard H. McIntire, the Colonial carpenter. House and garden. 51:108, 158, 162, 164. Feb. 1927. illus.

2731 Swan, Mabel M. Revised estimate of McIntire. Antiques. 20:338-43. Dec. 1931. illus.

MAZZUCHELLI, FATHER SAMUEL C. (b. 1806). *See also* 2500, 2502.

2732 Sister of Santa Clara college. An Iowa pioneer. Annals of Iowa. 3rd ser. 6:282-88. illus.

MILLS, ROBERT (1781-1855). *See also* 290, 1131, 1707, 1720, 1730, 1752, 1788, 1984, 1987, 2287, 2293.

2733 Evans, Richard Xavier (ed.). Daily journal of Robert Mills, Baltimore, 1816. Maryland historical magazine. 30:257-71. 1935.
Excerpts from the ms. in the Library of Congress.

2734 Gallagher, Mrs. H. M. Pierce. Robert Mills, America's first native architect. Architectural record. 65:387-93, 478-84. Apr., May 1929; 66:67-72. July 1929. illus.

2735 ———. Robert Mills, architect and engineer. Architectural record. 40: 584-86. Dec. 1916. illus.

2736 ———. Robert Mills, architect of the Washington monument, 1781-1855. N. Y., Columbia university press, 1935. 233p. illus.

2737 Newcomb, Rexford. Robert Mills, American Greek revivalist. Architect. 9:697-99. Mar. 1928. illus.

2738 WILSON, CHARLES C. Robert Mills, architect. Columbia, S. C., University of South Carolina. Bulletin 77. Feb. 1919.

MUNDAY, RICHARD (d. 1739). Active Rhode Island. *See* 128, 990, 993.

NIERNSEE, JOHN R. (1823-1885). Active South Carolina. *See* 2053.

ORMSBEE, CALEB (1752-1807). Active Rhode Island. *See* 990, 993.

PARRIS, ALEXANDER (1780-1852). Active New England. See *Dictionary of American Biography.*

PORTER, LEMUEL (1775-1830). Active Ohio. *See* 2575, 2589.

RAGUE, JOHN FRANCIS (1799-1877). *See* 2491, 2500-2502.

RAMÉE, JOSEPH JACQUES (1764-1842). *See* 1399.

RENWICK, JAMES (1818-1895). *See* 1334, 1380, 1673, 1729, 1741.

RHOADS, SAMUEL (1711-1784).

2739 KOCHER, A. LAWRENCE. Hand-books of Samuel Rhoads, carpenter-builder. Architectural record. 50:507-509. Dec. 1921.

ROGERS, ISAIAH (1800-1869). *See* 626, 1331.

SHERMAN, AARON. Active Massachusetts and Maine, early nineteenth century. *See* 492.

SHRYOCK, GIDEON (1802-1880). *See also* 1672, 1842-45, 1848, 1871, 1877.

2740 NEWCOMB, REXFORD. Gideon Shryock—pioneer Greek revivalist of the Middle West. Kentucky state historical society. Register. 26:221-35. Sept. 1928. illus.

2741 ————. Gideon Shryock—pioneer Greek revivalist of the West. Architect. 11:41-46. Oct. 1928. illus.

SLOAN, SAMUEL (1815-1884). *See* 2773 and *Godey's Lady's Book, ca.* 1859.

SMIBERT, JOHN (1684-1751). *See* 621, 632.

SMITH, ROBERT (*ca.* 1722-1777). *See* 1506, 1541, 1584.

STRICKLAND, WILLIAM (*ca.* 1787–1854). *See also* 290, 1523, 1524, 1580, 1590, 1591, 1601, 1602, 1603, 2117, 2118, 2273.

2742 ADDISON, AGNES. Progress of studies on William Strickland, architect. American society of architectural historians. Journal. 2:33-34. Apr. 1942.

2743 ————. Latrobe vs. Strickland. American society of architectural historians. Journal. 2:26-29. July 1942.

2744 GILLIAMS, E. LESLIE. A pioneer American architect. Architectural record. 23:123-35. Feb. 1908. illus.

2745 NEWCOMB, REXFORD. William Strickland, American Greek revivalist. Architect. 10:453-58. July 1928. illus.

2746 (Obituary.) American philosophical society. Proceedings. 6:28-32. 1859.

TEFFT, THOMAS ALEXANDER (1826-1859).

2747 WRISTON, BARBARA. The architecture of Thomas Tefft. Rhode Island school of design. Bulletin. 28:37-45. Nov. 1940. illus.

2748 ———. Thomas Tefft, progressive Rhode Islander. Rhode Island historical society. Collections. 34:60-61. Apr. 1941. illus.

THOMPSON, MARTIN (ca. 1786–1877). See 1349-53, 1365.

THORNTON, WILLIAM (1759-1828). See also 1676, 1678, 1680, 1697, 1700, 1712, 1713, 1724, 1728, 1756, 1785, 2008, 2178, 2226, 2242.

2749 BROWN, GLENN. Dr. William Thornton, architect. Architectural record. 6:53-70. July-Sept. 1896. illus.

2750 CLARK, ALLEN C. Dr. and Mrs. William Thornton. Washington, D. C., Columbia historical society. Records. 18:144-208. 1915.

2751 HUNT, G. H. William Thornton and John Fitch. Nation. 98:602-603. May 21, 1914.

2752 NEWCOMB, REXFORD. Doctor William Thornton, early American amateur architect. Architect. 9:559-63. Feb. 1928. illus.

2753 RUSK, WILLIAM SENER. William Thornton, architect. Pennsylvania history. 2:86-98. 1935.

TOWN, ITHIEL (1784-1844). See also 422, 461, 464, 1336-39, 1361, 2044, 2444.

2754 KELLY, JOHN FREDERICK. Forgotten incident in the life of Ithiel Town. Old time New England. 31:62-71. Jan. 1941. illus.

2755 NEWCOMB, REXFORD. Ithiel Town of New Haven and New York. Architect. 11:519-23. Feb. 1929. illus.

2756 NEWTON, ROGER HALE. Town and Davis, architects. N. Y., Columbia university press, 1942. 315p. illus.

2757 SEYMOUR, GEORGE DUDLEY. Ithiel Town—architect. Art and progress. 3:714-16. Sept. 1912. illus.

TRUMBULL, JOHN (1756-1843). See 459.

UPJOHN, RICHARD (1802-1878). See also 1370, 1379.

2758 (Obituary.) American architect and building news. Aug. 24, 1878.

2759 UPJOHN, EVERARD MILLER. Richard Upjohn, architect and churchman. N. Y., Columbia university press, 1939. 243p. illus.

VAN OSDEL, JOHN M. (1811-1892). Active Chicago. *See* 2427.

VAUX, CALVERT (1824-1895). Active New York City. See *White's Conspectus of American Biography.*

WALTER, THOMAS USTICK (1804-1887). *See also* 1523, 1524, 1581, 1593, 1600, 1606, 1610, 1747, 1760-92.

2760 MASON, C. G., JR. Memoir of the late Thomas Ustick Walter. American institute of architects. Proceedings, 1889.

2761 NEWCOMB, REXFORD. Thomas Ustick Walter. Architect. 10:585-89. Aug. 1928. illus.

2762 RUSK, WILLIAM SENER. Thomas U. Walter and his works. Americana. 33:151-79. Apr. 1939. illus.
   Includes bibliography.

WARREN, RUSSELL (1783-1860). Active Rhode Island and Charleston, South Carolina. *See* 990, 993, and *Dictionary of American Biography.*

WHITE, EDWARD BRICKELL (1806-1882). Active South Carolina. *See* 2053.

WILLARD, SOLOMAN (1783-1861). *See also* 622, 641.

2763 WHEILDEN, WILLIAM WILLDER. Memoir of Soloman Willard, architect and superintendent of the Bunker Hill monument. Boston, Bunker Hill monument association, 1865. 272p. illus.

WOODRUFF, JUDAH. Active Connecticut, late eighteenth century. *See* 267, 402.

YOUNG, AMMI B. (1799-1874). Active New England. *See* 545, 2756.

BIBLIOGRAPHIES

*In addition to those listed below extensive bibliographies appear in many
of the titles listed elsewhere in this list—e.g., 14, 20, 24, 70, 102, 973.*

See also the standard indices—e.g., *Art Index, Industrial Arts Index, Poole's
Index to Periodical Literature, Readers' Guide to Periodical Literature,*
and *Subject Index to Periodicals.*

2764 BACH, RICHARD FRANZ. Bibliography of the literature of Colonial architecture. Architectural record. 38:382. Sept. 1915; 39:92-93. Jan. 1916;
39:388-89. Apr. 1916; 40:188-89. Aug. 1916; 40:582-83. Dec.
1916; 41:189. Feb. 1917; 41:472-74. May 1917; 42:89-91. July
1917; 42:185-88. Aug. 1917; 42:283-84. Sept. 1917; Addenda to
close of 1917, 44: 177-80. Aug. 1918.

2765 ———. Books on Colonial architecture. Architectural record. 38:281-86.
Aug. 1915; 38:379-82. Sept. 1915; 38:592-94. Nov. 1915; 38:690-
93. Dec. 1915; 39:89-93. Jan. 1916; 39:186-90. Feb. 1916; 39:292-
94. Mar. 1916; 39:384-89. Apr. 1916; 39:568-74. June 1916; 40:
89-92. July 1916; 40:185-89. Aug. 1916; 40:279-81. Sept. 1916;
40:493-94. Nov. 1916; 40:578-83. Dec. 1916; 41:84-87. Jan. 1917;
41:187-89. Feb. 1917; 41:279-85. Mar. 1917; 41:373-74. Apr.
1917; 41:470-74. May 1917; 41:566-71. June 1917; 42:88-91. July
1917; 42:185-88. Aug. 1917; 42:283-84. Sept. 1917; 42:486-91.
Nov. 1917; Addenda for 1917, 44:85-90. July 1918; 44:175-80. Aug.
1918.

2766 ———. Early American architecture and the allied arts. Architectural record. 59:265-73. Mar. 1926; 59:328-34. Apr. 1926; 59:483-88. May
1926; 59:525-32. June 1926; 60:65-70. July 1926; 63:577-80. June
1928; 64:70-72. July 1928; 64:150-52. Aug. 1928; 64:190-92. Sept.
1928.
The allied arts here include glassware, metalwork, pottery, textiles, and furniture.

2767 BOSTON. PUBLIC LIBRARY. Catalogue of books referring to architecture, construction and decoration. Boston, The Trustees, 1894. 150p.

2768 BRADFORD, THOMAS LINDSLEY. The bibliographer's manual of American
history, containing an account of all state, territory, town and county
histories relating to the United States of North America, with verbatim
copies of their titles, and useful bibliographical notes . . . and with an
exhaustive index by titles, and an index by states. Philadelphia, Henkels,
1907. 2v.

2768A (Brown, Glenn, comp.). American institute of architects. Quarterly bulletin. v. 1-13. 1900-1912.

Contains an index of literature from the publications of architectural societies and periodicals on architecture and allied subjects.

2769 Columbia University. Avery Architectural Library. Catalogue of the Avery architectural library. N. Y., Library of Columbia college, 1895. 1139p.

2770 Cook, Ruth V. Current bibliography in architectural history. American society of architectural historians. Journal. v. 1, no. 1. Jan. 1941 and succeeding numbers.

An invaluable list including all important items, European and American. Cross indexed geographically and chronologically.

2771 Griffin, Grace Gardner (ed.). Writings on American history. American historical association. Annual report. 1902, 1903, 1906-1937.

The basic listing in this field. Appears about five years late.

2772 Hamlin, Talbot Faulkner. Bibliography of American architecture. N. Y., Avery library, ca. 1935.

2773, 2774 Hitchcock, Henry-Russell, Jr. American architectural books, a list of books, portfolios and pamphlets published in America before 1895 on architecture and related subjects. Middletown, Conn., privately circulated, 1938-1939. 169 mimeographed pages including errata.

Lists locations of the items. Review in Art Bulletin. 23:186-87. June 1941, by Frank Roos, Jr.

2775 Huth, Hans. Preservationism: a selected bibliography. American society of architectural historians. Journal. v. 1, no. 3-4. p. 33-45. July-Oct. 1941.

For all countries.

2776 Interior architecture and decoration; a selected list of references. New York. Public library. Bulletin. 43:87-112, 396-404. Feb., May 1939.

Also issued as a separate publication by American Institute of Decorators.

2777 Kocher, A. Lawrence. Library of the architect. Architectural record. 56:123-28. Aug. 1924; 56:218-24. Sept. 1924; 56:316-20. Oct. 1924; 56:517-20. Dec. 1924; 57:29-32. Jan. 1925; 57:125-28. Feb. 1925; 57:221-24. Mar. 1925; 57:317-20. Apr. 1925.

2778 Mumford, Lewis. Architecture. Chicago, American library association, 1926. 34p.

Reading with a Purpose series, no. 23.

2779 Peterson, Charles E. List of published writings of special interest in the study of historic architecture of the Mississippi Valley. St. Louis, Mo., United States Department of the interior, National park service, Historic American buildings survey, Central unit, 1940. 29p. mimeographed.

2780 UNITED STATES. NATIONAL PARK SERVICE. Park and recreation progress. Washington, D. C., Department of the interior, 1938 ———.
Yearbook, includes bibliography.

2781 WALL, ALEXANDER J. Books on architecture printed in America, 1775-1830. In Bibliographical essays, a tribute to Wilberforce Eames. Cambridge, Mass., Harvard University press, 1924. p. 299-311.

2782 YOUTZ, PHILIP N. American life in architecture. Chicago, American library association, 1932. 47p.
Reading with a Purpose series, no. 55.

INDEX

INDEX

NOTE.—Page numbers are in italics.

Assay office, New York City, 1365
Assembly house, Salem, Mass., 883
Astor hotel, New York City, 1331
Astor house, Mackinac Island, Mich., 2524
Atamasco, Baltimore, Md., 1982
Atkinson, Josephine, 1156
Atkinson, Mary J., 1157
Atkinson, Minnie, 500
Auburn, Mass., 567
Auburn, N. Y., 1198, 1199
Audubon house, New York City, 1304
Augusta County, Va., 2200
Augusta, Ga., 1823, 1829
Augusta, Me., 501-503
Austin, Henry, p. *14, 226*
Avery Architectural Library, *see* Columbia
      University
Avis, A., 2363

Babb, Margaret E., 2419
Bach, Richard Franz, p. *vii*; 56, 133, 2663,
      2687, 2764-2766
Bacon, Edgar Mayhew, 746, 1406, 1544
Bacon, Edwin M., 575
Bacon, Leonard, 386
Bacon, Mary Schell Hoke, 387
Bacon's Castle, Smithfield, Va., 196, 2378
Baer, Annie Wentworth, 522, 939, 984
Bagg, Ernest Newton, 535
Bailey, Rosalie Fellows, 1084
Baker, Abby Gunn, 1793
Baker, Geoffrey, 1673
Baker house, Jaffrey, N. H., 962
Balch, Alfred B., 2428
Baldwin, Frank Conger, 2157, 2346, 2359,
      2364
Baldwin house, Worcester, Mass., 934
Baldwin-Lyman house, Salem, Mass., 882
Bale, Florence Gratiot, 2430
Ball, Emma R., 2216
Baltimore, Md., 1976-1993
Bangor, Me., 504
Bangs, M. R., 695
Bank of Manhattan Company, 1265
Bank of Pennsylvania, Philadelphia, 1595
Bank of the United States, Philadelphia, 1580,
      1596
Banner, Peter, p. *226*
Bannister, Turpin C., p. *8; 1*
Bannister, William P., 146
Baraboo, Wis., 2641
Barbour house, Norfolk County, Va., 2352
Barclay, David, 1261
Bardstown, Ky., 1853, 1854
Bareis, George F., 2569
Bar Harbor, Me., 505
Barker, Charles R., 1502, 1503

NOTE.—Page numbers are in italics.

Barnstable, Mass., *see* Cape Cod *and* 568
Barnes, Case G., 2565
Barnett, George I., p. *226*
Barnett, Tom P., 2662
Barns, Pa., 1441, 1453
Barr, Alfred H., Jr., 3
Barratt, Norris Stanley, 1611
Barrell, *see* Sayward-Barrell house
Barrington, Lewis, 30
Barrows, John A., 2166
Bartholomew, H. S. K., 2461
Bartlett, George B., 703
Bartlett, Stuart, 340, 689, 690
Barton, A. O., 2639
Barton, George, 1505
Bartram houses, Philadelphia, 1544, 1553
Bassett, Norman L., 501
Batchelder, Samuel Francis, 2688
Bath, N. C., 2036
Bathurst, Essex County, Va., 2214
Baton Rouge, La., 1898
Battery, The, New York City, 1330
Battle Monument, Baltimore, 1976
Bauchle, May L., 2640
Baum, Dwight James, 827, 2052
Baxter, Sylvester, 737
Bayhan, Richard S., 1064
Bayles, William Harrison, 1332, 1333
Beacon Hill, Boston, 578, 594
Beacon Hill column, Boston, 619
Beard, Mrs. William Ewing, 2118
Beard, William Ewing, 2119
Beaufort, S. C., 2062-2064
Beauregard house, New Orleans, 1925
Beauvoir, Biloxi, Miss., 2016
Beck, Louise B., 1621
Beckett house, Salem, Mass., 855
Bedford County, Va., 2201
Bedford, Mass., 704
Beecher house, Guilford, Conn., 445
Beecher, *see* Wheeler-Beecher house
Beidleman, Ferdinand H., 1098
Belcher, Samuel, p. *226*
Belcher house, Elizabeth, N. J., 1134, 1135
Belknap, Henry Wykoff, 841
Belle Grove, Frederick County, Va., 2157
Belle Grove plantation, La., 1894
Bellows Falls, Vt., 1077
Bellows, Robert P., 388
Bells, church, 327
Belmont, Philadelphia, 1563, 1574
Belvoir, Fairfax County, Va., 2228, 2266
Bender, Horace, 264
Benedict, William H., 1158
Benjamin, Asher, p. *13, 14, 18, 19, 226*
Bennett, George Fletcher, 1099
Bennett house, Easton, Conn., 434
Bennett house, New Bedford, Mass., 811
Bennett, Wells, 1716, 1762, 1785

NOTE.—Page numbers are in italics.

NOTE.—Page numbers are in italics.

NOTE.—Page numbers are in italics.

NOTE.—Page numbers are in italics.

NOTE.—Page numbers are in italics.

NOTE.—Page numbers are in italics.

NOTE.—Page numbers are in italics.

NOTE.—Page numbers are in italics.

NOTE.—Page numbers are in italics.

NOTE.—Page numbers are in italics.

NOTE.—Page numbers are in italics.

NOTE.—Page numbers are in italics.

NOTE.—Page numbers are in italics.

NOTE.—Page numbers are in italics.

NOTE.—Page numbers are in italics.

NOTE.—Page numbers are in italics.

NOTE.—Page numbers are in italics.

NOTE.—Page numbers are in italics.

NOTE.—Page numbers are in italics.

NOTE.—Page numbers are in italics.

NOTE.—Page numbers are in italics.

NOTE.—Page numbers are in italics.

NOTE.—Page numbers are in italics.

NOTE.—Page numbers are in italics.

NOTE.—Page numbers are in italics.

Note.—Page numbers are in italics.